Meerkats on the lookout in the
Namib Desert, Namibia

NATIONAL GEOGRAPHIC
KiDS

ALMANAC
2024

NATIONAL GEOGRAPHIC
WASHINGTON, D.C.

National Geographic Kids Books
gratefully acknowledges the following people for their help with the *National Geographic Kids Almanac.*

Stacey McClain of the
National Geographic Explorer Programs

Amazing Animals

Suzanne Braden, Director, Pandas International

Dr. Rodolfo Coria, Paleontologist,
Plaza Huincul, Argentina

Dr. Sylvia Earle, National Geographic
Explorer-in-Residence

Dr. Thomas R. Holtz, Jr., Senior Lecturer,
Vertebrate Paleontology,
Department of Geology, University of Maryland

Dr. Luke Hunter, Executive Director, Panthera

Nizar Ibrahim, National Geographic Explorer

Dereck and Beverly Joubert,
National Geographic Explorers-in-Residence

"Dino" Don Lessem, President, Exhibits Rex

Kathy B. Maher, Research Editor (former),
National Geographic magazine

Kathleen Martin, Canadian Sea Turtle Network

Barbara Nielsen, Polar Bears International

Andy Prince, Austin Zoo

Julia Thorson, Translator, Zurich, Switzerland

Dennis vanEngelsdorp, Senior Extension Associate,
Pennsylvania Department of Agriculture

Space and Earth
Science and Technology

Tim Appenzeller, Chief Magazine Editor, *Nature*

Dr. Rick Fienberg, Press Officer and Director of Communications,
American Astronomical Society

Dr. José de Ondarza, Associate Professor,
Department of Biological Sciences, State University
of New York, College at Plattsburgh

Lesley B. Rogers, Managing Editor (former),
National Geographic magazine

Dr. Enric Sala, National Geographic Explorer-in-Residence

Abigail A. Tipton, Director of Research (former),
National Geographic magazine

Erin Vintinner, Biodiversity Specialist,
Center for Biodiversity and Conservation at the
American Museum of Natural History

Barbara L. Wyckoff, Research Editor (former),
National Geographic magazine

Culture Connection

Dr. Wade Davis, National Geographic
Explorer-in-Residence

Deirdre Mullervy, Managing Editor,
Gallaudet University Press

Wonders of Nature

Anatta, NOAA Public Affairs Officer

Dr. Robert Ballard,
National Geographic Explorer-in-Residence

Douglas H. Chadwick, Wildlife Biologist and Contributor
to *National Geographic* magazine

Susan K. Pell, Ph.D., Science and Public Programs Manager,
United States Botanic Garden

History Happens

Dr. Sylvie Beaudreau, Associate Professor,
Department of History, State University of New York

Elspeth Deir, Assistant Professor, Faculty of Education,
Queens University, Kingston, Ontario, Canada

Dr. Gregory Geddes, Professor, Global Studies,
State University of New York–Orange,
Middletown-Newburgh, New York

Dr. Fredrik Hiebert, National Geographic Visiting Fellow

Micheline Joanisse, Media Relations Officer,
Natural Resources Canada

Dr. Robert D. Johnston,
Associate Professor and Director of the
Teaching of History Program, University of Illinois at Chicago

Dickson Mansfield, Geography Instructor (retired),
Faculty of Education, Queens University,
Kingston, Ontario, Canada

Tina Norris, U.S. Census Bureau

Parliamentary Information and Research Service,
Library of Parliament, Ottawa, Canada

Karyn Pugliese, Acting Director, Communications,
Assembly of First Nations

Geography Rocks

Dr. Kristin Bietsch, Research Associate,
Population Reference Bureau

Carl Haub, Senior Demographer,
Conrad Taeuber Chair of Public Information,
Population Reference Bureau

Dr. Toshiko Kaneda, Senior Research Associate,
Population Reference Bureau

Dr. Walt Meier, National Snow and Ice Data Center

Dr. Richard W. Reynolds, NOAA's National Climatic Data Center

United States Census Bureau, Public Help Desk

Contents

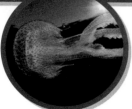

WONDERS OF NATURE 214

HISTORY HAPPENS 236

GEOGRAPHY ROCKS 268

NATIONAL GEOGRAPHIC KIDS
ALMANAC CHALLENGE 2024

THE RESULTS ARE IN!

Which tree autobiography won our 2023 Almanac Challenge?
See page 127.

Want to become part of the 2024 Almanac Challenge? Go to page 126 to find out more.

YOUR WORLD 2024

Whether you call it football or soccer, this sport is a worldwide favorite. Check out the 2024 Paris Olympic Games to see 16 countries play in the men's tournament and 12 countries play in the women's tournament.

ANIMALS RESCUED FROM WAR

In war-torn Ukraine, helpful humans have been working hard to rescue and relocate pets and even wild animals from danger. When Russian forces invaded Ukraine in 2022, many people had to quickly flee and leave everything behind, including their pets. At the same time, some animal shelters and zoos were also abandoned, leaving thousands of creatures stranded without food or water. But thanks to efforts from volunteers who have risked their own safety to return to embattled areas and rescue as many animals as they can, many of these critters now have a chance. One group has saved more than 300 animals, finding most of them new homes in safer spots. This includes a shelter near Kyiv, Ukraine, which has taken in dozens of left-behind wild animals—including lions, a leopard, a tiger, wolves, and more—with hopes of relocating them to zoos around the world.

Stellar Telescope

What does a swarm of thousands of ancient galaxies or a stellar nursery look like? Thanks to NASA's high-powered James Webb Space Telescope, we can now see "back in time" to when the first galaxies were forming. The telescope, which has been in development for three decades and cost some $10 billion to produce, has the capacity to look 13.6 billion light-years away. It recently picked up detailed, infrared, never-before-seen images of galaxies sparkling like confetti, stellar nurseries (regions of space where stars are formed), and even remote exoplanets. While so much is still left to learn and to explore in outer space, this telescope is helping to make it all a little less of a mystery.

New Frogs Found

They look like they're plucked straight out of a sci-fi movie: tiny frogs, no bigger than a U.S. quarter, with translucent underbelly skin, revealing a window into their internal organs. But these frogs aren't fictional—in fact, there are several species of see-through frogs, including two recently discovered types found in Ecuador's Andes Mountains. Known as Mashpi and Nouns' glass frogs, the amphibians— each with a lime green back with black spots arranged around yellow spots—are distinct species, despite looking nearly identical. Underneath, translucent skin on their bellies reveals their red hearts, white livers and digestive systems, and green eggs among the females. The transparent skin, scientists say, is an adaptation that might help the tree-dwelling creatures disguise their shape among leaves. One thing these unique creatures have in common: They're all at risk of extinction and under constant threat from habitat loss.

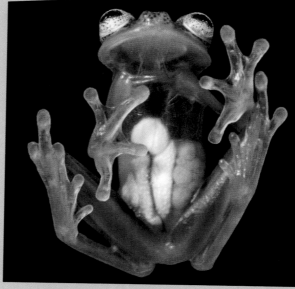

DOG INTERRUPTS Soccer Game

Sometimes, you just really need a belly rub! That was the case at a soccer game in Chile, when a friendly dog darted onto the field during a women's pro match and rolled around in front of one of the goalies, as if asking for some love. The game was paused, and the dog moved on to another player and eventually rolled in front of the referee before it was scooped up by an athlete and carried off the field. No one knew where the dog came from—or how it got onto the field. But footage of the puppy-on-the-pitch went viral, racking up hundreds of thousands of views online.

SEA DRAGON!

When a conservationist drained a water reserve in the United Kingdom, the last thing they thought they'd uncover were the remains of a giant prehistoric sea dragon. But that's just what happened when the crew came across an ichthyosaur fossil measuring around 33 feet (10 m) in length, including a 6-foot (1.8-m) skull—the largest fossil of its kind ever discovered in the U.K.! Dating back some 180 million years, the fossil offers a more complete picture of this ferocious underwater predator.

DARING Dining

Now here's a meal with a view!

A newly opened restaurant is suspended some 900 feet (280 m) above Tsalka (Dashbashi) Canyon, a deep mountain gorge in the country of Georgia. Accessible by a 787-foot (240-m)-long suspension walkway, the diamond-shaped, glass-and-steel structure is said to be the world's highest-hanging restaurant on a bridge. The unique vantage point offers diners sweeping views of the surrounding forest, including waterfalls and caves carved from volcanic rock. But it's not just food on the menu here: There's a zip line on which safely secured guests can bike across the canyon, as well as a cliff swing which allows brave visitors to soar over the gorge—all making this restaurant one extreme eatery.

Welcome to the MEKONG

MEGOPHRYS FRIGIDA

CAPPARIS MACRANTHA

TRACHYPITHECUS POPA

The Mekong region is having a moment. The vast swath of land covering 200 million acres (81 million ha) and spanning six countries (China, Myanmar, Laos, Thailand, Cambodia, and Vietnam) is already one of the most biologically diverse habitats in the world. Now it's known to be even more diverse, as more than 200 new species have been discovered in the area.

A recent study by the World Wildlife Fund (WWF) shows impressive findings among the species that call the area home. This increased count includes 155 plants, 35 reptiles, 17 amphibians, 16 fish, and one mammal, adding up to more than 3,000 new species in the region since 1997.

Among those newly identified animals? The Popa langur (*Trachypithecus popa*), the lone mammal on the Mekong list. Named after an extinct volcano in Myanmar, this fluffy, gray, leaf-eating monkey with white rings around its eyes is critically endangered. Then there's the orange-brown knobby newt, which sports devilish horns and a racing stripe, and a rock gecko with skin that WWF experts say looks like it has a "half-finished paint job." With yellow-orange on its upper body that fades into gray, experts say its unique coloring allows it to blend in with lichen and dry moss.

While finding new species is mostly positive news, experts stress that it's more important than ever before to protect the vulnerable Mekong region— and everything that lives there.

PAREAS GEMINATUS

13

CHIMPS USE
BUG "BANDAGES"

What does a chimpanzee do when it has a cut? It puts on a bandage, of course! Experts observing a group of about 45 apes in the wilds of Gabon—a country in Central Africa—noticed the chimps catching winged insects and then applying clumps of the bugs to open wounds. In one case, a female chimp rubbed crushed insects onto her young son's wounded foot; in another, an adult female caught an insect and handed it to a male chimp, who stuck it on his cut as she groomed him. Why insects? Researchers suspect that the particular type of bug that the chimps catch might have an anti-inflammatory effect that can soothe and help heal injuries. No matter why, scientists say that this first-aid feat supports the idea that chimps have the ability to express concern for others and to take care of them, too.

Rainforest CITY

For centuries, the city of Jakarta has served as the bustling capital of Indonesia. But the massive metropolis—which boasts a population of some 11 million—is feeling the effects of those crowded conditions. Groundwater extraction, climate change, and human impact are causing the nearby Java Sea to rise, leaving about 40 percent of Jakarta below sea level. In fact, it's one of the world's fastest-sinking cities—and Indonesian officials are scrambling to build a new capital for their country.

The plan? To relocate the capital to Kalimantan on the island of Borneo, some 800 miles (1,300 km) away from Jakarta. There, Nusantara, a brand-new high-tech smart city, will be built and completed around 2045. Experts hope the move will create an eco-friendly and more sustainable environment and will take some pressure off of Jakarta so it doesn't wind up washing away one day.

Of course, the capital city shift does not come without questions. Some people think that building a new city from scratch will only lead to more pollution. Another concern is that the rainforest will be cleared away, even though experts say that Nusantara is being built in a part of the rainforest that's already been cleared and covered mostly by eucalyptus plantations, which have less biodiversity than other areas. Only time will tell if it's the best solution for Indonesia and all of the people, plants, and animals that call the country home.

A ROAD CUTS THROUGH THE RAINFOREST IN KALIMANTAN, INDONESIA.

Giraffe Secret Revealed

Ever wonder why giraffes have such long necks—besides just being able to grab leaves high in trees? Fossils from the animals' early relatives could lend clues to their evolution. Scientists are studying fossils of giraffoids, goat-size mammals that roamed Earth 17 million years ago and had a habit of headbutting one another to assert dominance. Although giraffoids had short necks, researchers say those with longer, more muscular necks had an advantage in a headbutting battle. This may have triggered an evolution of the longer-necked species over two million years. And while they no longer headbutt, modern male giraffes still defend themselves with their necks, using them to throw powerful punches at opponents when competing for mates.

Space Tacos

LEFT: A NASA ASTRONAUT TENDS TO THE CHILI PEPPER PLANTS. RIGHT: AN ASTRONAUT ENJOYS PART OF THE CHILI PEPPER HARVEST IN A TACO.

Forget prepackaged and freeze-dried food: On the International Space Station (ISS), astronauts munch on tacos! To celebrate a chili pepper harvest—the very first time the spicy fruit had ever been grown in space—a crew of astronauts whipped up a special taco night. The meal—inspired by 26 chili peppers that were all planted, grown, and harvested on the space station—also included fajita beef, rehydrated tomatoes, and artichokes. The fiesta broke a record for feeding the most astronauts from a space-grown crop, a promising step forward for the future of agriculture in space—and a welcome treat for astronauts on the ISS who don't always get to eat fresh food. But this wasn't just a last-minute meal: NASA scientists spent more than two years researching pepper varieties before selecting the seeds to send to space. Then, it took 137 days for the plants to grow (about two weeks longer than chili plants on Earth), making it the longest plant experiment in the history of the space station.

15

Cool Events 2024

WORLD OCEANS DAY
SURF'S UP!
Today, we show love for the world's oceans—and the millions of plants and animals that call them home.
June 8

INTERNATIONAL WOMEN'S DAY
Celebrate all of the amazing women on Earth on this day aimed at raising awareness for the importance of gender equality.
March 8

2024 SUMMER OLYMPICS
Faster, higher, stronger—together. The world's best athletes head to Paris to compete on the biggest stage in sports and go for the gold.
July 26–August 11

INTERNATIONAL DAY OF MATHEMATICS
IT JUST ADDS UP: Math is an awesome (and important) subject! Do some extra equations to celebrate all things numbers.
March 14

INTERNATIONAL YOUTH DAY
HEY KID, YOU'RE PRETTY GREAT! Today is a day to celebrate being young and having fun!
August 12

WORLD POETRY DAY
ARE YOU A POET AND YOU DON'T EVEN KNOW IT? Try your hand at this expressive form of writing with your own sonnet, limerick, or haiku.
March 21

INTERNATIONAL ORANGUTAN DAY
Show these hairy orange-red apes big love and encourage others to help protect these endangered species in the wild.
August 19

WORLD WATER DAY
Honor the amazing resource that covers about 70 percent of our planet—**WE WOULDN'T BE HERE WITHOUT IT!**
March 22

WORLD SMILE DAY
GOT SOMETHING TO SMILE ABOUT?
Slap on a happy grin and shine your light toward others: Smiling is contagious!
October 4

Diver Finds
Medieval Sword

Talk about a buried treasure! A diver exploring the underwater environment off the coast of Israel swam upon a 900-year-old sword that likely belonged to a medieval knight. The four-foot (1.2-m) sword, thought to be made of iron, was found on the sandy bottom of the Mediterranean Sea. Covered in a thick casing of shells and other marine organisms from its centuries undersea, the sword is totally intact. The diver, who reported his find to authorities who specialize in antiquities, also came across other ancient artifacts in the same area. The sword is set to be cleaned, studied, and eventually put on display.

UNLIKELY
ROOMMATES

When a conservation manager at a nature reserve in Australia came across a gecko curled up in a nest of western pygmy possums, he assumed the reptile was just passing through. But when the gecko remained two weeks later, he realized the animals were actually living together. While an odd grouping, experts say it's not entirely unlikely. Because western pygmy possums eat nectar and insects, the gecko wouldn't be a meal for the mammals. And the gecko, which sticks to a diet of spiders and other bugs, was likely enjoying the warmth and safety of the nest. Whatever the reason, it all makes for one adorable living arrangement!

Comeback
TORTOISE

Native to the Galápagos Islands, Fernandina giant tortoises hadn't been seen in more than a hundred years. Hunted by pirates and traders, the tortoises also lost part of their habitat to volcanic eruptions. But when scientists spotted a peculiar pile of poop on Fernandina Island in the Galápagos, they linked it to the long-lost tortoise. Two days later, they discovered a Fernandina tortoise, which they brought to a rehabilitation center to keep healthy. Now the team plans to return the tortoise and look for other members of her species—hopefully a male. Maybe this species isn't lost after all.

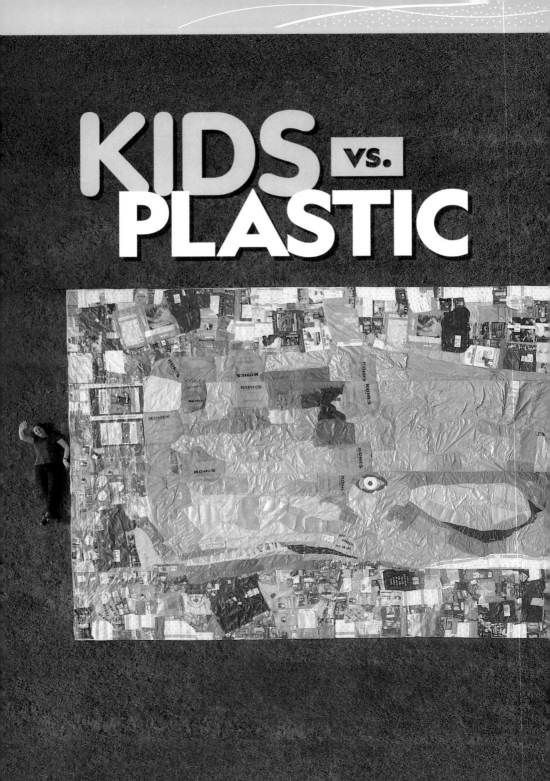

National Geographic Explorer Kat Owens (left) creates portraits of animals harmed by trash in the ocean by sewing together pieces of plastic that are difficult or impossible to recycle.

WHAT IS
PLASTIC?

Plastic can be molded, colored, and textured to make, well, just about anything. That begs the question: What precisely is this wonder product?

THE BASICS
Plastics are polymers, or long, flexible chains of molecules made of repeating links. This molecular structure makes plastic lightweight, hard to break, and easy to mold—all of which makes it extremely useful.

WHERE DO POLYMERS COME FROM?
Polymers can be found in nature, in things like the cell walls of plants, tar, tortoiseshell, and tree sap. In fact, nearly 3,500 years ago, people in what is today Central America used the sap from gum trees to make rubber balls for games. About 150 years ago, scientists began replicating the polymers in nature to improve on them—these are called synthetic polymers.

WHO INVENTED PLASTIC?
In 1869, an American named John Wesley Hyatt created the first useful synthetic polymer. At the time, the discovery was a big deal: For the first time, manufacturing was no longer limited by the resources supplied by nature like wood, clay, and stone. People could create their own materials.

WHAT IS SYNTHETIC PLASTIC MADE FROM?
Today, most plastic is made from oil and natural gas.

WHEN DID IT BECOME POPULAR?
During World War II, from 1939 to 1945, nylon, which is strong and light like silk but made of plastic, was used for parachutes, rope, body armor, and helmet liners. And airplanes used in battle had lightweight windows made of plastic glass, also known as Plexiglas. After the war, plastic became a popular material. Everything from dishes to radios to Mr. Potato Head hit the market. A few decades later, plastic soda bottles became a lightweight, nonbreakable alternative to glass bottles, and grocery stores switched from paper bags to cheaper thin plastic bags.

THAT BRINGS US TO TODAY.
Look around: Are you more than a few feet away from something plastic? Probably not! Plastic is all around us.

More than **700 SPECIES of MARINE ANIMALS** have been reported to **HAVE EATEN** or been **ENTANGLED** in **PLASTIC.**

WHERE DOES ALL THE PLASTIC GO?

Only a small percentage of all the plastic that has ever been made has been recycled to make other things. Most has been tossed out and left to slowly biodegrade in landfills, a process that can take hundreds of years. The other option for getting rid of plastic is to burn it. But because plastic is made from fossil fuels, burning it releases harmful pollutants into the air. Here is a breakdown of where all the plastic has gone since people started making it, and how long it takes to biodegrade if it does wind up in a landfill.

9% Recycled

19% Burned, releasing toxins into the air

72% Sent to landfills or winds up in the natural environment (like oceans)

THE LIFE SPAN OF PLASTIC

PLASTIC BAG
20 YEARS

PLASTIC-FOAM CUP
50 YEARS

Plastic that's sent to a landfill doesn't just disappear—it stays there for a really long time. Different types of plastic take different lengths of time to biodegrade.

STRAW
200 YEARS

BOTTLE
450 YEARS

SODA SIX-PACK RINGS
450 YEARS

FISHING LINE
600+ YEARS

DEADLY DEBRIS

THE INS AND OUTS OF THE (NOT SO) GREAT PACIFIC GARBAGE PATCH

On a map, the space between California and Hawaii, U.S.A., looks like an endless blue sea, but in person, you'll find a giant floating island—made up of plastic. Plastic can be found in all the oceans of the world, but currents and winds move marine debris around in certain patterns that create huge concentrations, or patches, of plastic in some spots. The biggest one is the Great Pacific Garbage Patch. Scientists estimate that there are about 1.8 trillion pieces of plastic in the patch, and 94 percent of them are microplastics. So don't try walking on it; it's definitely not solid! Some of the patch is made up of bulky items, including fishing gear like nets, rope, eel traps, crates, and baskets. The patch is also made up of debris washed into the sea during tsunamis. A tsunami is a series of waves caused by an earthquake or an undersea volcanic eruption. It can pull millions of tons of debris—from cars to household appliances to pieces of houses—off coastlines and into the ocean. Scientists and innovators are working on ways to clean up the patch. But with more plastic constantly entering waterways, the effort will inevitably be ongoing.

TANGLED NYLON ROPE THAT HAS WASHED ASHORE OFF THE COAST OF PHUKET, THAILAND

SMASHED-UP SHIPS EVENTUALLY MAKE THEIR WAY TO A SWIRLING MASS OF DEBRIS CALLED THE GREAT PACIFIC GARBAGE PATCH.

GARBAGE PATCH ZONES

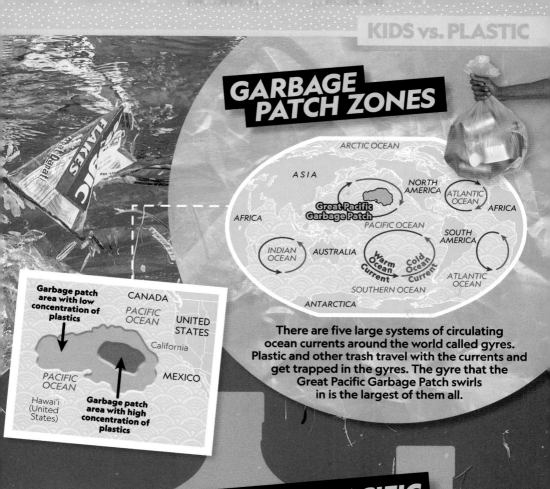

ARCTIC OCEAN

ASIA

NORTH AMERICA

ATLANTIC OCEAN

AFRICA

Great Pacific Garbage Patch

AFRICA

PACIFIC OCEAN

SOUTH AMERICA

INDIAN OCEAN

AUSTRALIA

Warm Ocean Current

Cold Ocean Current

ATLANTIC OCEAN

SOUTHERN OCEAN

ANTARCTICA

There are five large systems of circulating ocean currents around the world called gyres. Plastic and other trash travel with the currents and get trapped in the gyres. The gyre that the Great Pacific Garbage Patch swirls in is the largest of them all.

Garbage patch area with low concentration of plastics

CANADA

PACIFIC OCEAN

UNITED STATES

California

PACIFIC OCEAN

MEXICO

Hawai'i (United States)

Garbage patch area with high concentration of plastics

THE GREAT PACIFIC GARBAGE PATCH MEASURES 618,000 SQUARE MILES (1.6 MILLION SQ KM).

That's about:

3 TIMES THE SIZE OF FRANCE

2 TIMES THE SIZE OF TEXAS

There are 250 PIECES OF PLASTIC in the Great Pacific Garbage Patch for EVERY HUMAN on Earth.

YOUR **PLASTIC-FREE** GUIDE TO
SNACKS

Chew on these three ideas for plastic-free snacking.

1
TRAIL MIX

Just mix all your favorite treats from the bulk section of the grocery store together in a bowl, and then eat! You can even sprinkle your mixture with sea salt, cinnamon, or another of your favorite spices for more flavor. Check out these ideas for ingredient inspiration.

- [ ] Pretzels
- [ ] Nuts like almonds, pistachios, or peanuts
- [ ] Pumpkin or sunflower seeds
- [ ] Dried fruit like apricots, raisins, or banana chips
- [ ] Chocolate chips
- [ ] Whole-grain cereal
- [ ] Shredded coconut

2
STOVETOP POPCORN

You'll need a paper bag full of popcorn kernels from the bulk section of the grocery store, some cooking oil, and a big pot with a lid. Make sure to get an adult's help with this recipe.

- [ ] Pour a splash of oil into the pot, using just enough to cover the bottom.
- [ ] Grab an adult and heat the pot on the stovetop over medium heat.
- [ ] Pour in enough popcorn kernels to create one layer along the bottom of the pot.
- [ ] Cover the pot with the lid.
- [ ] After a few minutes, listen for popping sounds. When the popping slows, remove the pot from the burner, take off the lid, and put the popcorn in a bowl.
- [ ] Top off your treat with salt, melted butter, or spices.

3
BAKED APPLES

Turn this packaging-free fruit into a special snack with brown sugar, butter, and cinnamon. Make sure to get an adult's help with this recipe.

- [ ] Grab an adult and preheat the oven to 350°F (175°C). (You can also use the microwave.)
- [ ] Cut each apple in half, then scoop out its core.
- [ ] Put the apples in an ovenproof baking dish, and then spread a tablespoon of brown sugar and a tablespoon of butter on the inside of each apple half. Then sprinkle the apples with cinnamon.
- [ ] Bake the apples in the oven for about half an hour, or cook in the microwave for about three minutes or until the fruit softens.

kids
vs. PLASTIC

Do your part to help prevent single-use plastic items from reaching the ocean.
Parents and teachers:
For more information on this topic, you can visit **natgeokids.com/KidsVsPlastic** with your young readers.

CHOOSE THIS

NOT THAT

You can buy sneakers made from repurposed plastic bottles.

WHY?

Every minute, people around the planet use about a million plastic bottles—enough to wrap around Earth more than three times! Even worse? A large portion of those used bottles aren't recycled and wind up in the oceans or landfills. You can do your part by opting for a reusable bottle instead. Not only will you help reduce the staggering amount of plastic waste in the world, but you'll help protect the planet, too!

SIP ON THESE!

1 A special insulation keeps your drink hot or cold longer in a stainless steel bottle.

STAINLESS STEEL

2 It's light enough to toss into your backpack—and easy to clean in the dishwasher.

REUSABLE PLASTIC

3 Well-insulated and pretty to look at, glass bottles are also the most fragile.

GLASS

4 Durable and often bigger than other bottles, aluminum is great for a longer hike.

ALUMINUM

10 FACTS ABOUT PLASTIC MASTERPIECES

VISITORS TO THE ISLAND OF BOCAS DEL TORO, PANAMA, CAN STAY IN A FOUR-LEVEL, **50-FOOT** (14-M)-**TALL CASTLE** MADE FROM **40,000** PLASTIC BOTTLES.

Artists used recyclable plastic from landfills to create a series of **LARGE PINK SNAILS** for an art installation in St. Petersburg, Russia.

On one beach in Sri Lanka, there's a **life-size elephant built with plastic trash** collected from a local seashore.

A New York City artist used recycled single-use plastic bags, duct tape, and steel to create a series of GIANT DOG sculptures.

A Norwegian artist repurposed **hundreds of plastic grocery bags** and **chicken wire** to create **a polar bear mom and cub.**

To create awareness about plastic waste, **an American artist made a suit from see-through plastic bags** and **filled them** with all the **trash** he produced over the course of one month.

Builders in Canada **constructed a three-bedroom house** out of more than **600,000** plastic water bottles.

Made from **1.5 million plastic bottles,** the EcoARK building in Taipei, Taiwan, is sturdy enough **TO WITHSTAND AN EARTHQUAKE.**

Artists created a nearly **10-foot (3-m)-tall trash-breathing dragon** to protest the use of disposable plastic throughout Europe.

THE "GARBAGE FISH" SCULPTURE IN HELSINGØR, DENMARK, IS MADE OUT OF BOTTLES, BAGS, AND OTHER PLASTIC THAT HAS WASHED ASHORE FROM A NEARBY WATERWAY.

DOLPHIN RESCUE

DIVERS TAKE ACTION TO SAVE A DOLPHIN FROM FISHING LINE.

A dozen reef manta rays swim in a group in the open ocean near Hawaii, U.S.A., scooping up plankton in their mouths. Divers direct their lights toward the scene, watching the rays. Amid the action, a male bottlenose dolphin swims slowly through the group. The dolphin catches the divers' attention. He's alone, which is unusual since most dolphins travel in small pods, plus he doesn't seem to be afraid of the noises that the divers are making.

The dolphin passes back and forth in front of the divers a few times, as if to get their attention. "We usually don't interact with wild animals," underwater camera operator Martina Wing says. "But this dolphin was trying to show us that he had a problem." The dolphin, later given the name Notch, is tightly tangled in fishing line.

OPEN-OCEAN TRASH

Bottlenose dolphins live in almost all of the world's oceans. Plastic can be found at every level of *every*

ocean. Light plastic floats on the ocean's surface, while heavier plastic typically sinks to the very bottom—but a lot of plastic floats somewhere in the middle.

This garbage is carried through the oceans by wind and water currents, often ending up swirling in one of five garbage patches around the world created by circular ocean currents called gyres. The biggest of these is the Great Pacific Garbage Patch (see pages 22–23). By weight, the most common item in the garbage patch is abandoned fishing gear—the stuff that's entangling Notch.

SWIMMING FREE

The divers look closer and see that Notch has a hook stuck in his left fin and fishing line wrapped around his mouth. A diver tries to use his bare hands to unwind the plastic line from the dolphin's body, but the string is hard to remove. Luckily, the diver has a pair of scissors and uses them to snip the line. The dolphin waits patiently for the diver to carefully remove the hook next. "He seemed so relieved when he was finally free," Wing says.

A year later, a group of snorkelers spots a healthy-looking Notch swimming with a potential mate. "I'm so glad we were able to rescue him," Wing says. "And now maybe he's going to have a family of his own."

SNIP AND SAVE

DIVER KELLER LAROS USES SCISSORS TO CAREFULLY REMOVE PLASTIC FISHING LINE AND A HOOK LODGED IN THE DOLPHIN'S LEFT FIN.

Bottlenose dolphins shed their outermost layer of skin every two hours.

THE OCEAN COVERS MORE THAN 70 PERCENT OF EARTH'S SURFACE. ABOUT 97 PERCENT OF THE PLANET'S WATER IS IN THE OCEAN.

BOTTLENOSE DOLPHIN
Off the coast of Kailua-Kona, Hawaii

NORTH AMERICA
EUROPE
ASIA
ATLANTIC OCEAN
PACIFIC OCEAN
AFRICA
PACIFIC OCEAN
SOUTH AMERICA
INDIAN OCEAN
AUSTRALIA
SOUTHERN OCEAN
ANTARCTICA

POLLUTION SOLUTION

CATCH THE TRASH

HOW DO YOU SCOOP UP A LOT OF TRASH? With a really big contraption. Like, *really* big. The first Ocean Cleanup system was a 2,000-foot (610-m)-long U-shaped pipe with an attached netlike skirt. Set afloat in the Pacific Ocean in mid-2019, the system used ocean currents and wind to gather up trash from the surface down to 10 feet (3 m) below the structure. Eventually, boats will come to collect the trash from the skirt and bring it back to shore, where it can be recycled. The Ocean Cleanup organization hopes to launch more sea sweepers around the world to remove up to 90 percent of floating ocean plastic by 2040.

Experts think 8.8 million tons (8 million t) of plastic enter the ocean every year.

By 2050, scientists think that the amount of plastic in the ocean might triple.

FLOATING PLASTIC COLLECTOR

DIY Granola Bar Goodies

Plastic food wrappers, like the ones on store-bought granola bars, are a common sight at beach cleanups. Here's a sweet solution: Help keep Earth healthy by ditching the plastic-wrapped snacks and making your own granola bars instead.

PLANET PROTECTOR TIP
Wrap your granola bars in paper or cloth instead of plastic wrap for an on-the-go treat.

YOU'LL NEED

- Medium-size mixing bowl
- Spoon
- 1½ cups (190 g) old-fashioned oats
- 1½ cups (190 g) puffed rice cereal
- ½ cup (65 g) roasted, unsalted sunflower seeds
- ½ teaspoon (1.3 mL) cinnamon
- 1 cup (125 g) brown sugar
- ½ cup (65 g) honey
- Medium-size pot
- 3 tablespoons (45 mL) vegetable oil
- ¼ teaspoon (2.5 mL) salt
- ½ teaspoon (1.3 mL) vanilla extract
- ¼ cup (32 g) chocolate chips
- Wax paper
- Square glass baking pan
- Knife

STEP ONE
Put oats, puffed rice cereal, sunflower seeds, and cinnamon in a mixing bowl and stir with a spoon.

STEP TWO
Grab an adult and combine the brown sugar and honey in a pot.

STEP THREE

Heat the mixture on low and stir for two minutes, or until the mixture is smooth.

STEP FOUR

Mix in oil, salt, and vanilla. Next add the chocolate chips and stir until the chips have completely melted. Then turn off the stove.

STEP FIVE

When the wet mixture in the pot is still warm, pour it into the bowl with the dry ingredients. Stir until the wet and dry ingredients are all combined.

STEP SIX

Place a sheet of wax paper into the glass baking pan so that the paper hangs over the sides of the pan. Pour the mixture on top of the wax paper in the glass pan.

STEP SEVEN

Use your hands to press the granola firmly into the pan. Wait a few hours for the granola to completely cool. (You can put the pan in the refrigerator to cool it more quickly.)

STEP EIGHT

When the granola mixture is fully cooled, carefully lift the wax paper out of the glass pan. Then ask an adult to help cut the snack into bars or bite-size squares. **Enjoy!**

QUIZ WHIZ

What's your eco-friendly IQ? Find out with this quiz!

Write your answers on a piece of paper. Then check them below.

1 **True or false?** Roughly 2 percent of plastics are burned, instead of being recycled or sent to landfills.

2 **Which kind of reusable bottle has a special insulation to keep your drink hot or cold longer?**
a. stainless steel
b. reusable plastic
c. glass
d. aluminum

3 **_____, the most common item by weight in the Great Pacific Garbage Patch, can entangle dolphins as they swim underwater.**
a. single-use straws
b. disposable bags
c. fishing gear
d. milk jugs

4 **One artist made a suit from see-through plastic bags and filled them with all the trash he produced over the course of a _____.**
a. day
b. week
c. month
d. year

5 **True or false?** Wrapping homemade treats such as granola bars in paper or cloth instead of plastic wrap can help prevent plastic food wrappers from reaching the ocean.

Not **STUMPED** yet? Check out the _NATIONAL GEOGRAPHIC KIDS QUIZ WHIZ_ collection for more crazy **ENVIRONMENT** questions!

ANSWERS: 1. False: Roughly 19 percent of plastic is burned.; 2. a; 3. c; 4. c; 5. True

32

Write a Letter That Gets Results

Knowing how to write a good letter is a useful skill. It will come in handy when you want to persuade someone to understand your point of view. Whether you're emailing your congressperson or writing a letter for a school project or to your grandma, a great letter will help you get your message across. Most important, a well-written letter makes a good impression.

CHECK OUT THE EXAMPLE BELOW FOR THE ELEMENTS OF A GOOD LETTER.

Your address

Date

Salutation
Always use "Dear" followed by the person's name; use Mr., Mrs., Ms., or Dr. as appropriate.

Introductory paragraph
Give the reason you're writing the letter.

Body
The longest part of the letter, which provides evidence that supports your position. Be persuasive!

Closing paragraph
Sum up your argument.

Complimentary closing
Sign off with "Sincerely" or "Thank you."

Your signature

Maddie Smith
1234 Main Street
Peoria, Illinois 61525

April 22, 2024

Dear Owner of the Happy Hamburger,

I am writing to ask you to stop using single-use plastic at the Happy Hamburger.

This is my favorite restaurant. My family and I eat there almost every Saturday night. I always order the bacon cheeseburger with mac and cheese on the side. It's my favorite meal, ever!

The other day, my dad brought home a to-go order from your restaurant. The order contained a plastic fork, knife, and spoon, all wrapped in plastic. It also came in a plastic bag. Now that's a lot of plastic!

I am concerned because plastic is a huge problem for the planet. Did you know that nine million tons of plastic waste end up in the ocean every year? Even worse, scientists think that the amount of plastic might triple by 2050.

Some other restaurants in town have cut back on their single-use plastic. The Hotdog Hangout uses paper bags instead of plastic bags for takeout. And servers at the Weeping Onion ask customers if they'd like plastic cutlery, instead of automatically including it in to-go orders.

These are simple changes that I hope you can make at the Happy Hamburger. That way, not only would you be serving the best burgers around, but you'd also be helping to protect the planet.

Thank you very much for your time.

Sincerely,

Maddie Smith

Maddie Smith

COMPLIMENTARY CLOSINGS

Sincerely, Sincerely yours, Thank you, Regards, Best wishes, Respectfully

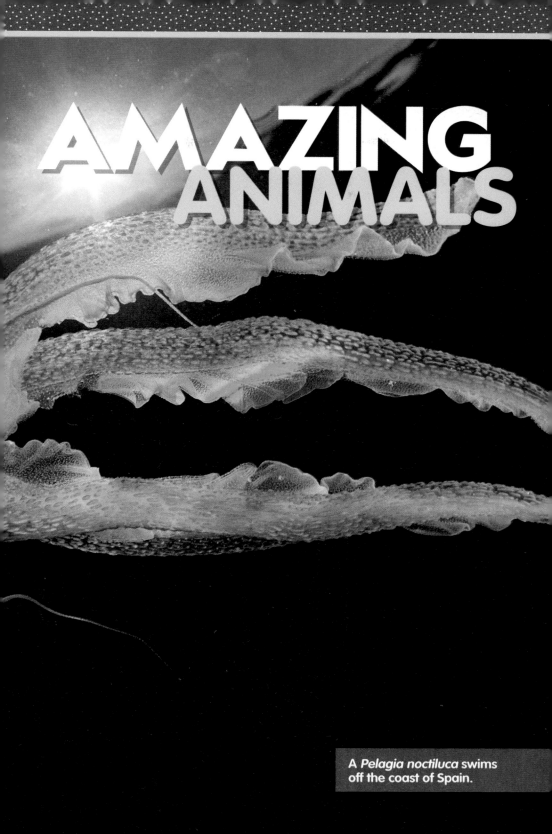

AMAZING ANIMALS

A *Pelagia noctiluca* swims off the coast of Spain.

EXTRAORDINARY ANIMALS

Dog Fetches Ocean Trash

Boca Raton, Florida, U.S.A.
Lila the Labrador jumps off her owner's boat and dives into the seawater. When she resurfaces, she has a glass bottle in her mouth. Good dog!

The Lab often joins her owner's cleanup crew when they pick up trash on local beaches and in the water. "I usually just say 'Go get it, Lila!' and she'll run off to pick up the trash," says owner Alex Schulze, who co-founded a company called 4ocean that sells bracelets made of recycled materials.

Lila usually collects a few pounds of trash when they walk the beach. On the boat, she barks to let Schulze know that she sees something before diving in.

As a puppy, Lila loved retrieving things, even swimming to the bottom of the family pool to try to fetch the drain cover, Schulze says. To train her, first he took a tennis ball in the pool and walked with it into deeper water to get her comfortable. Eventually, they played fetch. "And then she was catching toys way in the deep end."

MY EARS ARE POPPING.

LILA DIVES FOR A GLASS BOTTLE ON THE SEAFLOOR.

GLASS BOTTLE

LILA SWIMS BACK TO THE BOAT WITH A PIECE OF TRASH.

HOME IS WHERE THE SHELL IS.

THIS HERMIT CRAB IN THE ANDAMAN ISLANDS (NEAR THAILAND) USED A BROKEN GLASS BOTTLE FOR A SHELL.

A HERMIT CRAB HANGS OUT IN AN EMPTY SEA-SNAIL SHELL, ITS NATURAL HOME.

Shell-come Home, Hermit Crabs!

Mu Ko Lanta Marine National Park, Thailand
At first, hermit crabs thought this beach was *claw*-some. Tens of thousands of land hermit crabs swarmed the sand after tourists disappeared during the COVID-19 pandemic shutdown. But soon the crabs were in trouble. "Hermit crabs can't create their own shells," zoologist Niki Khan says. "So they use leftover shells from sea snails."

But with so many hermit crabs skittering on the beach, sea-snail shells became scarce.

Plus, earlier visitors had taken shells from the beach as souvenirs. So some hermit crabs were using plastic and other trash to protect themselves.

That's when park rangers and local residents came to the rescue. After rangers asked people to donate shells they had at home, about 440 pounds (200 kg) of new shell homes suddenly appeared under rocks, near tree trunks, and along the shoreline—right where the crabs could find them. Folks also organized beach cleanups to help the hermit crabs feel more at home. Nice *shell*-ter!

Monkey Takes Selfies

NO FILTER NEEDED!

Batu Pahat, Malaysia
One night, a thief sneaked through an open window at Zackrydz Rodzi's house and took one thing: his cell phone.

Rodzi used another phone to call his number and followed the ring into the forest beyond his backyard until he found his muddy phone on the ground. Then he opened the photo gallery to discover that the burglar had taken hundreds of pictures of itself. "I was shocked, and then I laughed," Rodzi says. The culprit? A long-tailed macaque. "Who knew a monkey could take a selfie?" he says.

Rodzi doesn't typically see monkeys near his house, but living so close to the jungle means that humans and animals share space. "Monkeys consider anywhere with trees their territory," says Cherish Smith of the Jungle Friends Primate Sanctuary. "And they like to play with human things like stuffed animals and toys." Now Rodzi has the coolest camera roll ever.

Rabbits Uncover Ancient Treasure

SORRY MY SMOOCHES ARE SANDY!

LINED ETCHINGS DECORATE THE POTTERY (TOP). THE STONE TOOL MIGHT'VE BEEN USED TO CRUSH SHELLFISH.

THESE ARTIFACTS WERE FOUND OUTSIDE THIS BURROW.

SKOKHOLM ISLAND, WALES

These bunnies are hopping right into the history books.

The European rabbits were digging out a burrow when they kicked up two ancient artifacts: a 3,750-year-old pottery shard from a burial urn and a 9,000-year-old tool that might've been used to prepare food. The island's wardens spied the goodies at the entrance of the burrow, then sent pictures to a local archaeologist. Turns out, the bunnies had made a big find.

"These are the first ancient tools found on this island," archaeologist Toby Driver says.

"So overnight, these rabbits changed our understanding to show that prehistoric people were visiting or living on this remote spot."

Rabbits dig burrows to protect themselves and their babies from predators and harsh weather. Experts think the bunnies accidentally dug into an ancient burial mound that was built on top of an even older hunter-gatherer site. But these hoppers aren't always hard workers. "They love to sunbathe on the grassy plains with their legs stretched out behind them," island warden Giselle Eagle says. Thanks, furry archaeologists!

ANIMAL MYTHS BUSTED

Some people mistakenly think adult opossums hang by their tails or that porcupines shoot their quills. What other misconceptions are out there? Here are some common animal myths.

MYTH Elephants are afraid of mice.

HOW IT MAY HAVE STARTED People used to think that mice liked to crawl into elephants' trunks, which could cause damage and terrible sneezing. So it makes sense that elephants would be afraid of the rodents.

WHY IT'S NOT TRUE An elephant's eyesight is so poor that it could barely even see a mouse. Plus, an elephant isn't afraid to live among predators such as tigers, rhinos, and crocodiles, so a mouse would be the least of its worries!

Who are you again?

MYTH Goldfish only have a three-second memory.

HOW IT MAY HAVE STARTED While an adult human's brain weighs about three pounds (1.4 kg), an average goldfish's brain weighs only a tiny fraction of that. So how could there be any room for memory in there?

WHY IT'S NOT TRUE Research has shown that goldfish are quite smart. Phil Gee of the University of Plymouth in the United Kingdom trained goldfish to push a lever that dropped food into their tank. "They remembered the time of day that the lever worked and waited until feeding time to press it," Gee says. One scientist even trained goldfish to tell the difference between classical and blues music!

MYTH Touching a frog or toad will give you warts.

HOW IT MAY HAVE STARTED Many frogs and toads have bumps on their skin that look like warts. Some people think the bumps are contagious.

WHY IT'S NOT TRUE "Warts are caused by a human virus, not frogs or toads," said dermatologist Jerry Litt. But the wart-like bumps behind a toad's ears *can* be dangerous. These parotoid glands contain a nasty poison that irritates the mouths of some predators and often the skin of humans. So toads may not cause warts, but they can cause other irritations. It's best not to handle these critters—warty or not!

BIG WART

WARTS

Cute Animal
SUPERLATIVES

Funky features. Super senses. Sensational speed. No doubt, all animals are cool. But whether they've got goofy grins, funky hair, or endless energy, some species are extra adorable. Here are 15 of the cutest creatures on Earth.

BEST FUZZ

What's all the fuzz about? A snowy egret chick is born with a cap of soft, frizzy feathers. As it grows, the fuzz transforms into long, feathery plumes in a bright white hue, which gives the large bird—native to the coastlands of North and South America—its name.

BEST BREAKTHROUGH

Here's the *tooth* about baby turtles: These reptiles are born with temporary appendages called carbuncles, or egg teeth. They're sharp enough to crack the shells and help turtles break free from their eggs on their own. Once the turtles hatch, they will eventually lose the egg teeth.

MOST COLORFUL

The rainbow finch's funky feathers make this bird a standout on the grasslands of Australia. The hue of its head, which can be black, yellow, red, and orange, varies from bird to bird.

BEST TEAMWORK

High five! Meerkat pups often bond soon after birth and spend most of their time together exploring their environment and playing. Native to Africa's Kalahari Desert, the extremely social animals are super supportive of one another, with a community working together to share the load of raising and protecting their pups.

BEST COAT

Blizzard in the forecast? *Snow* problem! The golden snub-nosed monkey, found high in the mountains of central China, has a thick, furry coat and tail. They keep it warm in winter, making this primate ready for any weather.

BEST SPIKES

The lowland streaked tenrec may be tiny, but its spiky exterior poses a big threat to predators. Found only in Madagascar, this mini mammal is about the size of a hedgehog and will shoot its barbs into an animal when under attack.

BEST NAPPER

Tigers love their catnaps! In fact, the animals snooze some 18 hours a day—snagging z's whenever and wherever they can. Why so sleepy? The big cats usually rest after a big meal, which helps them conserve energy for their next hunt. Once they're up, they're recharged and ready to go.

LONGEST DROP

Talk about a grand entrance: A baby giraffe falls about six feet (1.8 m) from its mom during birth before hitting the ground.

GREAT GLIDER

A Siberian flying squirrel can catch some major air. Using a flap of skin that stretches between its forelegs and hind legs like a parachute and its long, flat tail to balance, the squirrel can cover the length of a football field in one giant leap.

EARLY WALKER

Found in northern Canada, Greenland, Russia, Scandinavia, and Alaska, U.S.A., the sure-footed muskox can stand up, follow its mom, and keep up with its herd just hours after being born. This early start keeps the calf protected from potential predators.

BEST TRANSFORMATION

Think pink! The rosy maple moth may wind up with coloring that looks a lot like a fuzzy pink and yellow tennis ball, but it doesn't begin that way. It actually starts out as a caterpillar known as the greenstriped mapleworm.

BEST NUZZLER

Rabbits have the sweetest way to say they're sorry: nuzzling noses! Researchers say that if a pair of bonded bunnies has a falling out, one will rub noses with the other to apologize and end the spat. Bunnies also touch noses to communicate with one another or to sniff out a new scent.

BEST SPOTS

Ladybugs' spots aren't just there to look cool: Their colorful exteriors double as a warning for predators like birds, frogs, wasps, spiders, and dragonflies that they taste terrible. And they actually do, thanks to an icky fluid ladybugs release from their legs when threatened.

BEST GRIP

Tree frogs just love hanging around! When the agile amphibians leap from branch to branch in their rainforest habitat, they rely on their lightning-quick reflexes, long limbs, and super-strong grip to, well, hang on. A sticky substance on their toe pads also helps the frogs get a good grasp.

SWEETEST RIDE

When common loon chicks hatch, they're almost immediately on the go—Mom carries her little ones on her back to protect them from predators. Once grown, loons can dive nearly 250 feet (76 m) and hold their breath for up to eight minutes as they fish.

WHAT IS
Taxonomy?

Because our planet has billions and billions of living things called organisms, people need a way of classifying them. Scientists created a system called taxonomy, which helps to classify all living things into ordered groups. By putting organisms into categories, we are better able to understand how they are the same and how they are different. There are eight levels of taxonomic classification, beginning with the broadest group, called a domain, followed by kingdom, down to the most specific group, called a species.

Biologists divide life based on evolutionary history, and they place organisms into three domains depending on their genetic structure: Archaea, Bacteria, and Eukarya. (See page 197 for "The Three Domains of Life.")

Where do animals come in?

Animals are a part of the Eukarya domain, which means they are organisms made of cells with nuclei. More than one million species of animals, including humans, have been named. Like all living things, animals can be divided into smaller groups, called phyla. Most scientists believe there are more than 30 phyla into which animals can be grouped based on certain scientific criteria, such as body type or whether or not the animal has a backbone. It can be pretty complicated, so another, less complicated system is used to group animals into two categories: vertebrates and invertebrates.

HEDGEHOG

SAMPLE CLASSIFICATION
RED PANDA

Domain:	Eukarya
Kingdom:	Animalia
Phylum:	Chordata
Class:	Mammalia
Order:	Carnivora
Family:	Ailuridae
Genus:	*Ailurus*
Species:	*fulgens*

TIP:
Here's a sentence to help you remember the classification order:
Did King Phillip Come Over For Good Soup?

BY THE NUMBERS

There are 16,720 vulnerable or endangered animal species in the world. The list includes:

• **1,337 mammals,** such as the snow leopard, the polar bear, and the fishing cat

• **1,409 birds,** including the Steller's sea eagle and the black-banded plover

• **3,548 fish,** such as the Mekong giant catfish

• **1,845 reptiles,** including the Round Island day gecko

• **2,291 insects,** such as the Macedonian grayling

• **2,515 amphibians,** such as the emperor newt

• **And more,** including 251 arachnids, 745 crustaceans, 235 sea anemones and corals, 214 bivalves, and 2,384 snails and slugs

ROUND ISLAND DAY GECKO

Vertebrates
Animals WITH Backbones

Fish are cold-blooded and live in water. They breathe with gills, lay eggs, and usually have scales.

Amphibians are cold-blooded. Their young live in water and breathe with gills. Adults live on land and breathe with lungs.

Reptiles are cold-blooded and breathe with lungs. They live both on land and in water.

Birds are warm-blooded and have feathers and wings. They lay eggs, breathe with lungs, and are usually able to fly. Some birds live on land, some in water, and some on both.

Mammals are warm-blooded and feed on their mothers' milk. They also have skin that is usually covered with hair. Mammals live both on land and in water.

BIRD: MANDARIN DUCK

AMPHIBIAN: POISON DART FROG

Invertebrates
Animals WITHOUT Backbones

Sponges are a very basic form of animal life. They live in water and do not move on their own.

Echinoderms have external skeletons and live in seawater.

Mollusks have soft bodies and can live either in or out of shells, on land or in water.

Arthropods are the largest group of animals. They have external skeletons, called exoskeletons, and segmented bodies with appendages. Arthropods live in water and on land.

Worms are soft-bodied animals with no true legs. Worms live in soil.

Cnidaria live in water and have mouths surrounded by tentacles.

MOLLUSK: MAGNIFICENT CHROMODORIS NUDIBRANCH

SPONGE: SEA SPONGE

ARTHROPOD: PRAYING MANTIS

Cold-Blooded versus Warm-Blooded

Cold-blooded animals, also called ectotherms, get their heat from outside their bodies.

Warm-blooded animals, also called endotherms, keep their body temperatures level regardless of the temperature of their environment.

COMEBACK CRITTER:

GOLDEN LION TAMARIN

Scientists help these primates reclaim their forest home.

A family of golden lion tamarins is on the move. With two babies on his back and his mate beside him, the father tamarin reaches for a branch in Brazil's Atlantic Forest. Just a few years ago, this land was a treeless cattle pasture. But conservationists knew that if more forest was lost, then the golden lion tamarins—which live wild nowhere else on Earth—would be gone, too.

DISAPPEARING FORESTS

The Atlantic Forest was once about the size of Egypt. But in the 1500s, European traders and settlers started cutting down the trees to build ships and make room for settlements. Then, over the past century, farmers cut down more trees to clear land for crops until the forest was less than 10 percent of its original size.

Golden lion tamarins spend most of their time in the tree canopy, using branches to travel in search of food and mates. As the forest shrank, habitats became cut off from each other—and so did the primates. By the 1970s, concerned biologists estimated that only about 200 golden lion tamarins were left in the Atlantic Forest.

MONKEY BOOT CAMP

Conservationists gathered at the Smithsonian's National Zoo in Washington, D.C., in 1972 to develop a plan to save the species in the wild. Some zoos already had golden lion tamarins in captivity; all they had to do was breed more tamarins, then prepare some of the families to return to the wild. How? "We sent them to boot camp," says Kenton Kerns, assistant curator of small mammals at the National Zoo.

During several summers following 1972, zookeepers around the world let tamarins out of their enclosures to hang out in the trees. Staff provided each family with a nest to sleep in and sweet potatoes to munch on, and kept watch to

An adult golden lion tamarin is about the size of a squirrel.

GOLDEN LION TAMARIN FATHERS OFTEN CARRY THEIR BABIES ON THEIR BACKS IN BETWEEN FEEDINGS.

GOLDEN LION TAMARIN TWINS HANG ON TO THEIR FATHER AT GERMANY'S DUISBURG ZOO.

Where golden lion tamarins live

BRAZIL

BRAZIL

ATLANTIC OCEAN

ATLANTIC OCEAN

The golden lion tamarin is featured on a banknote in Brazil.

A GOLDEN LION TAMARIN LEAPS FROM ONE BRANCH TO ANOTHER IN ITS BRAZILIAN FOREST HOME.

make sure they didn't leave the grounds. "The free-range lifestyle taught the tamarins how to find insects and navigate branches," Kerns says. In 1983, the first group of tamarins was ready to return to Brazil's forests.

While the monkeys were in training, Brazil's Golden Lion Tamarin Association was busy restoring the tamarins' habitat. The group bought land from private owners and worked with farmers to plant trees on their property, connecting patches of forest and protecting more than 40 square miles (103 sq km) of habitat. The organization also gave local citizens jobs managing tree nurseries and trained teachers on environmental issues. "People were proud to have tamarins on their land," says Denise Rambaldi, former director of the Golden Lion Tamarin Association.

GOING GREEN

A few thousand golden lion tamarins now live in the Atlantic Forest. About a third of them are descended from 147 captive-born tamarins from the zoo program.

But conservationists aren't done. They continue to reforest the land and inspire young people to protect the animals. Says Lou Ann Dietz, founding director of Save the Golden Lion Tamarin: "Seeing tamarin families chirping and jumping around in the trees overhead, their fur reflecting the sunlight like fire, makes it all worth it."

Giraffe on a Raft

How conservationists rescued
giraffes stuck on
a flooding island

Trapped Eight near-threatened Rothschild's giraffes—a subspecies of northern giraffes—were living on a small island in the middle of a lake in Kenya, a country in East Africa. But heavy rains caused the lake's water level to rise rapidly and flood the island, leaving the giraffes with little land to roam. One female named Asiwa was marooned on a small sliver of land. "Since giraffes can't swim, Asiwa was stuck," says David O'Connor, president of the conservation organization Save Giraffes Now. The other giraffes weren't in as much danger. "Asiwa was the most vulnerable, so she was our first priority," he says.

Constructing a _Gir_-raft
Conservationists realized the only way to get Asiwa back to the mainland was by boat—or better yet, a custom-made raft that would be the perfect size to fit a giant animal. Local craftspeople went to work on something tall enough to hold an adult-size giraffe. The solution was a strong steel pen welded to the top of 60 floating barrels.

All Aboard Now the rescue team had to figure out how to convince Asiwa to get on the raft. They came up with a clever idea: delicious mangoes the workers hoped she would follow to the boat like a trail of bread crumbs. But Asiwa didn't follow them very far. "She was still wary of the barge," O'Connor says. So the team sedated the giraffe with a tranquilizer dart, blindfolded her to keep her calm, and then guided her with ropes onto the raft. "She walked like a puppy on a leash right onto the barge," O'Connor says.

FLOODED ISLAND

Setting Sail Asiwa had never been on a boat before (obviously!), so the rescuers were worried she might panic and kick during the one-hour trip. But it was smooth sailing. "She was well-behaved during the voyage," O'Connor says. "The sail across the lake was very peaceful."

Home Sweet Home After the raft reached the shore, workers removed Asiwa's blindfold and opened her pen. Then she walked into her new home—the Ruko Community Conservancy, which includes a 4,400-acre (1,781-ha) giraffe sanctuary. "To go from living on less than one acre to having 4,400 acres to roam is incredible," O'Connor says. "Asiwa's finally safe." More good news: All of her friends from the island have now joined her at the sanctuary.

So. Many. Penguins!

A newly discovered giant colony

helps scientists understand why **Adélies** rule the roost.

ADÉLIE PENGUINS LIVE IN ANTARCTICA, THE DRIEST, COLDEST, AND WINDIEST CONTINENT ON EARTH.

Just two penguin species live only in Antarctica: Adélies and emperor penguins.

Squawk! Gurgle! Honk!

Along the bustling "highways" crisscrossing Antarctica's Danger Islands, more than a million Adélie penguins waddle to and from the ocean. It's a lot of traffic and noise—but until recently scientists didn't even know this metropolis existed.

That is, until penguin poop helped them find it.

Few people have ever explored the Danger Islands. Researchers could never get close enough because of heavy sea ice that could trap their boats. So no one really knew how much wildlife was there.

Then satellite imagery from space spotted guano, or poop, stains on the islands, hinting that a large number of penguins might be present.

"Penguin guano is a pinkish red color and looks like practically nothing else in the Antarctic," ecologist Heather Lynch says. "Once we viewed the images, we figured there had to be penguins on the Danger Islands."

Then Lynch's team got another surprise: The Danger Islands are home to more than 1.5 million Adélie penguins.

Before the discovery, scientists had been concerned that Adélies were disappearing, possibly because of climate change. But now that they've uncovered this super colony, the known Adélie population in Antarctica is not only thriving, but super busy, too.

PENGUIN LIFE

Throughout the year, Adélies log more than 8,000 miles (12,875 km) on the "road" commuting back and forth from their nests to the ocean to hunt for krill, squid, lanternfish, or jellyfish for dinner. With so many residents on the move, traffic can be tricky.

"The Adélies have fairly distinct highways," seabird ecologist Barbara Wienecke says. "The paths get incredibly congested, so like humans, the birds sometimes have to take detours to avoid getting stuck in traffic."

And like a bustling city, the noise never stops. Adélie chicks and parents identify each other mostly by sound—not by sight. So they squawk on their commute to let their family know they're coming back from fishing for the day. And if they've been away on a long hunting trip, each bird sings a unique hum to make sure they've found the correct partner.

The chatter isn't all sweet, though.

"If a neighbor gets too close, an Adélie can sound a nest alarm by making loud, sharp calls, which basically mean 'This is my nest! Go away!'" Wienecke says.

And don't forget the splat sounds they make while pooping. Adélies go often, and even all over each other! They're not trying to hit each other, though—the wind tends to blow the guano toward other nests.

NOSY NEIGHBORS

All that noise can be distracting, but Adélies have to stay focused to prevent a big-city theft of their valuables—that is, their pebbles.

Penguins use the small rocks to build nests for their chicks. Because pebbles can be scarce on the island, one Adélie might swipe a few stones from another. In rare cases, if the parents and chicks are away from the nest, a nonbreeding neighbor might try to steal the entire nest and connect it to their own nest to build an even bigger home. The birds fight back against these intruders by biting them

ADÉLIES DIVE FOR FOOD TO FEED THEMSELVES AND THEIR CHICKS.

or slapping them with their wings to scare them off.

Despite squabbles, neighbors can be helpful. "When the nests are all built within pecking distance of each other, it makes it harder for predatory seabirds like south polar skuas and giant petrels to target the colony," Wienecke says. "If they did, they'd have a lot of Adélies banding together against them."

Scientists have gotten involved to protect Adélies, too. "Since our expedition, a proposed marine protected area was expanded to include the Danger Islands," Lynch says. "And in the meantime, the area's dangerous sea ice will likely keep out most of the people curious about the Adélie penguins."

That way, penguin cities can keep hustling, bustling, and making noise for years to come.

Emperors reach nearly four feet (1.2 m) tall and can weigh up to 50 pounds (23 kg); Adélies only stand up to two feet (0.6 m) tall and weigh about 10 pounds (5 kg).

MORE THAN 1.5 MILLION ADÉLIE PENGUINS LIVE IN THIS CROWDED COLONY ON THE DANGER ISLANDS.

Seals Solve Ocean Mysteries

ANTARCTICA

These researchers don't need beakers or lab coats—they're seals!

Scientists wanted to collect hard-to-get data that might provide clues to science mysteries, like how climate change is affecting the ocean and the animals that live there. So an international team enlisted the help of Weddell and southern elephant seals.

First, researchers harmlessly glued sensors to the seals' heads that monitored behavior, location, water temperature, and the amount of salt in the water. Then the seals swam away, diving up to 6,500 feet (1,981 km) under the sea ice for up to 90 minutes at a time while the sensors transmitted the data. (The trackers fell off later.)

"They can go where boats and scientists can't," Antarctic marine ecologist Sara Labrousse says.

The information has helped scientists learn more about how animals and their prey are affected by changes in the ocean—and even why mysterious holes in sea ice are appearing. "We don't have a lot of data beneath the sea ice, so it's very precious information," Labrousse says. We'd give these seals an A+ in science class.

DO I HAVE SOMETHING ON MY HEAD?

A WEDDELL SEAL SPORTS A SCIENTIFIC SENSOR.

WEDDELL SEAL

4 GNARLY NUDIBRANCHS

1 YOU ARE WHAT YOU EAT

Near the rocky shores of California, U.S.A., and Mexico's Baja California, a neon **Spanish shawl** nudibranch is hard to miss crawling on corals or fluttering through open water. This flashy finger-length slug gets its bright color by recycling pigments from its favorite food, tiny plantlike jellyfish known as hydroids.

LIKE OYSTERS AND CLAMS, NUDIBRANCHS ARE MOLLUSKS. BUT THESE SEA SLUGS DON'T HAVE SHELLS.

3 PATTERN PLAY

Fluorescent stripes and polka dots turn the **Nembrotha kubaryana**'s costume into a can't-miss warning sign for potential predators. Distinguished by its often orange edging, this nudibranch lives in tropical western Pacific and Indian Ocean waters and can grow up to 4.7 inches (12 cm) long.

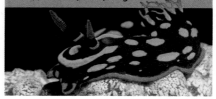

2 DEADLY SURFER

The thumbnail-size **blue dragon** cruises tropical oceans, using a stomach bubble to float on the surface while it searches for its favorite snack: Portuguese man-of-wars. But watch out! The dragon stores the poison it ingests from its prey in the tips of its frilly blue fingers.

4 SPOTS, HORNS, AND WINGS

Its frilly pigtails, mustache, and daisy-shaped spots make **Bornella anguilla** look more like a cartoon character than a pinkie finger–length sea slug. This nudibranch, named for its eel-like way of swimming (*anguilla* means "eel" in Latin), lives in the tropical waters of the western Pacific and Indian Oceans.

UNIC🌙RNS
OF THE SEA

SCIENTISTS TRY TO **SOLVE THE MYSTERY** OF THE NARWHAL'S **GIANT TUSK.**

Chilly water laps against an iceberg in the Arctic Ocean. Suddenly, a pod of narwhals—a species of whale that sports a unicorn-like horn on its head—emerges from the sea near the iceberg's edge.

Narwhals live in the Arctic Ocean. Like most whales, they're jumbo-size—up to 3,500 pounds (1,588 kg)—and surface to breathe. And like some whale species such as orcas, they live in pods. (Narwhals usually have 15 to 20 in a group.) But a narwhal has one thing that no other whale does: a giant tusk growing out of its noggin.

For centuries people have been trying to figure out what this tusk—actually an enlarged tooth—is used for. Scientists have come up with a couple theories that may help solve this gnawing puzzle.

TUSK, TUSK

A narwhal's swordlike tusk first pokes from its jaw through the animal's upper lip when it's about three months old. This is the only tooth the whale develops. Over time, the tusk can grow to be half the length of the whale's body. New research shows that narwhals may use these long appendages to snag prey like arctic cod, using quick jabs to stun the fish before they eat them.

TOOTH SLEUTHS

Another theory is that a male narwhal uses the tooth to attract a female. Similar to a peacock's flashy feathers, the tusk makes the male stand out to potential mates. The animals have been observed scraping their tusks together, as though they are in a fencing match. This may be a way for male members of the pod to identify one another.

There's still plenty that scientists don't know about narwhals, and they will continue to look for answers. In the meantime, it appears that these mysterious whales still have a few secrets up their tusks.

SURFACING ABOVE WATER, A GROUP OF NARWHALS TAKE A BREATH OF AIR.

THIS POD OF MALES SWIMS THROUGH ARCTIC WATERS.

A NARWHAL MOM TRAVELS WITH HER BABY.

GIANTS OF THE DEEP

Some of the world's largest animals live in the ocean.
But just how big can these animals get? Scientists aren't always sure, because some creatures are rare or in hard-to-reach parts of the ocean. Here are measurements for a few of the largest marine species ever discovered (plus a human for comparison).

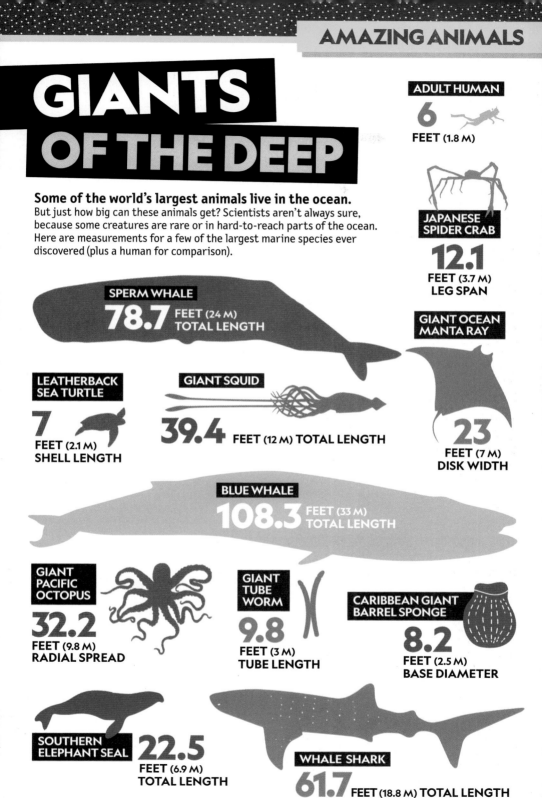

ADULT HUMAN
6 FEET (1.8 M)

JAPANESE SPIDER CRAB
12.1 FEET (3.7 M) LEG SPAN

SPERM WHALE
78.7 FEET (24 M) TOTAL LENGTH

GIANT OCEAN MANTA RAY
23 FEET (7 M) DISK WIDTH

LEATHERBACK SEA TURTLE
7 FEET (2.1 M) SHELL LENGTH

GIANT SQUID
39.4 FEET (12 M) TOTAL LENGTH

BLUE WHALE
108.3 FEET (33 M) TOTAL LENGTH

GIANT PACIFIC OCTOPUS
32.2 FEET (9.8 M) RADIAL SPREAD

GIANT TUBE WORM
9.8 FEET (3 M) TUBE LENGTH

CARIBBEAN GIANT BARREL SPONGE
8.2 FEET (2.5 M) BASE DIAMETER

SOUTHERN ELEPHANT SEAL
22.5 FEET (6.9 M) TOTAL LENGTH

WHALE SHARK
61.7 FEET (18.8 M) TOTAL LENGTH

SharkFest

Dive in to join the party with these 5 surprising sharks.

Not all sharks are gigantic, toothy eating machines. Among the 500 species, there are a few surprising sharks. Some have teeth so small that they can't take a bite out of anything. Others are practically vegetarian! Discover five species of sharks with mind-blowing traits.

A group of sharks is called a shiver.

TWO LEMON SHARKS HANG OUT NEAR THE BAHAMA ISLANDS.

1 Fishy Friends: Lemon Sharks

Love hanging out with your BFF? So do lemon sharks! Young lemon sharks often stick together for protection from larger sharks and other predators. Scientists say this species hangs out with the same friends for years. And when scientists studied the pups in a predator-free environment, these sharks still chose to swim together rather than alone. Maybe these fish need matching friendship bracelets.

2 Green Glowers: Chain Catsharks

WHAT YOU SEE

WHAT CHAIN CATSHARKS SEE

TO CAPTURE THIS IMAGE, SCIENTISTS BUILT A CAMERA THAT SEES THE WORLD LIKE THIS CATSHARK DOES.

Through your eyes, the chain catshark seems to have brownish yellow skin with black chain-shaped markings. But to another chain catshark swimming 1,600 to 2,000 feet (488 to 610 m) below the surface, the fish glows in the dark! Pigments in the sharks' skin absorb the blue light in the ocean and reflect it as green. These sharks have special cells in their eyes—called receptors—to see it. Because the glow patterns are different for males and females, scientists think these shy sharks use this ability to attract mates.

3 Salad Snackers: Bonnethead Sharks

Bonnethead sharks love their greens. Unlike almost all other sharks, which are carnivores, the bonnetheads' digestive system allows them to absorb nutrients from plants. Scientists aren't sure if bonnetheads intentionally snack on plants, or if they're accidentally ingested while scooping up shellfish hiding in the seagrass.

A BONNETHEAD SHARK EXPLORES THE WATERS OF THE FLORIDA KEYS, U.S.A.

4 Ocean Oldies: Greenland Sharks

A Greenland shark swimming through deep, freezing Arctic water today might have been born when George Washington became the first president of the United States! This shark species can live for nearly 300 years—and possibly as many as 500 years. That's the longest of any vertebrate (an animal with a backbone). Experts think their icy cold habitat and slow lifestyle (a Greenland shark's heart beats only once every 12 seconds; yours beats about once a second) might be their secret to growing seriously old.

A GREENLAND SHARK SWIMS BELOW THE ARCTIC OCEAN ICE, OFF THE COAST OF CANADA.

Sharks have been on Earth longer than trees.

5 Gentle Giants: Whale Sharks

Sharks are relatives of manta rays.

A whale shark's mouth is so wide that a 10-year-old kid could fit inside. But don't worry: These easygoing sharks stick to a diet of tiny shrimplike plankton about as small as a few grains of sand. The largest fish in the world, whale sharks can be longer than a school bus and weigh 50,000 pounds (22,680 kg). They feed by swimming slowly with their mouths open, filtering plants and animals from the water.

A WHALE SHARK WITH ITS MOUTH OPEN SWIMS AMONG REMORA FISH.

PINK POWER

Flamingos are some of the toughest birds on Earth!

Think flamingos are pushovers? Think again: They might be the most extreme birds in the animal kingdom!

"Their pink color and wobbly-looking legs can cause people to assume they're kind of dainty," says Felicity Arengo, a flamingo researcher at the American Museum of Natural History. "But flamingos are actually much tougher than they look." Check out these five adaptations to decide.

They Have a Leg Up

Lake Natron in Tanzania, a country in East Africa, is loaded with corrosive chemicals that could burn off human skin. It's a watery graveyard for many of the other birds that land there. (Animals that perish in the lake are gradually mummified.)

But flamingos can wade in the water all day. Their fragile-looking, stilt-like legs are covered in armor—hundreds of hard, flexible scales atop their thick, leathery skin. This thick covering protects the birds when they're in toxic waterways all over the world.

Their Beaks Have Impressive Bites

Like the ocean's largest whales, flamingos are filter feeders. But instead of swimming for their dinners, they just kick the mud where food—like brine shrimp, algae, and fly larvae—lives, dip their heads, and slurp up their meals. Unlike humans, both their lower and upper jaws move, allowing the birds to open and shut their mouths rapidly—as fast as 20 times a second—which pumps food-filled water inside their beaks. A short, comb-like structure running along the edge of their beaks keeps large

The black feathers under a flamingo's wings can be seen only when the birds are flying.

AN AMERICAN FLAMINGO PREPARES TO FEED ITS THREE-DAY-OLD CHICK.

A group of flamingos is called a flamboyance or a stand.

THREE AMERICAN FLAMINGOS WALK THROUGH A BREEDING COLONY NEAR THE GULF OF MEXICO.

particles out, while another strainer around their tongues captures the tasty tidbits. Yum!

They Can Drink Anything

Flamingos can be found on every continent except Australia and Antarctica. Most of the birds live in supersalty lakes, marshes, and lagoons. And some of those water habitats are fed by near-boiling hot springs. So what do flamingos drink? Salt water—minus the salt.

Located in their heads, tiny organs called salt glands filter out the salt from the water they sip, then the salt discharges through their nostrils. Even species that live in deserts, like the Chilean flamingo, have this adaptation to drink from pools in salt flats.

When it comes to freshwater, flamingos can safely guzzle from hot springs, which reach temperatures up to 140°F (60°C). How? Experts think it has something to do with extra-tough linings all flamingos have in their mouths and

throats. Scientists have also discovered blood vessels in the birds' heads that might help them regulate their body temperature by shedding the heat they swallow, sort of like how a car's radiator helps get rid of excess heat from the engine.

They Don't Get Cold Feet

If humans doze off in freezing water, they will suffer frostbite—or worse. Not flamingos. The birds simply break their feet free from the ice, then bury their beaks in the icy water to snack. In fact, some flamingos only leave for warmer areas when the ice gets too thick to feed. Experts think the same armor that protects the flamingos in corrosive water likely helps them handle icy conditions as well—as does their ability to regulate their body temperature.

Their Nests Are Like Little Castles

Flamingoes make dome-like mud nests in the middle of corrosive waters. This helps keep their single eggs—and later, their chicks—safe from predators. The mounds also keep everything mostly dry when rain raises the water level.

After chicks hatch, they're watched over by babysitters in flamingo nurseries so the parents can feed. Away from the nests, juvenile and adult flamingos stick together in large flocks, which confuses predators trying to pick a target among the wall of pink. Proving that these birds aren't just tough—they're smart, too.

A COLONY OF AMERICAN FLAMINGOS NESTS IN THE YUCATÁN PENINSULA IN MEXICO.

A RED-EYED TREE FROG SITS ON A PLANT SHOOT IN THE CENTRAL AMERICAN COUNTRY OF COSTA RICA.

Earth is home to more than 6,000 species of frogs, many of which aren't much bigger than a coin. But these small amphibians possess some big surprises. Check out how five frogs use everything from their ears to their webbed feet to live their best life.

FROG Squad

These awesome amphibian features will turn you into a frog fan.

EYE SURPRISE

Appearing to have its eyes closed, a red-eyed tree frog sits on a branch. The frog, which lives in rainforests ranging from southern Mexico all the way down to the northwestern tip of Colombia in South America, may look like it's asleep, but it is observing its surroundings, thanks to a translucent eyelid. This allows the amphibian to spy on its habitat and look out for predators, like birds, snakes, and large spiders. When the frog senses movement, it opens its special eyelids to reveal its bright red eyeballs—in hopes of startling a hungry predator.

Closed

SEE-THROUGH EYELIDS LET RED-EYED TREE FROGS CHECK OUT THEIR SURROUNDINGS WHILE THEY REST.

Open

OPEN WIDE! RED-EYED TREE FROGS REVEAL THEIR BRIGHT RED EYES TO ALARM PREDATORS.

TINY EARS, BIG NOSE

It's almost impossible to hear anything over a thundering waterfall—unless you're a hole-in-the-head frog living in a rainforest in Southeast Asia. This frog is named for markings that look like, well, holes in its head. But the *actual* holes are for ears that give it super hearing.

The hole-in-the-head frog is one of just two frog species that can croak out and hear ultrasonic calls, or calls at a pitch too high to be heard by humans and other animals. This adaptation likely allows the frogs to communicate above rumbling rivers and streams in their habitat.

HOLE-IN-THE-HEAD FROGS CAN ONLY BE FOUND IN ONE PLACE ON THE PLANET: THE SOUTHEAST ASIAN ISLAND OF BORNEO.

MEGAMOUTH

African bullfrogs have huge mouths! When open, their mouths stretch approximately five inches (13 cm) wide, or over half the size of their eight-inch (20-cm)-long bodies. And these bullfrogs can fit plenty inside those mouths: Using their strong tongues to pull in prey like rodents, birds, and lizards, they pierce animals with toothlike structures called odontodes, located on their lower jaws. Sharp teeth on the roof of a bullfrog's mouth keep the prey in place. Now the frog can take its time and enjoy the meal. Um, yum?

AN AFRICAN BULLFROG EYES ITS NEXT MEAL: A GIANT AFRICAN MILLIPEDE.

WEBBED FEET TO BEAT

In a rainforest in Southeast Asia, a Wallace's flying frog eyes a lower branch on a nearby tree. Rather than climbing down one tree and up the other to reach the branch, the frog simply takes flight. It splays out its four webbed feet as it leaps down. Membranes between its toes trap air from underneath to form tiny parachute-like shapes. Loose skin flaps on either side of the frog's body catch more air as it falls. It glides to the other tree before making a smooth landing.

Wide, sticky toe pads create cushions to soften the impact as Wallace's flying frogs land. These frogs have been spotted gliding 50 feet (15 m). "They probably glide that far to escape predators," said Phil Bishop, a scientific adviser for the Amphibian Survival Alliance. Traveling the extra distance beats becoming a snack.

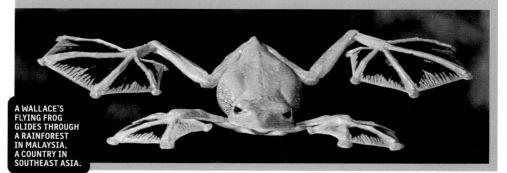

A WALLACE'S FLYING FROG GLIDES THROUGH A RAINFOREST IN MALAYSIA, A COUNTRY IN SOUTHEAST ASIA.

AT CLOSE RANGE, IT'S HARD TO MISS A DYEING POISON FROG'S BOLD COLOR PATTERN.

COOLEST SKIN FOR THE WIN

Up close, a dyeing poison frog's blue, yellow, and black hues are hard to miss. But this amphibian, found in the northeastern rainforests of South America, doesn't have to worry much about predators. Its skin is packed with poison that can paralyze or even kill other animals; the colors are a warning that the frog is toxic if eaten. The poison from certain species historically has been used on the tips of hunting darts, giving poison frogs their other common name, "poison dart frogs." *Yikes.*

10 QUIRKY FACTS ABOUT QUOKKAS

Quokkas
(pronounced KWA-kuhs)
are sometimes called the
"world's happiest animal"
because of their **cute** and **friendly** appearance.

Scientists are studying quokkas, **which can contract a disease called DUCHENNE MUSCULAR DYSTROPHY, to help find a cure for humans** with the same disease.

Quokkas **STORE FAT IN THEIR CHUBBY TAILS** to get by when food is scarce.

Quokkas swallow plants whole—then they **throw them up and chew on the partly digested food.**

After mistaking quokkas for **GIANT RATS,** early explorers named the place they'd seen the animals **ROTTNEST ISLAND,** which means **"the rat nest island"** in Dutch.

TO ESCAPE PREDATORS, QUOKKAS HOP ALONG PREMADE HIGHWAYS IN THE GRASS, FORMED FROM PATHS WHERE THE ANIMALS REGULARLY TRAVEL.

Nocturnal animals, **QUOKKAS** can spend most of the day sleeping in beds of **SPIKY SHRUBS.**

The **INDIGENOUS PEOPLE of Australia** have several words for quokkas, including *BAN-GUP* and *BUNGEUP.*

QUOKKAS ARE STRONG CLIMBERS, capable of quickly scaling trees TO LOOK FOR FOOD such as leaves and seeds.

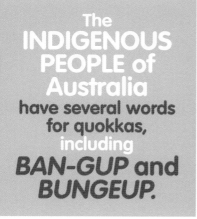

Similar to kangaroos, **the quokka is a MARSUPIAL** that hops on its hind legs **and** carries its babies— also called joeys— in a pouch for several months.

SUPER SNAKES

Snakes are masters of disguise, skilled hunters, and champion eaters. More than 3,000 species of these reptiles slither around the world. Check out these surprising facts about snakes.

AMAZON TREE BOA

AFRICAN SAW-SCALED VIPER

SNAKES SMELL WITH THEIR TONGUES.

Smell that mouse? A snake uses its tongue to smell. It flicks its long, forked tongue to pick up chemical molecules from the air, ground, or water. The tongue carries the smelly molecules back to two small openings—called the Jacobson's organ—in the roof of the snake's mouth. Cells in the Jacobson's organ analyze the scent. Mmm, lunch!

SNAKE VENOM CAN KILL.

By sinking two hollow, pointy fangs into their prey, many snakes inject venom to paralyze or kill victims before devouring them. Africa's puff adder is thought to be one of the world's deadliest snakes. Up to six feet (1.8 m) long and weighing as much as 13 pounds (6 kg), the puff adder strikes fast. Its venom can cause severe pain, tissue damage, and even death in humans. It's a snake to be respected ... from a distance.

PUFF ADDER

SNAKES CHANGE THEIR SKIN.

Snakes literally grow out of their skin. Every few months, most start rubbing against the ground or tree branches. Starting at the mouth, a snake slithers out of its too-tight skin. Like a sock, the skin comes off inside out. Voilà—the snake has a fresh, shiny look. Nice makeover.

GOLDEN TREE SNAKE

CONSTRICTORS GIVE WICKED HUGS.

Boas, anacondas, pythons, and other snakes called constrictors are amazing squeezers. This kind of snake wraps its muscular body around a victim and squeezes until the animal suffocates. The twisted talent comes from muscles attached to 200 or more vertebrae in a snake's backbone. (Humans are born with only 33 vertebrae.)

DIONE RAT SNAKE

DEADLY CUTIES

JAVAN SLOW LORIS

Nine species of slow lorises live throughout Southeast Asia.

This adorable animal has some seriously KILLER traits.

Don't be fooled by the crazy-cute slow loris. The snuggly looking creature is the only venomous primate on the planet—and its bite packs enough toxin to kill prey in just a few seconds. The toxin is also powerful enough to kill or severely harm humans, but it's very rare for the slow loris to bite people without first being provoked.

And venom isn't the only killer move the slow loris has. Check out three ways the adorable slow loris is actually downright dangerous.

KILLER LOOKS
A slow loris's sweet face markings might say "Oh, he-ey!" to you, but they say "Danger!" to other animals. To a potential predator like a large snake or hawk-eagle, the markings are like flashing red lights near the loris's mouth, warning that the loris could fight back with its deadly venom.

HIDDEN HUNTER
Huge eyes make slow lorises look harmlessly huggable. But these peepers also make them effective hunters. A special layer behind the retina called a tapetum lucidum (pronounced tuh-PEE-tum loo-SUH-dum) reflects light back through the retina and gives a loris better nighttime vision for nocturnal hunting.

TWICE AS TOXIC
Unlike other venomous animals that produce venom in one place, slow lorises produce toxins in two places: in their saliva and in glands in their underarms. When lorises lick these glands and mix its oils with their saliva, they cook up an even more toxic mixture they can inject with a single bite.

A JAVAN SLOW LORIS HANGS OUT IN THE TREE CANOPY OF JAVA, AN ISLAND IN INDONESIA.

Bet You Didn't Know!

7 Bee Facts to Buzz About

HONEYBEE

1 Bees have special **stomachs** for **carrying nectar.**

2 Some bees may **sleep** on **flowers.**

3 A bee beats its **wings** up to **12,000 times each minute.**

4 Male bees can't **sting.**

5 In summer, a single **hive** can house up to **80,000 honeybees.**

6 The **alkali bee** can visit up to **6,000 flowers** a day.

7 Sweat bees like the **taste** of human perspiration.

SPIDERWEB STATS

A single spider can eat up to 2,000 insects every year. How do spiders catch all those tasty treats? Using silk from special glands called spinnerets, spiders weave sticky webs to trap their delicious prey. But this silk can do much more than simply catch dinner. Stick around and learn more about the incredible spiderweb.

.00004–.00016

INCH (.001–.004 mm)
Thickness of silk a spider uses to build webs

-76°F
TO
302°F
(-60°C to 150°C)

The extreme range of temperatures that a spider's silk can withstand

82
FEET (25 m)

Diameter of webs woven by Darwin's bark spiders—the largest spiderwebs in the world

ORB WEAVER SPIDER

5
Number of times stronger a spider's silk is compared to steel of the same diameter

2—8
Pairs of spinnerets, the glands a spider uses to make silk

Age of oldest spiderweb ever found embedded in amber
140 MILLION
YEARS OLD

BIG CATS

Not all wild cats are big cats, so what are big cats? To wildlife experts, this group includes tigers, lions, leopards, snow leopards, jaguars, cougars, and cheetahs. As carnivores, they survive solely on the flesh of other animals. Thanks to powerful jaws; long, sharp claws; and daggerlike teeth, big cats are excellent hunters.

A young leopard rests in a tree in Botswana.

The National Geographic Big Cats Initiative's goal is to stop the decline of lions and other big cats in the wild through research, conservation, education, and global awareness.

Parents and teachers:
For more information on this initiative, you can visit natgeo.org/bigcats with your young readers.

WHO'S WHO?

BIG CATS IN THE *PANTHERA* GENUS MAY HAVE a lot of features in common, but if you know what to look for, you'll be able to tell who's who in no time.

FUR

SNOW LEOPARD

A snow leopard's thick, spotted fur helps the cat hide in its mountain habitat, no matter the season. In winter its fur is off-white to blend in with the snow, and in summer it's yellowish gray to blend in with plants and the mountains.

A jaguar's coat pattern looks similar to that of a leopard, as both have dark spots called rosettes. The difference? The rosettes on a jaguar's torso have irregularly shaped borders and at least one black dot in the center.

JAGUAR

Most tigers are orange-colored with vertical black stripes on their bodies. This coloring helps the cats blend in with tall grasses as they sneak up on prey. These markings are like fingerprints: No two stripe patterns are alike.

TIGER

Lions have light brown, or tawny, coats and a tuft of black hair at the end of their tails. When they reach their prime, most male lions have shaggy manes that help them look larger and more intimidating.

LION

LEOPARD

A leopard's yellowy coat has dark spots called rosettes on its back and sides. In leopards, the rosettes' edges are smooth and circular. This color combo helps leopards blend into their surroundings.

BENGAL TIGER
240 to 500 pounds
(109 TO 227 KG)
5 to 6 feet long
(1.5 TO 1.8 M)

JAGUAR
100 to 250 pounds
(45 TO 113 KG)
5 to 6 feet long
(1.5 TO 1.8 M)

LEOPARD
66 to 176 pounds
(30 TO 80 KG)
4.25 to 6.25 feet long
(1.3 TO 1.9 M)

SNOW LEOPARD
60 to 120 pounds (27 TO 54 KG)
4 to 5 feet long (1.2 TO 1.5 M)

AFRICAN LION
265 to 420 pounds
(120 TO 191 KG)
4.5 to 6.5 feet long
(1.4 TO 2 M)

Weirdest.
Cat.
Ever.

THE SERVAL MIGHT LOOK STRANGE, BUT THAT'S A GOOD THING WHEN IT COMES TO HUNTING.

SERVAL KITTENS STAY WITH MOM UP TO TWO YEARS BEFORE LIVING ON THEIR OWN.

SERVALS CAN CATCH UP TO 30 FROGS IN THREE HOURS WHILE HUNTING IN WATER.

Servals can chirp, purr, hiss, snarl, and growl.

ALL EARS

The serval's big ears are key to the animal's hunting success. Servals rely on sound more than any other sense when they're on the prowl. Thanks to their jumbo ears—the biggest of any wild cat's relative to body size—servals can hear just about any peep on the savanna. (If a person had ears like a serval's, they'd be as big as dinner plates!) To make the most of their super hearing, servals avoid creating noise while hunting. So instead of stalking prey like some cats do, servals squat in clearings and sit still—sometimes for several hours—as they listen for food.

A serval sits patiently in a grassy field, swiveling its head back and forth like a watchful owl. The predator is scanning the savanna for a meal not with its eyes, but with its oversize ears.

An unseen rodent stirs under the thick brush, and the wild cat tenses. It crouches on its legs and feet before launching up and over the tall grass. Guided only by sound, the serval lands directly on the once invisible rat.

Thanks to its extra-long legs, stretched-out neck, and huge ears, the serval is sometimes called the "cat of spare parts." This wild cat might look weird to some people. "But put together, their bizarre-looking body parts make them really successful hunters," says Christine Thiel-Bender, a biologist who studies servals in their African home.

In fact, servals catch prey in more than half their attempts, making them one of the best hunters in the wild cat kingdom. That's about 20 percent better than lions hunting together in a pride.

Journey
of the
JAGUAR

These spotted cats are on the move to find new homes.

The jaguar once prowled through more than seven million square miles (18 million sq km) stretching through North and South America. But in the past century, things like cattle ranching and the growth of cities have cut this territory in half. Few jaguars have been seen in the United States, and their southern range now barely extends into Argentina. The separation of these pockets of jaguars means fewer mates will meet—and fewer cubs will be born each year.

A jaguar's eyesight is nearly twice as powerful at night to help it stalk prey in the dark.

SAFE PASSAGE
Over the past decade or so, special corridors of land were set aside to allow jaguars to get from one habitat to another. But as humans have cleared trees, shrubs, and grass along these corridors, they've become more dangerous for the jaguars as they have nowhere to hide. As a result, wildlife ecologist Alan Rabinowitz launched the Jaguar Corridor Initiative (JCI) to protect the "superhighway" that the jaguars were using—and therefore their entire range.

HOME OF THE RANCH
Another key to keeping the jaguars safe? Educating farmers who live along the corridors. In the past, when jaguars traveled past a pasture of cattle, they may have tried to eat the easy prey, which would make the cats targets for ranchers protecting their herds. But thanks to new guidelines on keeping farm animals fenced in at night, both the cats and the livestock are safer.

A JAGUAR SWIMS ACROSS THE PARAGUAY RIVER IN BRAZIL.

Jaguar moms typically give birth to two to four cubs at a time.

A JAGUAR STALKS PREY IN BRAZIL'S CUIABÁ RIVER.

Return of the
MISSING LYNX

How the Eurasian lynx could make a comeback in Scotland

The British Isles include Great Britain—home to Scotland, England, and Wales—Ireland, and other nearby islands.

EURASIAN LYNX, LIKE THIS ONE IN GERMANY, OFTEN REST IN TREES.

The last Eurasian lynx in the British Isles lived a life of danger as it dodged campfires, sprinted from vicious dogs, and hid in caves.

Since around A.D. 500, people here chopped down forests to clear land for their pastures and farms, leaving these shy cats with few places to hide—and fewer prey to stalk.

Around 6,000 years ago, these islands were covered in forests full of wolves, brown bears, and lynx. But because of disappearing woodlands, lack of prey, and hunting, these large predators started to vanish from these isles. But conservationists hope to one day bring the Eurasian lynx back to Scotland, which would be a win for the species—and the planet, too.

BALANCING ACT

What if you popped the hood of your parents' car and started pulling out parts? It wouldn't take long for the engine to sputter or belch smoke because the car was missing a crucial part. The landscape of Scotland went similarly out of whack when the Eurasian lynx disappeared.

Once they began pouncing on sheep and goats, lynx became public enemy number one, and people started hunting them. Without cats and other predators to hunt them, deer populations skyrocketed. Those animals nibbled on the leaves of trees and bushes for food, and soon large areas of the Scottish forest disappeared since it couldn't grow fast enough to keep up with the deer's appetites. Birds and rodents that relied on shelter in the lower level of forest vegetation fell prey to foxes, which lynx also hunt.

Groups trying to restore the forests have to put up fences to keep deer from nibbling the saplings. But with lynx roaming the woods, experts think these cats would keep the deer from overgrazing on the young trees, helping the forests make a comeback.

And that would have even bigger impacts. Earth is losing forestland as people cut down

AT ONE YEAR OLD, LYNX KITTENS ARE INDEPENDENT.

Eurasian lynx mothers give birth to up to five kittens at a time.

trees to make room for farming and cattle, and to sell the wood for products like furniture and toilet paper. In 2020 alone, Earth lost as many trees as would cover an area larger than Michigan, U.S.A.

So restoring forests in places like Scotland can help provide more space for wildlife and even fight climate change. That's because trees absorb carbon dioxide, the gas that traps the sun's heat and warms our planet.

"When you restore forests, you lock carbon away, you get an amazing habitat for more wildlife, and you also get more nature for humans to enjoy," says Steve Micklewright, a leader of the Scottish Rewilding Alliance, a group that's trying to restore Scotland's nature. "Everybody wins!"

CAT CHAT

A recent poll found that though about 75 percent of the local population support restoring Scotland's forests, people are less excited about bringing back lynx. That's mostly because farmers are worried that these wild cats will eat their livestock. Although scientists say that's unlikely—lynx prefer the forest, and farm animals live in pastures—conservationists want to address farmers' concerns before reintroducing the carnivore.

That means interviewing hundreds of people—sheep farmers, hunters, timber growers, and land managers—who live near what could be the lynxes' new home to get a better understanding of humans' relationship with wildlife.

For example, past proposals have offered farmers money for each animal that the lynx might take. But David Bavin, who's leading the study, says that doesn't consider things like how much farmers care about their animals, or if they feel their way of life is being disrespected. So conservationists want to make sure everyone is heard.

"We believe that lots of people have to agree it's the right thing to do, so we're taking our time, talking to people, and trying to find the right place where lynx would be welcome," Micklewright says.

Eventually, the next step would be for scientists to bring a few lynx from other parts of Europe to Scotland, fit them with tracking tags, and study where they go and what they do for five years. Researchers would also monitor how the landscape changes—for instance, if more young trees sprout when lynx prey on the leaf-nibbling deer—and whether the lynx hunted any sheep.

LAND OF THE LYNX?

Recent research found that mainland Scotland has enough habitat and prey to support about 450 lynx, and conservationists hope that reintroduced cats will restore balance to the wild forests and help more new trees grow. Bringing back this top predator to the landscape won't be easy, but conservationists think it's worth it, no matter how long it takes.

"They belong here just like any other creature that's already here, and it's our fault that they're gone," Micklewright says. "We have a home in Scotland waiting for the lynx, and we're just so excited to bring them back."

A Eurasian lynx is about as big as a Labrador retriever.

LYNX DEVELOP THEIR SPOTS BY THE TIME THEY'RE 14 WEEKS OLD.

Naughty PETS

POCKETS ARE PURR-FECT FOR CATNAPS.

WHOA. HOW'D ALL THIS FIT INTO THAT LITTLE POUCH?

NAME Snickers

FAVORITE ACTIVITY Back-to-school clothes shopping

FAVORITE TOY Belt made of yarn

PET PEEVE School uniforms

I'M SOOO LIVING MY BEST DOG LIFE.

GOOD THING I COATED THE SINK WITH TOOTHPASTE.

NAME Chewy

FAVORITE ACTIVITY Exploring the insides of pillows

FAVORITE TOY Stuffed teddy bear

PET PEEVE Zippers

NAME Queso

FAVORITE ACTIVITY Turning on the faucet while the cat is sleeping in the sink

FAVORITE TOY Soap bubbles

PET PEEVE Cat beds

NAME Sabacca

FAVORITE ACTIVITY Watching humans perform tricks in the pool

FAVORITE TOY Pool raft

PET PEEVE Not being allowed to drink the pool water

PET TALES

JUST CALL ME SUPER STELLA.

STELLA SNIFFS A HIKER'S BANDANNA SO SHE'S FAMILIAR WITH THEIR SCENT.

STELLA THE BLOODHOUND FOLLOWS THE HIKER'S SCENT THROUGH THE WOODS.

Dog Rescues Kid

RICHMOND, VIRGINIA, U.S.A.
Stella the bloodhound is napping next to her partner, Virginia State Police officer Enzo Diaz, when Diaz gets a call on his car radio late one night. A 13-year-old girl with a disability is missing.

Even a helicopter pilot flying over the area hasn't found any clues. But police hope Stella can. As a search-and-rescue dog, she's trained to find missing people using her incredible sense of smell.

Arriving at the girl's house, Diaz puts on Stella's harness and clips on a 15-foot (5-m) leash. The dog sniffs a pillowcase from the missing girl's bedroom so she's familiar with her scent. Then Diaz gives Stella the command to start searching: "Find her."

Stella leads Diaz into the nearby woods, where a neighbor last spotted the girl. Guided only by her nose and Diaz's flashlight, Stella navigates the woods by sniffing the ground. Suddenly, she goes into a full sprint and doesn't stop running until she's directly in front of the girl sitting quietly under a tree. The young girl is cold and a little wet, but otherwise she's OK. Stella sits next to her until police officers arrive to reunite the girl with her family.

Back in the car, Diaz gives the hound some wet food as a treat. "Stella soaks up the moment," Diaz says. "And then she goes right back to her nap."

The gene that gives cats black fur might also help them fight infections.

CAT SAVES OWNER

SWADLINCOTE, ENGLAND
Walter the black cat is anything but unlucky. He's saved his owner's life more than 50 times!

Walter's owner, Hazel Parkyn, has a disease called type 1 diabetes, which means her body can't control its blood sugar levels. If Parkyn's blood sugar level drops when she's asleep, she could have a seizure. Yet Walter always seems to know when Parkyn is in danger.

When blood sugar levels drop, chemical changes happen in the body that release a certain scent. When Walter smells the scent in his owner, he leaps onto Parkyn's chest and swats at her face with his paws until he wakes her. Then Parkyn can take her medicine to stabilize her blood sugar level.

Walter's more than just a pet—he's Parkyn's lifeguard.

Cats vs. Dogs

Check out the figures on these lovable pets to decide for yourself.

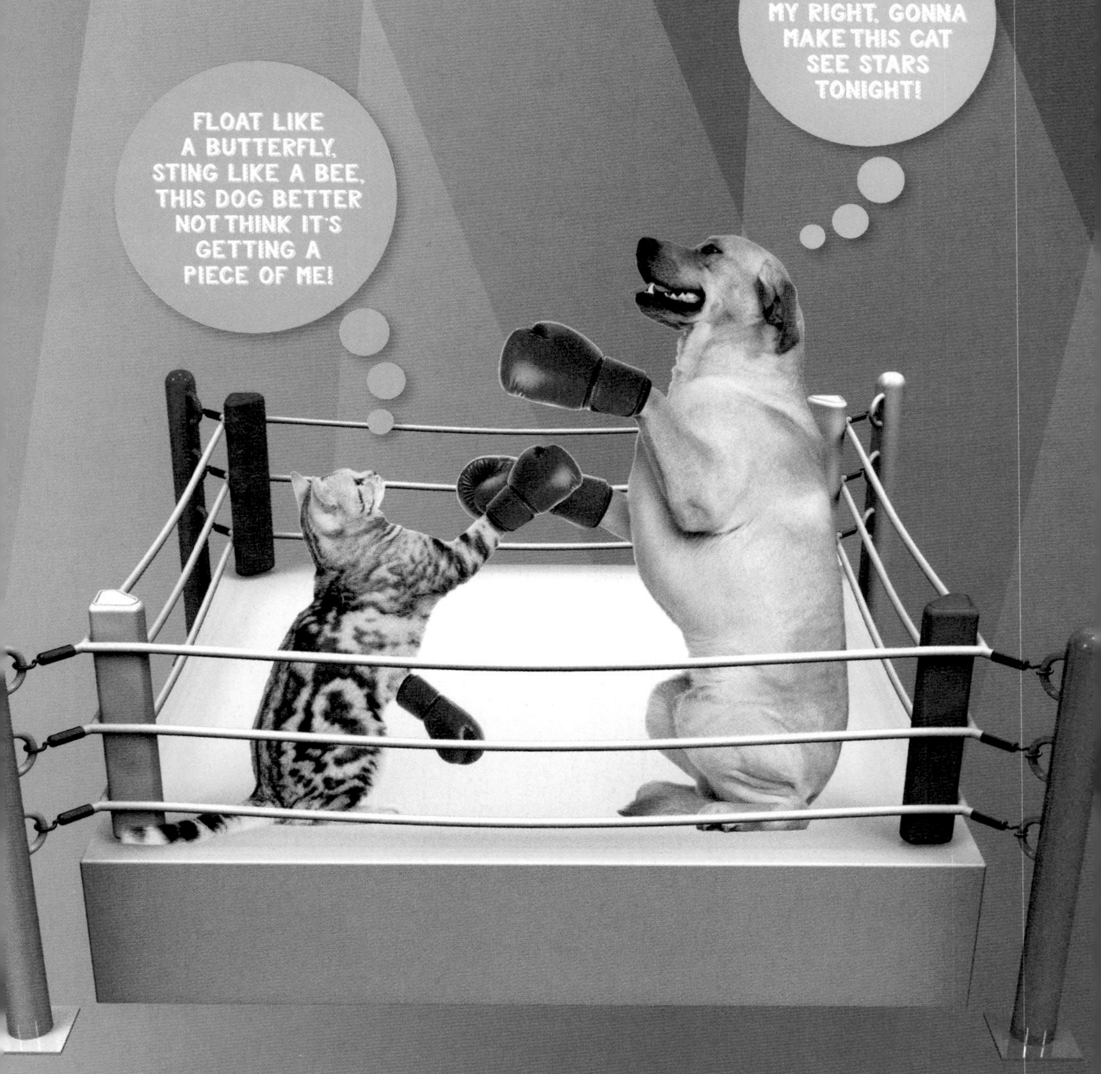

PET CATS ARE RELATED TO COUGARS.

MEOW!

Cats have been domesticated for at least **4,000 years.**

The average life span of an indoor cat is **13 to 17 years.**

The average cat litter has **3 to 5 kittens.**

Most adult cats can jump up to **6 times their height.**

Cats can hear sounds almost **1.5 times higher** than dogs can.

Cats sleep about **15 hours a day.**

ALL KITTENS ARE BORN WITH BLUE EYES.

DOGS ARE RELATED TO WOLVES.

WOOF!

Dogs have been domesticated for at least **14,000 years.**

The average life span of a dog is **8 to 16 years.**

The average dog litter has **5 or 6 puppies.**

Most adult dogs can jump up to **3 times their height.**

Dogs have about **220 million** scent cells—20 times more than cats.

NEWBORN PUPPIES DON'T WAG THEIR TAILS.

Dogs sleep about **14 hours a day.**

Prehistoric TIMELINE

HUMANS HAVE WALKED on Earth for some 300,000 years, a mere blip in the planet's 4.5-billion-year history. A lot has happened during that time. Earth formed, and oxygen levels rose in the millions of years of the Precambrian time. The productive Paleozoic era gave rise to hard-shell organisms, vertebrates, amphibians, and reptiles.

Dinosaurs ruled Earth in the mighty Mesozoic. And 66 million years after dinosaurs became extinct, modern humans emerged in the Cenozoic era. From the first tiny mollusks to the dinosaur giants of the Jurassic and beyond, Earth has seen a lot of transformation.

THE PRECAMBRIAN TIME

4.5 billion to 541 million years ago

- Earth (and other planets) formed from gas and dust left over from a giant cloud that collapsed to form the sun. The giant cloud's collapse was triggered when nearby stars exploded.
- Low levels of oxygen made Earth a suffocating place.
- Early life-forms appeared.

THE PALEOZOIC ERA

541 million to 252 million years ago

- The first insects and other animals appeared on land.
- 450 million years ago (mya), the ancestors of sharks began to swim in the oceans.
- 430 mya, plants began to take root on land.
- More than 360 mya, amphibians emerged from the water.
- Slowly, the major landmasses began to come together, creating Pangaea, a single supercontinent.
- By 300 mya, reptiles had begun to dominate the land.

What Killed the Dinosaurs?

It's a mystery that's boggled the minds of scientists for centuries: What happened to the dinosaurs? Although various theories have bounced around, a recent study confirms that the most likely culprit is an asteroid or comet that created a giant crater. Researchers say that the impact set off a series of natural disasters like tsunamis, earthquakes, and temperature swings that plagued the dinosaurs' ecosystems and disrupted their food chains. This, paired with intense volcanic eruptions that caused drastic climate changes, is thought to be why half of the world's species—including the dinosaurs—died in a mass extinction.

DINO TIMES

THE MESOZOIC ERA

252 million to 66 million years ago

The Mesozoic era, or the age of the reptiles, consisted of three consecutive time periods (shown below). This is when the first dinosaurs began to appear. They would reign supreme for more than 150 million years.

TRIASSIC PERIOD

252 million to 201 million years ago

- The first mammals appeared. They were rodent-size.
- The first dinosaurs appeared.
- Ferns were the dominant plants on land.
- The giant supercontinent of Pangaea began breaking up toward the end of the Triassic.

JURASSIC PERIOD

201 million to 145 million years ago

- Giant dinosaurs dominated the land.
- Pangaea continued its breakup, and oceans formed in the spaces between the drifting landmasses, allowing sea life, including sharks and marine crocodiles, to thrive.
- Conifer trees spread across the land.

CRETACEOUS PERIOD

145 million to 66 million years ago

- The modern continents developed.
- The largest dinosaurs developed.
- Flowering plants spread across the landscape.
- Mammals flourished, and giant pterosaurs ruled the skies over small birds.
- Temperatures grew more extreme. Dinosaurs lived in deserts, swamps, and forests from the Antarctic to the Arctic.

THE CENOZOIC ERA—TERTIARY PERIOD

66 million to 2.6 million years ago

- Following the dinosaur extinction, mammals rose as the dominant species.
- Birds continued to flourish.
- Volcanic activity was widespread.
- Temperatures began to cool, eventually ending in an ice age.
- The period ended with land bridges forming, which allowed plants and animals to spread to new areas.

DINO Classification

Classifying dinosaurs and all other living things can be a complicated matter, so scientists have devised a system to help with the process. Dinosaurs are put into groups based on a very large range of characteristics.

Scientists put dinosaurs into two major groups: the bird-hipped ornithischians and the lizard-hipped saurischians.

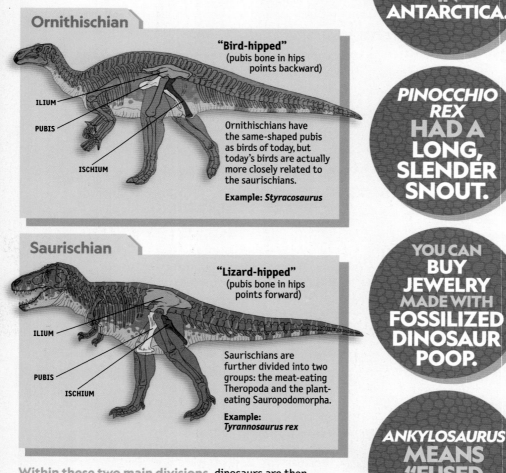

Ornithischian

"Bird-hipped"
(pubis bone in hips points backward)

ILIUM

PUBIS

ISCHIUM

Ornithischians have the same-shaped pubis as birds of today, but today's birds are actually more closely related to the saurischians.

Example: *Styracosaurus*

Saurischian

"Lizard-hipped"
(pubis bone in hips points forward)

ILIUM

PUBIS

ISCHIUM

Saurischians are further divided into two groups: the meat-eating Theropoda and the plant-eating Sauropodomorpha.

**Example:
*Tyrannosaurus rex***

Within these two main divisions, dinosaurs are then separated into orders and then families, such as Stegosauria. Like other members of the Stegosauria, *Stegosaurus* had spines and plates along its back, neck, and tail.

THERE WERE **DINOSAURS** IN **ANTARCTICA.**

PINOCCHIO REX **HAD A LONG, SLENDER SNOUT.**

YOU CAN **BUY JEWELRY** MADE WITH **FOSSILIZED DINOSAUR POOP.**

ANKYLOSAURUS **MEANS "FUSED LIZARD."**

4 NEWLY DISCOVERED DINOS

Humans have been searching for—and discovering—dinosaur remains for hundreds of years. In that time, at least 1,000 species of dinos have been found all over the world, and thousands more may still be out there waiting to be unearthed. Recent finds include nearly 200-million-year-old fossils in China, the earliest well-preserved armored dinosaur found in Asia to date.

1

Stegouros elengassen
(Ornithischian)

Name Meaning: Roofed tail

Length: 6 feet (1.8 m)

Time Range: Late Cretaceous period

Where: Patagonia, Chile

2

Australotitan cooperensis
(Saurischian)

Name Meaning: "Cooper" after a creek near the fossil's discovery site

Length: 80–100 feet (25–30 m)

Time Range: Late Cretaceous period

Where: Australia

3

Ulughbegsaurus uzbekistanensis
(Saurischian)

Name Meaning: "Ulugh Beg's reptile," after the 15th-century Middle Eastern astronomer and mathematician

Length: 30 feet (9.1 m)

Time Range: Late Cretaceous period

Where: Uzbekistan

4

Yuxisaurus kopchicki
(Ornithischian)

Name Meaning: Yuxi lizard, after the city in China

Length: 18 feet (5.5 m)

Time Range: Early Jurassic period

Where: China

DINO SECRETS REVEALED

Cool technology shows surprising discoveries about dinosaurs.

It's been 66 million years since the dinosaurs went extinct. And we're *still* learning new things about them, thanks to cutting-edge technology like lasers, 3D models, x-rays, and even robotics. For instance, experts are able to run fossilized bones through a computer program to reconstruct missing bits and better understand how these animals actually functioned. Want to find out more? Check out three surprising dino discoveries that modern technology has helped scientists unearth.

SPINOSAURUS HUNT PREHISTORIC SAWFISH.

River Beast

The Sahara seems like a strange place for a river-dwelling dinosaur. But more than 95 million years ago in what is now Morocco, a country in northern Africa, today's giant desert was actually lush with waterways deep enough for car-size fish to swim in. That's where *Spinosaurus*—a predator longer than *T. rex*—made its home.

At first, scientists believed that the sail-backed creature had some kind of watery lifestyle, perhaps hunting fish like a bear would. But after finding a partial skeleton in 2014, experts assessed that the dinosaur probably spent a lot of time in water.

And the paleontologists didn't stop there. Returning to the site in 2018, they dug up a 17-foot (5-m) *Spinosaurus* tail—one vertebra at a time. (These are the same bones that make up your spine.) Using high-speed cameras and robots, they created an eight-inch (20-cm)-long mechanical tail, which they watched paddle in an enclosed waterway.

They discovered that the beast swam through rivers like a crocodile and could propel itself with eight times more power than related land dinosaurs. In fact, *Spinosaurus* is the first large dino found that had a tail designed for swimming.

A YOUNG *MUSSAURUS* CHECKS OUT TWO RHYNCHOSAURS (PRONOUNCED REEN-KOH-SOARS) AS AN ADULT LOOKS ON.

Baby Steps

Dinosaurs lumbered on all fours like a *Stegosaurus* or scrambled around on two legs like a *Tyrannosaurus*. But not all dinosaurs moved the same way as they grew up.

Paleontologist Alejandro Otero found that out by using a high-tech machine called a CT scanner to take x-rays of *Mussaurus* bones (pronounced moo-SOAR-us). He turned the x-rays into 3D models using a computer program and then simulated how the dinosaur stood at different ages.

What did the simulations show? It turns out that, like human babies, *Mussaurus* hatchlings walked on all fours—but started walking on their two hind

A NEWLY HATCHED *DEINONYCHUS* CHICK IS WATCHED OVER BY DAD.

Cracking the Case

A fossilized dinosaur egg looks kind of like a rock. So scientists were surprised to discover that the eggs of *Deinonychus* (pronounced die-NAHN-uh-kus) were probably blue!

When exposed to heat and pressure, microscopic dino remains can transform into stuff that can last for millions of years. This lets scientists take a closer look. When paleobiologist Jasmina Wiemann struck the *Deinonychus* eggs with a laser, the light reflecting back revealed compounds that give modern eggs bright colors and speckling.

This helped her figure out the blue color, but it also suggested something else: Like modern birds with similarly colorful eggs, *Deinonychus* likely sat on open-air

QUIZ WHIZ

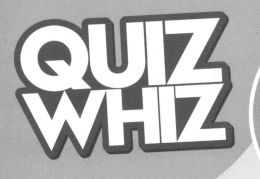

Explore just how much you know about animals with this quiz!

Write your answers on a piece of paper. Then check them below.

1 Early explorers mistakenly identified the quokka as what kind of animal?
- **a.** tiny bear
- **b.** giant rat
- **c.** smiling hamster
- **d.** friendly cat

2 **True or false?** A group of flamingos is sometimes called a flamboyance.

3 Conservationists are working to bring back the Eurasian lynx to forests in _____.
- **a.** Thailand
- **b.** Greece
- **c.** India
- **d.** Scotland

4 Dogs have 220 million scent cells, which is about _____ times more than cats.
- **a.** 2
- **b.** 20
- **c.** 200
- **d.** 2,000

5 **True or false?** Hermit crabs can create their own shells when they outgrow older ones.

Not **STUMPED** yet? Check out the *NATIONAL GEOGRAPHIC KIDS QUIZ WHIZ* collection for more crazy **ANIMAL** questions!

ANSWERS: 1. b; 2. True; 3. d; 4. b; 5. false

HOMEWORK HELP

Wildly Good Animal Reports

Seahorse

Your teacher wants a written report on the seahorse. Not to worry. Use these organizational tools so you can stay afloat while writing a report.

STEPS TO SUCCESS: Your report will follow the format of a descriptive or expository essay (see page 129 for "How to Write a Perfect Essay") and should consist of a main idea, followed by supporting details and a conclusion. Use this basic structure for each paragraph, as well as the whole report, and you'll be on the right track.

1. Introduction
State your **main idea.**

Seahorses are fascinating fish with many unique characteristics.

2. Body
Provide **supporting points** for your main idea.

Seahorses are very small fish.
Seahorses are named for their head shape.
Seahorses display behavior that is rare among almost all other animals on Earth.

Then **expand** on those points with further description, explanation, or discussion.

Seahorses are very small fish.
Seahorses are about the size of an M&M at birth, and most adult seahorses would fit in a teacup.
Seahorses are named for their head shape.
With long, tubelike snouts, seahorses are named for their resemblance to horses.
A group of seahorses is called a herd.
Seahorses display behavior that is rare among almost all other animals on Earth.
Unlike most other fish, seahorses stay with one mate their entire lives. They are also among the only species in which dads, not moms, give birth to the babies.

3. Conclusion
Wrap it up with a **summary** of your whole paper.

Because of their unique shape and unusual behavior, seahorses are among the most fascinating and easily distinguishable animals in the ocean.

KEY INFORMATION

Here are some things you should consider including in your report:

What does your animal look like?
To what other species is it related?
How does it move?
Where does it live?
What does it eat?
What are its predators?
How long does it live?
Is it endangered?
Why do you find it interesting?

SEPARATE FACT FROM FICTION: Your animal may have been featured in a movie or in myths and legends. Compare and contrast how the animal has been portrayed with how it behaves in reality. For example, penguins can't dance the way they do in the movie *Happy Feet.*

PROOFREAD AND REVISE: As you would do with any essay, when you're finished, check for misspellings, grammatical mistakes, and punctuation errors. It often helps to have someone else proofread your work, too, as that person may catch things you have missed. Also, look for ways to make your sentences and paragraphs even better. Add more descriptive language, choosing just the right verbs, adverbs, and adjectives to make your writing come alive.

BE CREATIVE: Use visual aids to make your report come to life. Include an animal photo file with interesting images found in magazines or printed from websites. Or draw your own! You can also build a miniature animal habitat diorama. Use creativity to help communicate your passion for the subject.

THE FINAL RESULT: Put it all together in one final, polished draft. Make it neat and clean, and remember to cite your references.

Taken by the James Webb Space Telescope, this image shows the edge of an area where stars form in the Carina Nebula. It is located about 7,600 light-years from Earth.

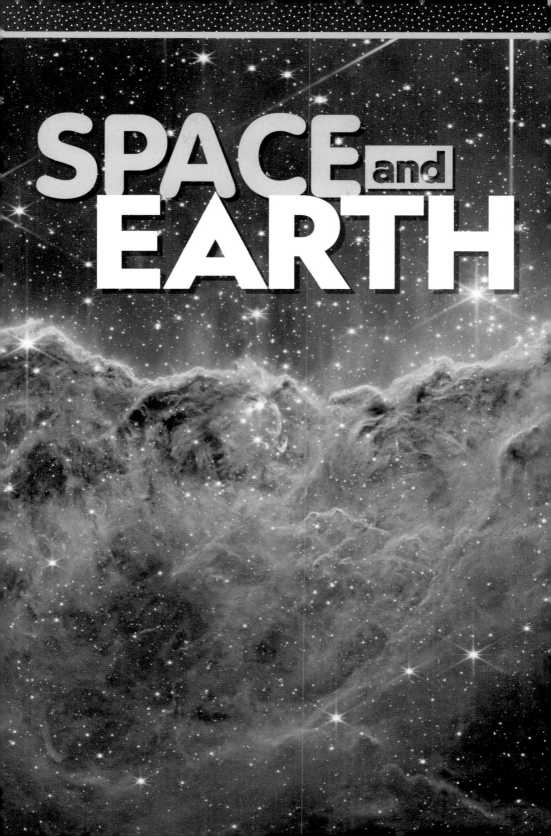

SPACE and EARTH

5 SPECTACULAR **SPACE** SIGHTS

THESE GALACTICALLY COOL COSMIC SHOTS
ARE UNIVERSALLY OUT-OF-THIS-WORLD.

1 SUPERSTELLAR

Ancient Chinese and Japanese astronomers witnessed the supernova explosion that created the Crab Nebula in A.D. 1054. This detailed mosaic image of the six-light-year-wide dead star is the work of NASA's Hubble Space Telescope.

2 HIDE-AND-SEEK

One of gas giant Jupiter's 50 (yes, 50!) confirmed moons is just about to hide behind its planet. The largest moon in the entire solar system, **Ganymede** is even larger than the planet Mercury.

3 FLYING FREE

It's just what it looks like! Mission Specialist Bruce McCandless II performed an **untethered space walk**, going farther unattached to his shuttle than any astronaut had before.

4 RED SUPERGIANT

V838 Monocerotis lives at the outer edge of the Milky Way, 20,000 light-years away. When the star suddenly brightened for a few weeks in 2002, the "light echo" revealed previously unseen dust patterns in its surrounding cloud structures.

5 EXTRA-LARGE CONE

Though the **Cone Nebula** is in total seven light-years long, this image shows only its upper 2.5 light-years—a height equaling 23 million round trips to the moon! It is surrounded eerily by the red glow of hydrogen gas.

CELESTIAL COUNTS

Have you ever wondered what's floating around out there in space?

Our solar system is made up of the sun and all of the objects that orbit around it. Read on to meet the planets, asteroids, and comets that make up our galactic neighborhood.

147
MOONS

5
DWARF
PLANETS

715,000+
ASTEROIDS

1
STAR
(That's the sun!)

8
PLANETS
Mercury, Venus, Earth,
Mars, Jupiter, Saturn,
Uranus, Neptune

3,400+
COMETS

300+
space
exploration
missions

PLANETS

CERES

MARS

EARTH

VENUS

MERCURY

JUPITER

SUN

MERCURY

Average distance from the sun:
   35,980,000 miles (57,900,000 km)
Position from the sun in orbit: 1st
Equatorial diameter: 3,030 miles
   (4,878 km)
Length of day: 59 Earth days
Length of year: 88 Earth days
Known moons: 0

VENUS

Average distance from the sun:
   67,230,000 miles (108,200,000 km)
Position from the sun in orbit: 2nd
Equatorial diameter: 7,520 miles
   (12,100 km)
Length of day: 243 Earth days
Length of year: 224.7 Earth days
Known moons: 0

EARTH

Average distance from the sun:
   93,000,000 miles (149,600,000 km)
Position from the sun in orbit: 3rd
Equatorial diameter: 7,900 miles
   (12,750 km)
Length of day: 24 hours
Length of year: 365 days
Known moons: 1

MARS

Average distance from the sun:
   141,633,000 miles (227,936,000 km)
Position from the sun in orbit: 4th
Equatorial diameter: 4,221 miles
   (6,794 km)
Length of day: 25 Earth hours
Length of year: 1.9 Earth years
Known moons: 2

This artwork shows the eight planets and five known dwarf planets in our solar system. The relative sizes and positions of the planets are shown, but not the relative distances between them.

SATURN

URANUS

NEPTUNE

PLUTO
HAUMEA
MAKEMAKE
ERIS

JUPITER

Average distance from the sun:
483,682,000 miles (778,412,000 km)

Position from the sun in orbit: 6th

Equatorial diameter: 88,840 miles
(142,980 km)

Length of day: 9.9 Earth hours

Length of year: 11.9 Earth years

Known moons: 79*

SATURN

Average distance from the sun:
890,800,000 miles (1,433,600,000 km)

Position from the sun in orbit: 7th

Equatorial diameter: 74,900 miles
(120,540 km)

Length of day: 10.7 Earth hours

Length of year: 29.5 Earth years

Known moons: 82*

*Includes provisional moons, which await confirmation
and naming from the International Astronomical Union.

URANUS

Average distance from the sun:
1,784,000,000 miles (2,871,000,000 km)

Position from the sun in orbit: 8th

Equatorial diameter: 31,760 miles
(51,120 km)

Length of day: 17.2 Earth hours

Length of year: 84 Earth years

Known moons: 27

NEPTUNE

Average distance from the sun:
2,795,000,000 miles (4,498,000,000 km)

Position from the sun in orbit: 9th

Equatorial diameter: 30,775 miles
(49,528 km)

Length of day: 16 Earth hours

Length of year: 164.8 Earth years

Known moons: 14

For information about dwarf planets,
see page 92.

DWARF PLANETS

Haumea

Eris

Pluto

Thanks to advanced technology, astronomers have been spotting many never-before-seen celestial bodies with their telescopes. One recent discovery? A population of icy objects orbiting the sun beyond Pluto. The largest, like Pluto itself, are classified as dwarf planets. Smaller than the moon but still massive enough to pull themselves into a ball, dwarf planets nevertheless lack the gravitational "oomph" to clear their neighborhood of other sizable objects. So, although larger, more massive planets pretty much have their orbits to themselves, dwarf planets orbit the sun in swarms that include other dwarf planets, as well as smaller chunks of rock or ice.

So far, astronomers have identified five dwarf planets in our solar system: Ceres, Pluto, Haumea, Makemake, and Eris. There are many more newly discovered dwarf planets that will need additional study before they are named. Astronomers are observing hundreds of newly found objects in the frigid outer solar system. As time and technology advance, the family of known dwarf planets will surely continue to grow.

CERES
Position from the sun in orbit: 5th
Length of day: 9.1 Earth hours
Length of year: 4.6 Earth years
Known moons: 0

PLUTO
Position from the sun in orbit: 10th
Length of day: 6.4 Earth days
Length of year: 248 Earth years
Known moons: 5

HAUMEA
Position from the sun in orbit: 11th
Length of day: 3.9 Earth hours
Length of year: 282 Earth years
Known moons: 2

MAKEMAKE
Position from the sun in orbit: 12th
Length of day: 22.5 Earth hours
Length of year: 305 Earth years
Known moons: 1*

ERIS
Position from the sun in orbit: 13th
Length of day: 25.9 Earth hours
Length of year: 561 Earth years
Known moons: 1

*Includes provisional moons, which await confirmation and naming from the International Astronomical Union.

BLACK HOLES

A black hole really seems like a hole in space. Most black holes form when the core of a massive star collapses, falling into oblivion. A black hole has a stronger gravitational pull than anything else in the known universe. It's like a bottomless pit, swallowing anything that gets close enough to it to be pulled in. It's black because it pulls in light. Black holes come in different sizes. The smallest known black hole has a mass about three times that of the sun. The biggest one scientists have found so far has a mass about 66 billion times greater than the sun's. Really big black holes at the center of galaxies probably form by swallowing enormous amounts of gas over time. In 2019, scientists released the first image of a black hole's silhouette (left). The image, previously thought impossible to record, was captured using a network of telescopes.

BLACK HOLE →

What if the sun suddenly disappeared?

Light from the sun takes about eight minutes to reach Earth. So if the sun winked out of existence, its final rays would reach us in eight minutes. Then, darkness. The moon would go black once sunlight stopped reflecting off its surface, and the only light on Earth would be starlight and artificial light—electric light, gaslight, and campfires. To survive the below-freezing temperatures, humans would need to move their cities deep underground near Earth's internal heat, or geothermal energy. Luckily, the sun disappearing is impossible. But its core *will* run out of hydrogen fuel ... in about a billion years.

10 STELLAR FACTS ABOUT STARS

SM0313, one of the **OLDEST STARS** in the universe, was born **13.6 billion** years ago.

It takes about **50 million years** for a star the size of our sun to form.

POLLUX

THE POLLUX STAR, **LOCATED IN THE GEMINI CONSTELLATION, HAS A RADIUS THAT'S NEARLY NINE TIMES BIGGER THAN THE SUN'S.**

Stars sparkle in shades of blue, red, orange, yellow, and white.

Between **100 and 400 billion** stars are in the Milky Way galaxy — but only about 9,000 are visible to the naked eye from Earth.

Most stars are shaped like balls, but in 2021, researchers discovered a rare **teardrop-shaped star.**

Heavy metal elements like **PLATINUM** and **GOLD** are created **when neutron stars collide.**

NASA's Hubble Space Telescope recently detected a star that's so far away, its light takes **12.9 billion years** to reach Earth.

Humans' fascination with the night sky goes way back! A roughly 17,000-year-old painting found in a cave in France is believed to be a map of the stars.

THE SUN accounts for more than **99 percent** of the solar system's total mass.

95

DESTINATION *ASTEROID*

Scientists attempt to land a robot on an ancient space rock.

For two years, an unmanned spacecraft traveled through space, headed toward the asteroid Bennu. This chunk of rock is tiny compared to other objects in the solar system, barely taller than New York City's Empire State Building. But scientists think it holds big secrets.

"Bennu is a leftover piece from when the sun, the planets, and the rest of the solar system formed 4.5 billion years ago," says planetary scientist Jason Dworkin, who's on the team that sent the NASA spacecraft—called OSIRIS-REx—on its mission. Studying pieces of Bennu might reveal new information about how the solar system was formed ... and maybe even how life started on Earth.

AN ILLUSTRATION OF THE SPACECRAFT OSIRIS-REx PREPARING TO LAND ON THE ASTEROID BENNU

SPINNING ROCK PILE

After a 205-million-mile (330-million-km) journey, OSIRIS-REx approached Bennu in 2018. Scientists wanted the robotic spacecraft to obtain a sample—but they knew it was going to be tricky. Before they could try, scientists needed to study the asteroid from Earth to figure out the best way to do it. Using a combination of remote cameras, lasers, and other tools aboard OSIRIS-REx, scientists discovered some surprising things about Bennu.

The asteroid's insides appear to have some empty spaces—sort of like Swiss cheese. And its surface has rocks the size of jumbo jets. Suddenly, scientists had to worry about the spacecraft smashing into a big rock or getting buried in rubble.

TRICKY LANDING

By fall 2020, scientists were ready to try snagging a sample. They sent instructions to the craft. Once the spacecraft touched down on Bennu, it had only a few seconds to vacuum up a sample before bouncing back into space. But ... success! Images from OSIRIS-REx showed the spacecraft had carried out its mission.

Scientists will study some of the sample and stow away the rest. That way future scientists can make their own discoveries.

PROTECTING EARTH FROM ASTEROIDS

Bennu's orbit crosses Earth's. And there's a very small chance—about 1 in 2,700—that it could hit our planet in the late 22nd century. Scientists hope that studying Bennu's samples will help them figure out new ways to protect Earth from a deadly asteroid strike.

Some ideas include blowing it up with a nuclear bomb and ramming it with a spacecraft. Or scientists could spray part of a small asteroid like Bennu with something that reflects light, such as zinc oxide. As light bounces off the asteroid's surface, it would push it out of our planet's path.

BENNU

OSIRIS-REx's name is partly inspired by the Egyptian god Osiris. ("REx" refers to the type of x-ray technology used by the spacecraft.)

96

Sky Calendar 2024

LOOK UP! From lunar eclipses to meteor showers—which are often named after a nearby star or constellation—here are some of the major events dazzling the night sky in 2024.

- **JANUARY 3–4**
  QUADRANTIDS METEOR SHOWER PEAK. Featuring up to 40 meteors an hour, this is the first meteor shower of every new year and radiates from the Herdsman (Boötes) constellation in the Northern Hemisphere.

- **JANUARY 12**
  MERCURY AT GREATEST WESTERN ELONGATION. Just before sunrise, Mercury will be at its highest point above the horizon: Look for the planet in the eastern sky.

- **MARCH 20**
  MARCH EQUINOX. On this day, there will be nearly equal amounts of darkness and light because of Earth's position in relation to the sun.

- **MARCH 25**
  PENUMBRAL LUNAR ECLIPSE. Visible throughout North America, Central America, and South America, the moon will darken slightly as it passes through Earth's partial shadow.

- **APRIL 8**
  TOTAL SOLAR ECLIPSE. The moon will completely block the sun. The total eclipse will be visible in the eastern United States, parts of Mexico, and Nova Scotia, Canada. The next eclipse won't be visible from this part of the world until 2044.

- **MAY 4**
  ETA AQUARIDS METEOR SHOWER PEAK. This meteor shower, which radiates from the Aquarius constellation, peaks at about 30 meteors an hour.

- **AUGUST 11–12**
  PERSEIDS METEOR SHOWER PEAK. See up to 90 meteors an hour! Best viewing is in the direction of the constellation Perseus.

- **SEPTEMBER 18**
  SUPERMOON AND PARTIAL LUNAR ECLIPSE. Look for part of the moon to darken as it passes through Earth's penumbra, or partial shadow. It will be visible in most of North America, Central America, South America, Europe, and Africa.

- **OCTOBER 2**
  ANNULAR SOLAR ECLIPSE. The moon is too far away to completely cover the sun, so this eclipse appears as a ring of light around a dark circle created by the moon. It will be visible off the Pacific coast of South America and parts of southern Chile and Argentina. A partial eclipse can be viewed throughout most of southern South America.

- **OCTOBER 21–22**
  ORIONID METEOR SHOWER PEAK. View up to 20 meteors an hour. Look toward the constellation Orion for the best show.

- **NOVEMBER 17**
  URANUS AT OPPOSITION. This is your best chance to view Uranus in 2024. The planet will be fully illuminated by the sun, appearing as a tiny blue-green dot in a telescope.

- **DECEMBER 13–14**
  GEMINID METEOR SHOWER PEAK. Emanating from the Gemini constellation, this spectacular show features up to 120 multicolored meteors an hour!

- **2024—VARIOUS DATES**
  VIEW THE INTERNATIONAL SPACE STATION (ISS). Parents and teachers: You can visit spotthestation.nasa.gov to find out when the ISS will be flying over your neighborhood.

Note: Dates are in UTC; may vary slightly depending on your location. Check with a local planetarium for the best viewing times in your area.

A LOOK INSIDE

The distance from Earth's surface to its center is some 4,000 miles (6,437 km) at the Equator. There are four layers: a thin, rigid crust; the rocky mantle; the outer core, which is a layer of molten iron and nickel; and finally the inner core, which is believed to be mostly solid iron and nickel.

The **CRUST** includes tectonic plates, land-masses, and the ocean. Its average thickness varies from 5 to 25 miles (8 to 40 km).

The **MANTLE** is about 1,800 miles (2,900 km) of hot, thick, solid rock.

The **OUTER CORE** is liquid molten rock made mostly of iron and nickel.

The **INNER CORE** is a solid center made mostly of iron and nickel.

What if you could dig to the other side of Earth?

Got a magma-proof suit and a magical drill that can cut through any surface? Then you're ready to dig some 7,900 miles (12,714 km) to Earth's other side. First you'd need to drill about 25 miles (40 km) through the planet's ultra-tough crust to its mantle. The heat and pressure at the mantle are intense enough to turn carbon into diamonds—and to, um, crush you. If you were able to survive, you'd still have to bore 1,800 more miles (2,897 km) to hit Earth's Mars-size core that can reach 11,000°F (6093°C). Now just keep drilling through the core and then the mantle and crust on the opposite side until you resurface on the planet's other side. But exit your tunnel fast. A hole dug through Earth would close quickly as surrounding rock filled in the empty space. The closing of the tunnel might cause small earthquakes, and your path home would definitely be blocked. Happy digging!

ROCK STARS

Rocks and minerals are everywhere on Earth! And it can be a challenge to tell one from the other. So what's the difference between a rock and a mineral? A rock is a naturally occurring solid object made mostly from minerals. Minerals are solid, nonliving substances that occur in nature—and the basic components of most rocks. Rocks can be made of just one mineral or, like granite, of many minerals. But not all rocks are made of minerals: Coal comes from plant material, while amber is formed from ancient tree resin.

Igneous

Named for the Greek word meaning "from fire," igneous rocks form when hot, molten liquid called magma cools. Pools of magma form deep underground and slowly work their way to Earth's surface. If they make it all the way, the liquid rock erupts and is called lava. As the layers of lava build up, they form a mountain called a volcano. Typical igneous rocks include obsidian, basalt, and pumice, which is so chock-full of gas bubbles that it actually floats in water.

ANDESITE

GRANITE PORPHYRY

Metamorphic

Metamorphic rocks are the masters of change! These rocks were once igneous or sedimentary, but thanks to intense heat and pressure deep within Earth, they have undergone a total transformation from their original form. These rocks never truly melt; instead, the heat twists and bends them until their shapes substantially change. Metamorphic rocks include slate as well as marble, which is used for buildings, monuments, and sculptures.

MICA SCHIST

BANDED GNEISS

Sedimentary

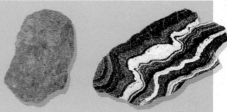

When wind, water, and ice constantly wear away and weather rocks, smaller pieces called sediment are left behind. These are sedimentary rocks, also known as gravel, sand, silt, and clay. As water flows downhill, it carries the sedimentary grains into lakes and oceans, where they are deposited. As the loose sediment piles up, the grains eventually get compacted or cemented back together again. The result is new sedimentary rock. Sandstone, gypsum, limestone, and shale are sedimentary rocks that are formed this way.

LIMESTONE

HALITE

Identifying Minerals

With so many different minerals in the world, how do we know what makes each one unique? Fortunately, each mineral has physical characteristics that geologists and amateur rock collectors use to tell them apart. Check out the physical characteristics below: color, luster, streak, cleavage, fracture, and hardness.

Color

When you look at a mineral, the first thing you see is its color. In some minerals, this is a key factor because their colors are almost always the same. For example, azurite, below, is always blue. But in other cases, impurities can change the natural color of a mineral. For instance, fluorite, above, can be green, red, violet, and other colors as well. This makes it a challenge to identify by color alone.

FLUORITE

AZURITE

Luster

"Luster" refers to the way light reflects from the surface of a mineral. Does a mineral appear metallic, like gold or silver? Or is it pearly like orpiment, or brilliant like diamond? "Earthy," "glassy," "silky," and "dull" are a few other terms used to describe luster.

ORPIMENT

DIAMOND

Streak

The "streak" is the color of a mineral's powder. When minerals are ground into powder, they often have a different color than when they are in crystal form. For example, the mineral pyrite usually looks gold, but when it is rubbed against a ceramic tile called a "streak plate," the mark it leaves is black.

PYRITE

Cleavage

"Cleavage" describes the way a mineral breaks. Because the structure of a specific mineral is always the same, it tends to break in the same pattern. Not all minerals have cleavage, but the minerals that do, like this microcline, break evenly in one or more directions. These minerals are usually described as having "perfect cleavage." But if the break isn't smooth and clean, cleavage can be considered "good" or "poor."

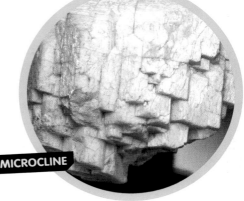

MICROCLINE

GOLD

Fracture

Some minerals, such as gold, do not break with cleavage. Instead, geologists say that they "fracture." There are different types of fractures, and, depending on the mineral, the fracture may be described as jagged, splintery, even, or uneven.

Hardness

The level of ease or difficulty with which a mineral can be scratched refers to its "hardness." Hardness is measured using a special chart called the Mohs Hardness Scale. The Mohs scale goes from 1 to 10. Softer minerals, which appear on the lower end of the scale, can be scratched by the harder minerals on the upper end of the scale.

RATING	MINERAL NAME	EXAMPLES
1	TALC	BAR OF SOAP
2	GYPSUM	FINGERNAIL
3	CALCITE	COPPER PENNY
4	FLUORITE	SOFT IRON NAIL
5	APATITE	STEEL POCKETKNIFE BLADE
6	ORTHOCLASE	WINDOW GLASS
7	QUARTZ	HARDENED STEEL FILE
8	TOPAZ	TOPAZ
9	CORUNDUM	RUBY, SAPPHIRE
10	DIAMOND	DIAMOND

MOHS HARDNESS SCALE

A HOT TOPIC

WHAT GOES ON
INSIDE A STEAMING, BREWING VOLCANO?

If you could look inside a volcano, you'd see something that looks like a long pipe, called a conduit. This leads from inside the magma chamber under the crust up to a vent, or opening, at the top of the mountain. Some conduits have branches that shoot off to the side, called fissures.

When pressure builds from gases inside the volcano, the gases must find an escape, and they head up toward the surface! An eruption occurs when lava, gases, ash, and rocks explode out of the vent.

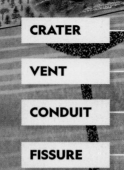

CRATER

VENT

CONDUIT

FISSURE

MAGMA CHAMBER

HARDENED LAVA AND ASH LAYERS

TYPES OF VOLCANOES

CINDER CONE VOLCANO
Eve Cone, Canada

Cinder cone volcanoes look like an upside-down bowl. They spew cinder and hot ash. Some of these volcanoes smoke and erupt for years at a time.

COMPOSITE VOLCANO
Licancábur, Chile

Composite volcanoes, or stratovolcanoes, form as lava, ash, and cinder from previous eruptions harden and build up over time. These volcanoes spit out pyroclastic flows, or thick explosions of hot ash and gas that travel at hundreds of miles an hour.

SHIELD VOLCANO
Mauna Loa, Hawaii, U.S.A.

The gentle, broad slopes of a shield volcano look like an ancient warrior's shield. Its eruptions are often slower. Lava splatters and bubbles rather than shooting forcefully into the air.

LAVA DOME VOLCANO
Mount St. Helens, Washington, U.S.A.

Dome volcanoes have steep sides. Hardened lava often plugs the vent at the top of a dome volcano. Pressure builds beneath the surface until the top blows.

RING OF FIRE

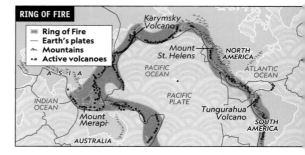

RING OF FIRE
- Ring of Fire
- Earth's plates
- Mountains
- Active volcanoes

Karymsky Volcano
Mount St. Helens
NORTH AMERICA
PACIFIC OCEAN
ATLANTIC OCEAN
A S I A
PACIFIC PLATE
INDIAN OCEAN
Mount Merapi
Tungurahua Volcano
SOUTH AMERICA
AUSTRALIA

Although volcanoes are found on every continent, most are located along an arc known as the Ring of Fire. This area, which forms a horseshoe shape in the Pacific Ocean, stretches some 24,900 miles (40,000 km). Several of the large, rigid plates that make up Earth's surface are found here, and they are prone to shifting toward each other and colliding. The result? Volcanic eruptions and earthquakes—and plenty of them. In fact, the Ring of Fire hosts 90 percent of the world's recorded earthquakes and about 75 percent of its active volcanoes.

Bet You Didn't Know!

7 Explosive Facts About Volcanoes

1 Volcanic eruptions on **Io,** one of **Jupiter's moons,** can **blast** up to **310 miles** (499 km).

One eruption 74,000 years ago was so **big** that its ash might've **blocked out the sun** enough to cause a **10-year ice age.** **2**

3 **Ash** from volcanic explosions on Earth can make the **moon** appear **blue.**

4 In 1883, a volcano erupting in Indonesia was **so loud** that it could be **heard in Australia.**

5 A volcano in Tanzania called Ol Doinyo Lengai **spews lava** that turns **white.**

6 Volcanoes on the **dwarf planet** Ceres are thought to **ooze** a mixture of **ice and salt.**

7 Scientists believe that **more than a million** volcanoes **might be under the ocean.**

[V]OLCANIC STATS

[...] below Earth's surface, pressure is building
[poo]ls of hot liquid rock and gas called magma.
[As] the pressure builds, magma bursts up through
[the w]orld's volcanoes. More than 80 percent of
[Earth'] surface was formed by these eruptions.

16[?]
Number of active volca[noes]
in the United States

[2,]000°F (1093°C)
[Maximu]m temperature of molten lava
[ejected] from an erupting volcano

75%
Percent of Earth's volcanoes
located in the Ring of Fire
around the Pacific Ocean

1,500
Number of potentially
active volcanoes on Earth

3[5]
Number of years Kilaue[a,]
Hawaii, U.S.A., continuo[usly]
erupted. It's one of the [most]
active volcanoes on Ear[th.]

[2]2,563 FEET (6,877 m)
[Height] of Ojos del Salado, the world's highest
[active v]olcano, in the Andes Mountains

50[0]
Estimated number of histo[rically]
recorded volcanic eruption[s]

QUIZ WHIZ

Are your space and Earth smarts out of this world? Take this quiz!

Write your answers on a piece of paper. Then check them below.

1 **True or false?** Impurities can change the natural color of a mineral, making it challenging to identify a mineral solely by color.

2 In 2021, researchers discovered a rare star shaped like a _____.
a. teardrop   **c.** pancake
b. heart   **d.** smiley face

3 Molten lava flowing from an erupting volcano can reach temperatures up to _____.
a. 500°F (260°C)   **c.** 1500°F (816°C)
b. 1000°F (538°C)   **d.** 2000°F (1093°C)

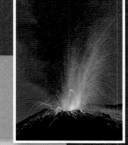

4 Mission specialist Bruce McCandless II once performed an untethered space walk, which meant he was unattached to his _____ while floating in space.
a. oxygen tank   **c.** space shuttle
b. water supply   **d.** Wi-Fi

5 Ganymede, the largest moon in our solar system, belongs to which planet?
a. Mars   **c.** Saturn
b. Jupiter   **d.** Neptune

Not **STUMPED** yet? Check out the *NATIONAL GEOGRAPHIC KIDS QUIZ WHIZ* book collection for more crazy **SPACE AND EARTH** questions!

HOMEWORK HELP

ACE YOUR SCIENCE FAIR

You can learn a lot about science from books, but to really experience it firsthand, you need to get into the lab and "do" some science. Whether you're entering a science fair or just want to learn more on your own, there are many scientific projects you can do. So put on your goggles and lab coat, and start experimenting.

Most likely, the topic of the project will be up to you. So remember to choose something that is interesting to you.

THE BASIS OF ALL SCIENTIFIC INVESTIGATION AND DISCOVERY IS THE SCIENTIFIC METHOD. CONDUCT YOUR EXPERIMENT USING THESE STEPS:

Observation/Research—Ask a question or identify a problem.

Hypothesis—Once you've asked a question, do some thinking and come up with some possible answers.

Experimentation—How can you determine if your hypothesis is correct? You test it. You perform an experiment. Make sure the experiment you design will produce an answer to your question.

Analysis—Gather your results, and use a consistent process to carefully measure the results.

Conclusion—Do the results support your hypothesis?

Report Your Findings—Communicate your results in the form of a paper that summarizes your entire experiment.

Bonus!

Take your project one step further. Your school may have an annual science fair, but there are also local, state, regional, and national science fair competitions. Compete with other students for awards, prizes, and scholarships!

EXPERIMENT DESIGN
There are three types of experiments you can do.

MODEL KIT—a display, such as an "erupting volcano" model. Simple and to the point.

DEMONSTRATION—shows the scientific principles in action, such as a tornado in a wind tunnel.

INVESTIGATION—the home run of science projects, and just the type of project for science fairs. This kind demonstrates proper scientific experimentation and uses the scientific method to reveal answers to questions.

SuperAviator, a two-person submarine, travels through coral reefs in the Florida Keys, Florida, U.S.A.

AWESOME
EXPLORATION

When she was just 15 years old, National Geographic Young Explorer Tiassa Mutunkei launched a campaign to protect, restore, and create awareness about Africa's wildlife. Here she shares how you, too, can become a wildlife hero, no matter how old you are.

10 WAYS YOU CAN BE A WILDLIFE HERO

START OR JOIN A WILDLIFE CLUB.

"You may already have a wildlife club at school or in your town. If not? Start one on your own! Talk to a trusted adult about how to set something up, and get your friends involved."

THROW A WILDLIFE PARTY.

"Visit a nearby animal shelter and learn how you can help. Have friends dress up as their favorite animals and come with some fun facts."

ORGANIZE A FUNDRAISER.

"Have a bake sale or a lemonade stand and donate the money to a wildlife organization."

TALK TO FRIENDS AND FAMILY.

"Don't be shy about sharing your ideas and concerns with others. You may gain a new perspective, and you never know when someone may be willing to help."

"ADOPT" AN ANIMAL.

"You can symbolically 'adopt' a wild animal through some organizations. You may not be able to take it home, but you can give it the resources it needs to survive and thrive."

PLANT AND GROW TREES.

"By doing so, you are creating and nurturing homes for birds and insects. And it's so easy to do!"

SET SMALL GOALS.

"Protecting wildlife can be an overwhelming task. So think about small changes you can make, and write them down. Remember: Any way you can help makes a difference for the future of all wildlife and our planet."

USE YOUR TALENTS TO RAISE AWARENESS.

"Do you love photography? Take pictures of animals you see and share them with others. That way, you can blend two passions into one cause."

VISIT NATIONAL PARKS AND ANIMAL SANCTUARIES.

"Really taking in a new-to-you environment may teach you so much about the animals that live there. The more you know, the more you can share with others."

TAKE CARE OF YOUR IMMEDIATE ENVIRONMENT.

"When you recycle, pick up trash, or make sure not to litter, you're actively protecting the habitat of the animals that live around you, including marine life."

The Explorer's Lens

LANNA WITH AN ARUÁ, ALSO KNOWN AS THE GIANT BRAZILIAN LAND SNAIL

Born and raised in Brazil's rural countryside, Leonardo Moutinho Lanna has been surrounded by beautiful nature since he was a kid. But he was far too focused on pursuing a career in business to really take in all the beauty around him. It wasn't until he joined a bird-watching tour with a friend that Lanna recognized an untapped passion and made a complete career change. Now a researcher, conservation biologist, and wildlife photographer, Lanna uses his work specifically to highlight insects, particularly the praying mantis. Here's more about this National Geographic Explorer!

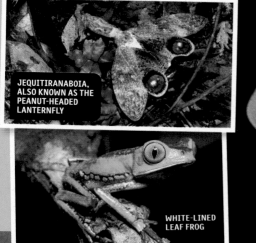

JEQUITIRANABOIA, ALSO KNOWN AS THE PEANUT-HEADED LANTERNFLY

WHITE-LINED LEAF FROG

HOODED MANTIS

NGK: Have you always been into nature and biology?

Leo: As a kid, I liked nature, but I was never a nerd about bugs or birds like I am now. I was actually focused on a career in business and marketing until I realized that there was something missing in my life. After going bird-watching with friends, I became fascinated by nature. I decided soon after that I was going to change direction and go into biology. I started school all over again, but it was truly worth it.

NGK: What is a standout moment you've had in the field?

Leo: Oh, there are so many! But truly, nothing beats being in the Amazon. It's hard to put the experience into words. There are so many textures, colors, shapes, and things you can't even imagine! I work a lot at night, which is when life in the Amazon comes alive. I used to be scared of the dark, but now I can't wait to go out there. It's like discovering a new planet every time I go into the field.

NGK: How did you overcome your fear of the dark?

Leo: It's hard to be afraid of the dark when you're inside this world that is just so alive. And the thing is, there is nothing that can harm you if you are careful and don't disturb nature. As I walk in the jungle, I see spiders and snakes everywhere, and I've heard jaguars—but I know I will be safe if I keep my distance and remember that I am a guest in their world.

NGK: What is one myth you'd like to bust about the praying mantis?

Leo: That they will attack you. People think they are harmful because their legs are full of spines and they have this violent reputation. There is no praying mantis on the planet that will hurt you—they have no poison and cannot bite or sting. But you should always leave them alone. Also, they are not strict carnivores: We recently documented a mantis eating plant sap, meaning they may use other food sources in nature.

ROTHSCHILD'S SILK MOTH

WAX-TAIL HOPPER

SOUTH AMERICAN DWARF DEAD LEAF MANTIS

VELVET SWAMPSNAKE

NGK: What is the coolest thing about your job?

Leo: I love connecting people to nature through insects. I am also a photographer and artist, and I enjoy blending science and art to help others appreciate this amazing planet that is full of limitless life.

NGK: Much of your work focuses on the praying mantis. What draws you to these insects?

Leo: It's funny, when I first went into biology, I didn't want anything to do with insects! I thought they were a bit boring. But insects are the most diverse group of species on this planet, and they are so fascinating. Also, the praying mantis is not studied widely in Brazil. We think there are more than 300 types of mantises to discover in Brazil alone, yet no one was doing much research. So I decided to.

NGK: What advice do you have for kids who are interested in following in your explorer footsteps?

Leo: First step is to just observe the world around you! Look at the bark of a tree. What is growing there? How does it change over the seasons? Take photos, draw pictures, or write it down. There is amazing nature all around us, even in big cities. So go out and embrace it!

EPiC SCIENCE FAiLS

Nat Geo Explorers spill their most embarrassing moments.

Even supersmart scientists mess up sometimes! These Nat Geo Explorers reveal some of their wildest slipups—and what they learned from them.

MONKEY BUSINESS

THE SCIENTIST:
Roberto Zariquiey
COOL JOB:
Linguist
THE LOCATION:
Ucayali, Peru

A NANCY MA'S NIGHT MONKEY IN VENEZUELA

"I spent a few weeks in a village in the Amazon rainforest taping hours of conversations with native speakers. Using a brand-new recording device, I was going to study and preserve the Indigenous (also called Native) languages of these people.

"But on the last day, a Nancy Ma's night monkey jumped on the table with my computer ... and knocked it onto the floor! When I turned the machine back on, all of the recordings were gone—and we hadn't made backups. We usually make two copies of the files and store them on separate computers. But we hadn't learned how to make backups with the new recorder yet.

"That monkey was definitely naughty. But I learned never to use equipment without fully knowing how it works."

TRAMPLED BY A TURTLE

THE SCIENTIST: Vanessa Bézy
COOL JOB: Marine biologist
THE LOCATION: Ostional, Costa Rica

"I study how and why thousands of olive ridley sea turtles come to nest on one beach at the same time. The nesting happens all night for about a week, so I don't get much sleep.

"One night I was waiting for some new volunteers to arrive, and I thought I'd catch a quick snooze. I found an old log on the beach, pressed my back up against it, and drifted off. After a few minutes, a 130-pound (59-kg) turtle came up over the log and clambered onto my shoulder—ouch! These sea turtles are cute, but they're also smelly, super loud, and really heavy.

"I pushed it off me and scrambled to my feet. The turtle was in a sort of zombie mode trying to find a spot to lay her eggs, so she just got off me and kept cruising.

"Now I always have a buddy nearby, get as much rest as I can in the day (even though it's really hot!), and bring a portable hammock, just in case."

VANESSA BÉZY RESEARCHES NESTING OLIVE RIDLEY SEA TURTLES IN COSTA RICA.

SO LONG, SCIENCE!

THE SCIENTIST:
Lydia Gibson

COOL JOB:
Ecologist and anthropologist

THE LOCATION:
Jamaica

"One day I was placing a temperature-reading device in a stream; it would gather data from the water every hour and keep tracking for years. (Cool tech, right?) But I forgot to bring string to attach the tracker to a tree and keep it from floating away. I thought, I'm an explorer in the jungle! I should use vines!

"So I tied a willowy, supple vine to the tracker and moved on to my next task. A few rainy months went by, and something told me I should check on that tracker. I went back, and it was long gone. I said goodbye to $250 and about two years' worth of data, since I'd used this tracker before. I should've just come back with the string!"

LYDIA GIBSON USES AN UNDERWATER DRONE TO LOOK FOR AQUATIC LIFE IN JAMAICA; (RIGHT) THE NOW LOST TRACKER ON THE VINE.

MAURICE ONIANG'O'S STEADY HANDS TOOK THIS PHOTO OF A VENOMOUS MOUNT KENYA BUSH VIPER.

"I'm terrified of snakes. But Kenya has two nearly extinct snake species that are found nowhere else. I felt I had to help Kenyans understand these animals.

"Feeling very nervous, I went into the forest with an expert to take photos of the Mount Kenya bush viper. This species is so rare because poachers sell them as pets in other countries, and locals kill them. The expert spotted one on a branch—and I went totally numb. With my hands shaking, I took about 500 pictures ... and most of them were very blurry. But after a few hours, I started to relax and got a few good photos.

"I'm still scared of snakes sometimes—I can't look at pictures of them eating or striking. But I learned to overcome my fear to help them survive in the wild."

FEAR FACTOR

THE EXPLORER:
Maurice Oniang'o

COOL JOB:
Conservationist and journalist

THE LOCATION:
Chuka, Kenya

TREE TRICK

THE SCIENTIST: Nareerat Boonchai

COOL JOB: Paleobotanist

THE LOCATION: Tak, Thailand

NAREERAT BOONCHAI STUDIES FOSSILIZED TREES LIKE THIS 127-FOOT (39-M) TREE IN THAILAND.

"I take samples of fossilized trees and compare them to modern ones to observe how the climate has changed. To protect the fossil after we uncover it, we build a shelter around it, then coat a small area of the tree with a clear liquid that prevents the sample from crumbling.

"On one expedition, my team was researching a 150,000-year-old, 127-foot (39-m)-long fossilized tree when a volunteer called. He said the chemical must have reacted badly because the tree was covered in a white substance! Worried that the tree was damaged, we rushed to the site.

"Then I realized what had happened: In Thailand, some people believe that spirits live in the trees and might bring people luck. Overnight, locals had rubbed a mixture of baby powder and water on the tree, hoping to see a lucky number on the wood. The tree was fine (the powder washed off in the rain), and I learned to always think about the local customs when I'm working on a project—and add fences around my specimens!"

Keep Earth WiLD

A National Geographic photographer gives you a behind-the-scenes look at his quest to save animals.

Joel Sartore has squealed like a pig, protected his camera from a parakeet, and suffered through a stink attack—all to help save animals through photography. "I hope people will look these animals in their eyes and then be inspired to protect them," says Sartore, a National Geographic photographer.

Sartore is on a mission to take pictures of more than 15,000 animal species living in captivity through his project, the National Geographic Photo Ark. During each photo shoot, he works with zookeepers, aquarists, and wildlife rehabbers to keep his subjects safe and comfortable. Read on for some of Sartore's most memorable moments.

Moment of SNOOZE

GIANT PANDAS, *native to China*

Zoo Atlanta, Atlanta, Georgia, U.S.A.

These giant pandas were just a few months old when I put the football-size twins in a small, white photo tent and snapped a few pics as they tumbled on top of each other. But the youngsters were tiring out, and I knew I was losing my chance to get a memorable photo before they drifted off to sleep. One cub put his head on the back of the other, and I managed to capture an awesome shot just seconds before the two cubs fell asleep.

> Some arctic fox dens are 300 years old.

Moment of HA

ARCTIC FOX, *native to the Arctic regions of Eurasia, North America, Greenland, and Iceland*

Great Bend Brit Spaugh Zoo, Great Bend, Kansas, U.S.A.

Todd the arctic fox wanted to sniff everything, but he was moving too quickly for me to get a good picture. I needed to do something surprising to get his attention, so I squealed like a pig! The weird sound made the fox stop, sit down, and tilt his head as if he were thinking, What's the matter with you? Good thing I was fast, because the pig noise only worked once. The next time I squealed, Todd completely ignored me.

More WILDNESS! Photo Ark spotlights all kinds of animals. Meet some of Joel Sartore's strangest subjects.

BUDGETT'S FROG

ORANGE SPOTTED FILEFISH

MEDITERRANEAN RED BUG

NORTH AMERICAN PORCUPINE

Sartore uses black or white backgrounds because he wants the focus to be on the animals. That way a mouse is as important as an elephant.

Newborn giant pandas are about the size of a stick of butter.

A single colony of gray-headed flying foxes can include a million bats.

Giraffes sometimes use their tongues to clean their ears.

Moment of YAY

GRAY-HEADED FLYING FOX, *native to southeastern Australia*

Australian Bat Clinic, Advancetown, Australia

When I arrived at the clinic, I was amazed to see all sorts of bats just hanging from laundry racks all over the rescue center. They sleepily watched me as I walked through the room and asked a staff member for a friendly flying fox to photograph. She scooped up a sweet bat and placed its feet on a wire rack in front of my backdrop. The calm bat didn't seem to mind being in front of the camera. The best part? This clinic rehabilitates bats that have torn their wings, and my subject was eventually released back into the wild.

Moment of YUM

RETICULATED GIRAFFE, *native to Africa*

Gladys Porter Zoo, Brownsville, Texas, U.S.A.

You definitely can't make a giraffe do anything it doesn't want to do. So to get this animal to be part of our photo shoot, we combined the activity with one of the giraffe's favorite things: lunch. We hung the huge black backdrop from the rafters in the part of the giraffe's enclosure where it gets fed. The giraffe ambled in, not minding me at all. For about ten minutes, while the animal munched on bamboo leaves, I could take all the pictures I wanted. But as soon as lunch was over, the giraffe walked out, and our photo shoot was done.

117

GETTING THE SHOT

Capturing good photographs of wild animals can be tough. To get amazing pictures of them, nature photographers often tap into their wild side, thinking and even acting like the creatures they're snapping. Whether tracking deadly snakes or swimming with penguins, the artists must be daring—but they also need to know when to keep their distance. Three amazing photographers tell their behind-the-scenes stories of how they got these incredible shots.

Check out this book!

GUIDE TO PHOTOGRAPHY

FANG FOCUS

PHOTOGRAPHER: Mattias Klum
ANIMAL: Jameson's mamba
SHOOT SITE: Cameroon, Africa

"The Jameson's mamba is beautiful but dangerous. It produces highly toxic venom. My team searched for weeks for the reptile, asking locals about the best spots to see one. At last we came across a Jameson's mamba peeking out from tree leaves. Carefully, I inched closer. It's important to make this kind of snake think that you don't see it. Otherwise it might feel threatened and strike you. At about four and a half feet (1.4 m) away, I took the picture. Then I backed up and the snake slid off."

SECRETS FROM AMAZING WILDLIFE PHOTOGRAPHERS

Usually solitary creatures, oceanic whitetip sharks have been observed swimming with pods of pilot whales.

SHARK TALE

PHOTOGRAPHER: Brian Skerry
ANIMAL: Oceanic whitetip shark
SHOOT SITE: The Bahamas

"I wanted to photograph an endangered oceanic whitetip shark. So I set sail with a group of scientists to an area where some had been sighted. Days later, the dorsal fin of a whitetip rose from the water near our boat. One scientist was lowered in a metal cage into the water to observe the fish. Then I dived in. Because I wasn't behind the protective bars, I had to be very careful. These nine-foot (2.7-m) sharks can be aggressive, but this one was just curious. She swam around us for two hours and allowed me to take pictures of her. She was the perfect model."

LEAPS and BOUNDS

PHOTOGRAPHER: Nick Nichols
ANIMAL: Bengal tiger
SHOOT SITE: Bandhavgarh National Park, India

"While following a tiger along a cliff, I saw him leap from the edge to his secret watering hole and take a drink. I wanted a close-up of the cat, but it wouldn't have been safe to approach him. Figuring he'd return to the spot, I set up a camera on the cliff that shoots off an infrared beam. Walking into the beam triggers the camera to click. The device was there for three months, but this was the only shot I got of the cat. Being near tigers makes the hair stand up on my arm. It was a gift to encounter such a magnificent creature."

PHOTO SECRETS REVEALED—

Harbor seal pups sometimes hang on to their mothers' backs in the water.

HARBOR SEAL

Some harbor seals can also be found in freshwater lakes and rivers.

A PATIENT PHOTOGRAPHER TALKS ABOUT MEETING A NEW "FRIEND."

PHOTOGRAPHER Ralph Pace
LOCATION Monterey, California, U.S.A.

"When I jump into water that's full of animals, they usually all swim away. To them, I'm just a big, goofy thing that's blowing lots of bubbles and making strange noises. So I've learned to be patient and wait for the perfect shot.

"I was snapping photos of kelp and sea urchins when I felt a pressure on my back. It surprised me, so I quickly turned around. It was a harbor seal, and it was swimming away! A few minutes later, I felt it climbing on my back again, and when I turned, it zoomed off, almost like it was shy. Harbor seals are curious and playful, so I figured it might come back. I thought, Next time it comes, I'll just stay patient and see what it does.

"After a few minutes, the seal crawled up my back, nibbled a bit on my hair, and then popped over the top of my head. Then the seal stopped—it must have caught a glimpse of itself in my camera because it just floated in the water, totally still. I felt like it was thinking, Whoa.

"The kelp forests where these harbor seals live are home to about 800 species of animals, but this habitat is in danger because of ocean heat waves caused by climate change. Connecting with an animal like this reminds me why it's so important to protect the kelp forests—let's save this habitat together!"

Although they mainly eat fish, harbor seals also eat squid, octopus, clams, and crabs.

ARCTIC OCEAN
NORTH AMERICA
EUROPE
ASIA
ATLANTIC OCEAN
AFRICA
PACIFIC OCEAN
PACIFIC OCEAN
SOUTH AMERICA
INDIAN OCEAN
AUSTRALIA
SOUTHERN OCEAN
ANTARCTICA

Where harbor seals live

121

WILD VET ADVENTURE

WITH ONE WILDLIFE DOCTOR

Animals can't tell their doctors when they aren't feeling well. So that makes the job of a wildlife veterinarian a little ... well, wild. Meet Gabby Wild, who travels the world to provide medical care for animals in zoos, shelters, national parks, and rescue centers. Here, the wildlife vet tells you how she treated one animal in need of a little medicine—and a lot of care.

KHUN CHAI (LEFT) NEEDED TO DRINK MILK FIVE TIMES A DAY.

ELEPHANT CALF GETS SOME TLC

"In Thailand, a country in Southeast Asia, people sometimes use elephants as work animals to help on their farms. One farmer illegally stole an elephant calf from the forest, which he thought would be cheaper than buying an adult elephant. But soon the calf was close to dying. The farmer realized the young elephant needed medical help.

"He brought the youngster to a wildlife hospital where I was working, and we named the calf Khun Chai, which means 'prince' in Thai. We observed that he didn't want to play with the other elephants and refused to drink the milk we offered him.

"I had studied some elephant behavior, and I thought that maybe he just didn't want to be bothered. So when I went into his enclosure, I sat quietly on the ground and only looked at him out of the corner of my eye. About a half hour later, I could feel a light tap on my shoulder—Khun Chai was patting me with his trunk!

"From that moment on, Khun Chai followed me all around the rescue center. I fed him milk five times a day, walked him three times a day, and bathed him a few times a week. As he ate and gained weight, he became a healthy elephant.

"We decided that because people had raised Khun Chai, it would be dangerous to release him back into the forest. So eventually we moved him to a local conservation center where he could live with other elephants. I'm glad I could help him grow up to be healthy and happy."

A male Asian elephant usually lives with its mother for about five years.

Extreme Job!

There's not much normal about John Stevenson's job. A volcanologist, Stevenson evaluates eruptions, follows lava flows, and travels to remote locations to learn more about volcanoes. Read on for more details on his risky but rewarding career.

TESTING NEW RESEARCH EQUIPMENT

SCIENCE-MINDED "As a kid, I really liked science and nature, and in college I pursued chemical engineering but studied geology as well. Having a background in all of the sciences gave me a better understanding of the bigger picture, from volcano monitoring to understanding eruptions."

BIG DIG "I once spent ten days collecting pumice and ash samples from a 4,200-year-old eruption in Iceland. We'd dig in the soil until we found the layer of ash that we wanted, then spend up to two hours photographing and taking samples. At night, we'd find a nice spot by a stream, eat dinner, and camp out."

DANGER IN THE AIR "Being exposed to the edge of a lava flow can be dangerous. The air is hot and can be thick with poisonous sulfur dioxide gas. Once, while working at the active Bárðarbunga volcano in Iceland, we had to wear gas masks and use an electronic gas meter as dust swirled around us."

RAINING ASH "When I worked at Volcán de Colima in Mexico, we camped a few miles from the crater. One night, I woke up to a whooshing sound. This quickly changed to a *patter-patter-patter* that sounded like heavy rain falling on the tent. When I put my hand out to feel the rain, it was covered in coarse gray sand. The volcano had erupted, and ash was raining down on us. We quickly packed up our stuff and headed to a safer spot."

JOB PERKS "I get to play with fun gadgets in cool locations. If I didn't have to work, I would still go hiking and camping and play with gadgets and computers in my spare time anyway. I enjoy trying to solve the problems of getting the right data and finding a way to process it so that it can tell us about how the world works."

WORKING IN THE FIELD

1 FLYING HIGH

On May 21, 1932, **Amelia Earhart** became the first woman to fly solo across the Atlantic Ocean when she landed her Lockheed Vega plane in Northern Ireland. During her 15-hour flight, Earhart drank tomato juice and ate chocolate to keep herself fueled.

AS A CHILD, EARHART HAD A LARGE BLACK DOG NAMED JAMES FEROCIOUS.

8 EXTRAORDINARY JOURNEYS

THESE BRAVE AND GRITTY EXPLORERS BATTLED HIGH SEAS, UNFORGIVING ICE, AND LONG STRETCHES OF FOREIGN TERRAIN ON THEIR EPIC ADVENTURES.

2 HEADING WEST

Sacagawea showed **Meriwether Lewis and William Clark** the way during their epic journey across thousands of miles of the American West. In November 1804, Sacagawea, a Shoshone Indian, and her French-Canadian husband joined up to translate for the group as they encountered American Indians.

3 MOON SHOT

Neil Armstrong took this picture of **Edwin "Buzz" Aldrin** during the 1969 Apollo 11 mission to the moon. The NASA astronauts were the first of only 12 people ever to walk on the moon.

4

FANTASTIC VOYAGES

To extend naval power, Chinese admiral **Zheng He** (circa 1371–1433) sailed the Indian Ocean during seven far-reaching expeditions. On his first journey, in 1405, he took 62 ships and 27,800 people to India and Sri Lanka.

PHOTOGRAPHER FRANK HURLEY DOCUMENTED THE FRIGID ADVENTURE USING BOTH A FILM AND A MOVIE CAMERA.

5

EXTREME ENDURANCE

Polar explorer **Ernest Shackleton's** ice-encrusted boat, *Endurance,* became stuck in January 1915 during his attempt to lead the first team to cross Antarctica. The ship sank, but the entire crew was saved after a year and a half, thanks to Shackleton's heroic efforts.

SCOTT'S TEAM ARRIVED JUST ONE MONTH AFTER AMUNDSEN'S—AND PERISHED ON THEIR TREK BACK TO BASE CAMP.

ROAMING RAFT

7

In 1947, Norwegian explorer **Thor Heyerdahl** set out from Peru in a simple, balsa-wood raft to show how ancient peoples could have crossed the Pacific Ocean. The voyage ended after 101 days at sea when the raft, the *Kon-Tiki,* shipwrecked the crew on a Polynesian island. (They were rescued.)

6

DRESSED FOR ACTION

The race to reach the South Pole between Norwegian **Roald Amundsen** (pictured) and British explorer **Robert Falcon Scott** was a tale for the ages. Amundsen and his team reached the South Pole first, on December 14, 1911.

WORLD TRAVELER

Even before airplanes, distance was no object for **Ibn Battuta**, a 14th-century Arab explorer. He traveled over some 75,000 miles (120,000 km) throughout the Middle East, along the African coast, and into India and China. His travel records help historians understand the Muslim world of his time.

8

125

ELEPHANT-STAGRAM
STORIES

As an ecologist— someone who studies all aspects of life in an ecosystem, like animal behavior— Dominique Gonçalves has an exceptional relationship with elephants. Her mission? To help restore and conserve the elephant population in Gorongosa National Park near her home in Mozambique (a country in southeastern Africa). As part of her job studying elephants, Dominique tracks and photographs them and monitors their movements, growth, health, and behavior. And, yep, sometimes this means getting up close and personal with the park's elephants. "It's not every day you see your own reflection in the eye of an elephant," she says of a recent run-in with one of the animals she observes. "In the wild, you really realize how majestic and powerful they are." Here, Dominique shares more fascinating facts about elephants!

They are curious. When Dominique came face-to-trunk with a male elephant she'd been tracking for a while, she first felt fear— until she realized that the elephant was only curious, even bending his head as if to get a better look. After a quiet, peaceful moment, he lifted his head, looked around, and slowly led the other elephants to a nearby lagoon. "He was so close, I couldn't even breathe," she recalls. "Then he just walked away."

They express emotions. Through her studies, Dominique has seen firsthand how each elephant is an individual, with complex relationships and emotions. In fact, studies show that an elephant's range of emotions can include joy, love, grief, rage, and compassion. "They have great intelligence, power, and strength ... but are also warm and compassionate to each other," says Dominique.

They're protective parents. Mama elephants are known to be fiercely protective of their young. Dominique once observed a female knocking down trees and hitting herself on the back with a branch as she tried to guard her injured baby from nearby humans, who she sensed were a threat. "They do anything to protect their family, especially the matriarchs and the females," says Dominique.

THIS YEAR'S CHALLENGE

Elephants are extremely intelligent and socially complex animals. Sadly, these amazing creatures are endangered because of poaching and habitat loss. People like Dominique Gonçalves are trying to raise awareness to help save elephants and their habitat.

Humans are very social, too. One of the ways we communicate is through social media. It allows people to interact with friends, share interests, and be part of a community. Social media is also a great tool to connect with others and raise awareness for an important cause.

But what if elephants had social media? What do you think they would say?

Create a social media profile for an elephant, including a few posts raising awareness for their species. Here are some things to think about as you create their profile:

- What would they post about?
- What information would they want to share with their friends and followers?
- How would they use their platform to make a positive change?

You can print and use a template from our website or make your own! We'll feature several elephant profiles on the National Geographic Kids website next year so you can see what kids from around the country have created. The winner will be featured in next year's Almanac and in *National Geographic Kids* magazine.

➜ Get details and the official rules at **natgeokids.com/almanac.**

LAST YEAR'S CHALLENGE

We asked you to imagine yourself as a tree, and you created an amazing, unique forest of trees from all around the world! You let us know how important trees are to the animals and ecosystems where they live, and you shared your concerns about challenges threatening different tree species.

- Artwork and autobiographies were submitted about trees from across the globe, including North America, Europe, Africa, and Asia.
- The oak tree had the most entries, followed by many varieties of fruit tree (especially cherry), then maple, redwood, pine, and willow.
- Many of you sent us fascinating, less familiar trees, including ʻōhiʻa, baobab, red sanders, jacaranda, neem, and banyan.

Congratulations and thank you to all of our "Me as a Tree" participants for your time, energy, information, and creativity. This year, for the first time ever, two entries tied for the Grand Prize. Amazingly, they are both about the same kind of tree: coastal redwood.

Adam Amir Belmezouar, age 11
Abby Kress, age 12

See more entries online at **natgeokids.com/almanac.**

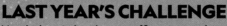

QUIZ WHIZ

Discover just how much you know about exploration with this quiz!

Write your answers on a piece of paper. Then check them below.

1 Upon landing in Northern Ireland after a 15-hour flight in 1932, Amelia Earhart became the first woman to fly solo across which body of water?

a. Atlantic Ocean
b. Pacific Ocean
c. Indian Ocean
d. Arctic Ocean

2 **True or false?** Harbor seals live in the Northern Hemisphere.

3 A single colony of gray-headed flying foxes can include how many bats?

a. 100
b. 1,000
c. 100,000
d. 1 million

4 Scientists studying fossilized trees take samples, then compare them to modern trees to observe _____.

a. how long they lived
b. how the climate has changed
c. why they grew
d. why they fell down

5 **True or false?** All praying mantises are strict carnivores, munching only on other insects.

Not **STUMPED** yet? Check out the *NATIONAL GEOGRAPHIC KIDS QUIZ WHIZ* collection for more crazy **EXPLORATION** questions!

ANSWERS: 1. a; 2. True; 3. d; 4. b; 5. False: Some eat plants.

HOMEWORK HELP

How to Write a Perfect Essay

Need to write an essay? Does the assignment feel as big as climbing Mount Everest? Fear not. You're up to the challenge! The following step-by-step tips will help you with this monumental task.

1 **BRAINSTORM.** Sometimes the subject matter of your essay is assigned to you, sometimes it's not. Either way, you have to decide what you want to say. Start by brainstorming some ideas, writing down any thoughts you have about the subject. Then read over everything you've come up with and consider which idea you think is the strongest. Ask yourself what you want to write about the most. Keep in mind the goal of your essay. Can you achieve the goal of the assignment with this topic? If so, you're good to go.

2 **WRITE A TOPIC SENTENCE.** This is the main idea of your essay, a statement of your thoughts on the subject. Again, consider the goal of your essay. Think of the topic sentence as an introduction that tells your readers what the rest of your essay will be about.

3 **OUTLINE YOUR IDEAS.** Once you have a good topic sentence, you then need to support that main idea with more detailed information, facts, thoughts, and examples. These supporting points answer one question about your topic sentence—"Why"? This is where research and perhaps more brainstorming come in. Then organize these points in the way you think makes the most sense, probably in order of importance. Now you have an outline for your essay.

4 **ON YOUR MARK, GET SET, WRITE!** Follow your outline, using each of your supporting points as the topic sentence of its own paragraph. Use descriptive words to get your ideas across to readers. Go into detail, using specific information to tell your story or make your point. Stay on track, making sure that everything you include is somehow related to the main idea of your essay. Use transitions to make your writing flow.

5 **WRAP IT UP.** Finish your essay with a conclusion that summarizes your entire essay and restates your main idea.

6 **PROOFREAD AND REVISE.** Check for errors in spelling, capitalization, punctuation, and grammar. Look for ways to make your writing clear, understandable, and interesting. Use descriptive verbs, adjectives, and adverbs when possible. It also helps to have someone else read your work to point out things you might have missed. Then make the necessary corrections and changes in a second draft. Repeat this revision process once more to make your final draft as good as you can.

FUN and GAMES

Burrowing owlets, like this one seen in Florida, U.S.A., mimic rattlesnake sounds to scare predators away from their nests.

ANIMAL FUN HOUSE

These animal photos have been given the fun house mirror treatment. On a separate sheet of paper, unscramble the letters to identify what's in each picture.

ANSWERS ON PAGE 354

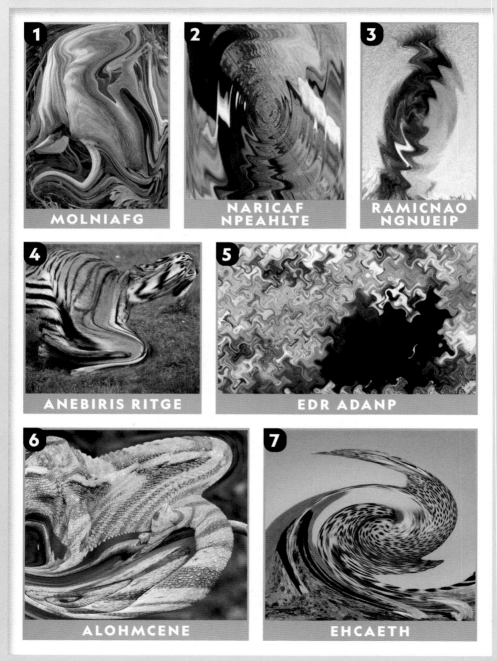

1 MOLNIAFG

2 NARICAF NPEAHLTE

3 RAMICNAO NGNUEIP

4 ANEBIRIS RITGE

5 EDR ADANP

6 ALOHMCENE

7 EHCAETH

FUNNY FILL-IN

Ask a friend to give you words to fill in the blanks in this story and write them on a separate sheet of paper. Then read the story out loud and fill in the words for a laugh.

_____ and I were exploring the bottom of the _____ when we found a shipwreck.
(friend's name) .... (body of water)

And not just any shipwreck—the _____ , which disappeared in the _____ . We swam
.... (celebrity) .... (historical era)

through the _____ to see what we could find. My favorite part was an old ballroom with
.... (liquid)

a(n) _____ hanging from the ceiling, lots of old-fashioned _____ , and plenty of
.... (piece of furniture) .... (noun, plural)

_____ swimming around. Best of all, we found a large wooden _____ . We struggled to
(animal, plural) .... (noun)

open it, and _____ billowed out when we finally lifted off the top. But inside were lots of
.... (something gross)

_____ _____ and sparkly jewelry. While we were _____ our discovery,
(color) (noun, plural) .... (verb ending in -ing)

we heard a noise. A giant _____ had _____ wrapped its _____
.... (animal) .... (adverb ending in -ly) .... (body part, plural)

around the fortune! Uh-oh. Looks like this treasure's already been claimed.

133

WHAT IN THE WORLD?

HEADS OR TAILS?

These photographs show close-up and faraway views of animal body parts. On a separate sheet of paper, unscramble the letters to identify what's in each picture.

ANSWERS ON PAGE 354

TCA KHEWSSIR

ECLMA MUPH

SOEOM REATNL

KASEN ETUOGN

HAWEL AITL

KOEGC TOFO

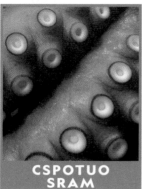

CSPOTUO SRAM

LUEB-OTDEOF OYBBO OFTO

EOSTRRO MBCO

FROM THE PAGES OF *QUIZ WHIZ:*

STUMP
YOUR PARENTS

Answer the questions on a separate sheet of paper. If your parents can't answer these questions, maybe they should go to school instead of you!

ANSWERS ON PAGE 354

THE FORMULA ROSSA RIDE— *BEFORE* PEOPLE WERE REQUIRED TO WEAR THE ANSWER BELOW!

1 **At what temperature does sand melt?**
A. 300°F (149°C)   C. 2300°F (1260°C)
B. 1300°F (705°C)   D. 3000°F (1649°C)

2 **In your lifetime, how many spiders will you eat while sleeping?**
A. 4 to 8
B. 10 to 15
C. 1,000 to 2,000
D. Zero. Spiders typically don't let themselves get eaten.

3 **What causes the bulge in the middle of Earth?**
A. the weight of the people and animals living near the Equator
B. the force created as Earth spins on its axis
C. heavy ice at the poles pressing down on Earth
D. oceans near the Equator

4 **The basenji, a dog from Africa, is also called the barkless dog. What does this dog do instead of barking?**
A. scratches
B. spins in a circle
C. yodels
D. nods yes or no

5 **What is the largest shoe size in NBA history?**
A. 13.5
B. 22
C. 30
D. 16.5

6 **Riders on the superfast Formula Rossa roller coaster, located in Abu Dhabi, United Arab Emirates, are required to wear _____ .**
A. helmets   C. bow ties
B. mouth guards   D. goggles

7 **In the Middle Ages, what did women in Florence, Italy, consider fashionable?**
A. dyeing their hair purple
B. wearing braces on their teeth
C. shaving off their eyebrows
D. growing long beards

8 **The strawberry is a member of which plant family?**
A. cherry   C. pumpkin
B. rose   D. Venus flytrap

9 **Seahorses move mainly by doing what?**
A. waiting for the ocean current to propel them forward
B. flapping small fins on their backs
C. curling their tails and using them like pogo sticks
D. catching a ride with SpongeBob

10 **To see a sunrise on this planet, you'd need to look west instead of east.**
A. Venus   C. Mars
B. Earth   D. Saturn

135

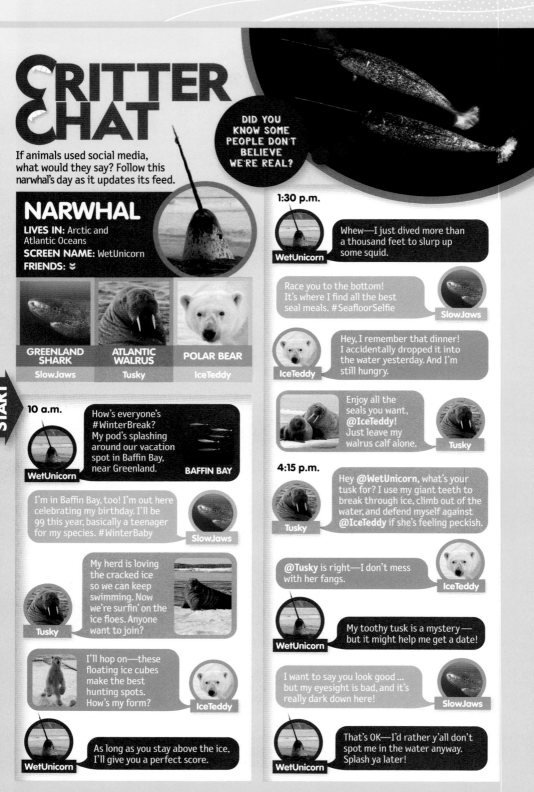

CRITTER CHAT

If animals used social media, what would they say? Follow this narwhal's day as it updates its feed.

DID YOU KNOW SOME PEOPLE DON'T BELIEVE WE'RE REAL?

NARWHAL

LIVES IN: Arctic and Atlantic Oceans
SCREEN NAME: WetUnicorn
FRIENDS: ⌄

GREENLAND SHARK
SlowJaws

ATLANTIC WALRUS
Tusky

POLAR BEAR
IceTeddy

START

10 a.m.

WetUnicorn: How's everyone's #WinterBreak? My pod's splashing around our vacation spot in Baffin Bay, near Greenland.

BAFFIN BAY

SlowJaws: I'm in Baffin Bay, too! I'm out here celebrating my birthday. I'll be 99 this year, basically a teenager for my species. #WinterBaby

Tusky: My herd is loving the cracked ice so we can keep swimming. Now we're surfin' on the ice floes. Anyone want to join?

IceTeddy: I'll hop on—these floating ice cubes make the best hunting spots. How's my form?

WetUnicorn: As long as you stay above the ice, I'll give you a perfect score.

1:30 p.m.

WetUnicorn: Whew—I just dived more than a thousand feet to slurp up some squid.

SlowJaws: Race you to the bottom! It's where I find all the best seal meals. #SeafloorSelfie

IceTeddy: Hey, I remember that dinner! I accidentally dropped it into the water yesterday. And I'm still hungry.

Tusky: Enjoy all the seals you want, @IceTeddy! Just leave my walrus calf alone.

4:15 p.m.

Tusky: Hey @WetUnicorn, what's your tusk for? I use my giant teeth to break through ice, climb out of the water, and defend myself against @IceTeddy if she's feeling peckish.

IceTeddy: @Tusky is right—I don't mess with her fangs.

WetUnicorn: My toothy tusk is a mystery—but it might help me get a date!

SlowJaws: I want to say you look good ... but my eyesight is bad, and it's really dark down here!

WetUnicorn: That's OK—I'd rather y'all don't spot me in the water anyway. Splash ya later!

FIND THE HIDDEN ANIMALS

Animals often blend in with their environment for protection. Find each animal listed below in one of the pictures. On a separate sheet of paper, write the letter of the correct picture and the animal's name.

ANSWERS ON PAGE 354

1. **ghost crab**
2. **agile frog**
3. **day octopus**
4. **crab spider**
5. **western screech owl**
6. **red-shouldered macaws**

A

B

C

D

E

F

WHAT IN THE WORLD?

BELOW SEA LEVEL

These photographs show close-up views of underwater creatures. On a separate sheet of paper, unscramble the letters to identify what's in each picture.

ANSWERS ON PAGE 354

ASE RSAST

CSOUPTO

HAEERSOS

INGALHSEF

ARNTSYIG

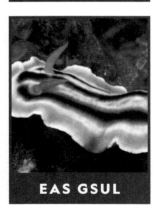

EAS GSUL

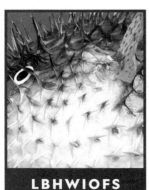

LBHWIOFS

AES HIURNC

OSTLREB

FUNNY FILL-IN

SCUBA SURPRISE

Ask a friend to give you words to fill in the blanks in this story and write them on a separate sheet of paper. Then read the story out loud and fill in the words for a laugh.

My family and I went to _____ for a beach vacation. On our last day we all went scuba
faraway place

_____ . We _____ off the _____ wearing _____ _____ .
verb ending in –ing   past-tense verb   noun   adjective   article of clothing, plural

Under the _____ water, I swam ahead of my family—and came face-to-face with
adjective

a(n) _____ creature with the head of a(n) _____ and the body of a(n) _____!
adjective   land animal   water animal

It had _____ _____ covered in _____ stripes. "Hi," the creature said.
large number   body part, plural   color

"My name is _____." Then it _____ at me. I turned to get my family's
celebrity   past-tense verb

attention, but the creature swam away faster than a(n) _____! No one believed my story,
noun

but that's OK. Maybe I discovered a new species.

139

SIGNS OF THE TIMES

Seeing isn't always believing. Two of these funny signs are not real. Can you spot which two are fake?

ANSWERS ON PAGE 354

1. SERIOUSLY THE ROAD IS CLOSED STOP DRIVING AROUND THE SIGNS

2. THIS SIGN WILL ACCOMPLISH NOTHING

3. OLD FISHERMAN XING

4. WHOA

5. HIGH RISK AREA NEXT 15 km

6. Serious / Funny

7. SELF PARKING

WHAT IN THE WORLD?

HOT AND COLD

These photographs show close-up views of hot and cold objects. On a separate sheet of paper, unscramble the letters to identify what's in each picture.

ANSWERS ON PAGE 354

CEI MRECA

NSU

YNOSW ERKEC

AALV

REONFZ FITUR

VEOST RUENRB

LECARGI

HIICL PEEPSRP

EIC NKIR

STUMP
YOUR PARENTS

DID YOU HEAR THAT?

Answer the questions on a separate sheet of paper. If your parents can't answer these questions, maybe they should go to school instead of you!

ANSWERS ON PAGE 354

1 **What's inside the fingertips of astronauts' gloves?**
A. magnets   C. twinkle lights
B. heaters   D. screwdrivers

2 **Why is the tallest building (1,016 feet [310 m]) in the United Kingdom nicknamed "The Shard?"**
A. It's named after the architect Joseph Shard.
B. It's shaped like a long, thin, pointed piece of glass called a shard.
C. "Shard" is an old English word meaning "great height."
D. Someone misspelled "shark."

3 **Which flower is safe for people to eat?**
A. orange daylily   C. violet
B. pink clover   D. all of the above

4 **If a pig stays out too long in the sun, it might _____.**
A. get a sunburn
B. turn purple
C. climb a tree
D. lose its hair

5 **A sand dollar is a(n) _____.**
A. plant
B. animal
C. rock formation
D. alien visitor

6 **Pygmy elephants, native to the island of _____, are smaller than their relatives but boast extra-long ears and tails.**
A. Borneo   C. Barbados
B. Bermuda   D. Bahrain

7 **A dog's eye has how many eyelids?**
A. 3   C. 1
B. 2   D. 422

8 **Which U.S. national park has the world's most massive tree?**
A. Acadia National Park in Maine
B. Shenandoah National Park in Virginia
C. Sequoia National Park in California
D. Redwood National Park in California

9 **Which step happens first to a caterpillar inside a chrysalis?**
A. It grows wings.
B. Its legs fall off.
C. Its eyes get bigger.
D. It dissolves into goo.

10 **It takes _____ for light to get from the sun to Earth's surface.**
A. less than one second
B. about eight minutes
C. exactly three days
D. more than two years

CRITTER CHAT

If animals used social media, what would they say? Follow this dhole's day as it updates its feed.

WHO'S A GOOD BOY? I AM!

DHOLE

LIVES IN: India, with smaller populations in Central and East Asia
SCREEN NAME: RedDog
FRIENDS: ≫

RHESUS MACAQUE
MonkeyAround

ASIAN HAWK-EAGLE
MoHawk

BENGAL MONITOR
LongLizard

START

7:30 a.m.

RedDog
My siblings and I are doing a #PupPepRally to get hyped up for our big hunt! #WoofWoof

Did your pack sleep in? I've been hiding in my secret tree spot all morning, and I've already snatched a treat. #TheEarlyHawk GetsTheLizard
MoHawk

You might be able to take out little lizards, but don't try me. I'm a five-foot (1.5 m)-long, 15-pound (6.8-kg) 'zilla. And now I'm tongue-sniffing for prey.
LongLizard

Yikes! Guess I'll stick with my 200-monkey troop for safety in numbers. #FruitSaladForUs

MonkeyAround

1:15 p.m.

RedDog
Score—we caught a wild pig! Now we're headed to the stream for a sip and a swim. Who's in?

OK—just as long as everybody's already eaten. Cannonball!
MonkeyAround

I call a breath-holding contest! I know I can stay underwater for about 15 minutes. #SwimTeamChamp

LongLizard

I'm no waterbird, but my nest is close to the stream so my chick and I can ref.

MoHawk

4:00 p.m.

RedDog
I just ran into my friend, and I can't stop wagging my tail!

Me, too. Then I picked and ate the fleas off of their fur. #ThatsWhatFriendsAreFur

MonkeyAround

Who needs friends? The only face I'm excited to see is the sun's. I'll be soaking up some rays if you need me. #SoloLife

LongLizard

Yeah, I don't need eagle friends other than my mate. We whistle at each other. #KwipKwipKwipKwi Kweee (That means "I like you!")
MoHawk

Sweet! I whistle, cluck, and scream at my pack mates—you know they love to hear it.
RedDog

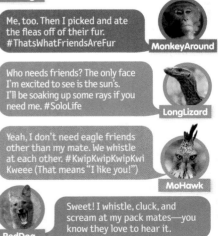

FUNNY FILL-IN

BABYSITTING BLUES

Ask a friend to give you words to fill in the blanks in this story and write them on a separate sheet of paper. Then read the story out loud and fill in the words for a laugh.

Last weekend I babysat _____ while her parents went to a(n) _____ concert.
                        female celebrity   *type of music*

They told me to feed her _____ for dinner and put her to bed. But as soon as
                          something gross

they left, she _____ over a(n) _____ _____ and began _____ toys
                past-tense verb   *adjective*   *noun*   *verb ending in –ing*

everywhere. She even _____ on the walls with _____! Then she disappeared, and
                      past-tense verb   *noun, plural*

the _____ _____. I opened the door to find a(n) _____ holding _____
     noun   *past-tense verb*   *type of job*   *large number*

_____ of _____ the girl had naughtily ordered. Finally, I found her hiding under
 noun, plural   *type of food*

the _____. Together we _____ the house and brushed her _____.
     piece of furniture   *past-tense verb*   *noun*

When her parents returned, she was fast asleep. Who says _____ is easy?
                                                          verb ending in –ing

144

WHAT IN THE WORLD?

IN THE SPOTLIGHT

These photographs show close-up and faraway views of objects that produce light. On a separate sheet of paper, unscramble the letters to identify what's in each picture. Lost in the dark? **ANSWERS ON PAGE 354**

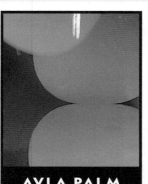

AVLA PALM

ENNO GSNI

YIFFERL

NGGLTIIHN

RLSRKPAES

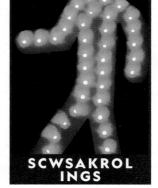

SCWSAKROL INGS

ITHLGBBLU

TORNRNEH GLISTH

ITGNH-TIHLG

FIND THE HIDDEN ANIMALS

Animals often blend in with their environment to hide. Find each animal listed below in one of the pictures. On a separate sheet of paper, write the letter of the correct picture and the animal's name.

ANSWERS ON PAGE 354

1. common potoo (a type of bird)
2. green huntsman spider
3. Peringuey's adder
4. lappet moth
5. leaf-tailed gecko
6. frogfish

A

B

C

D

E

F

SIGNS OF THE TIMES

Seeing isn't always believing. Two of these funny signs are not real. Can you figure out which two are fake?
ANSWERS ON PAGE 354

1. No Drama

2. ← HOSPITAL
   SKIING →

3. PENGUINS CROSSING SLOW

4. SPEED LIMIT 14½

5. ALIEN PARKING

6. GREAT SNORING

7. NO CARS BEYOND THIS POINT DUCKS ONLY

147

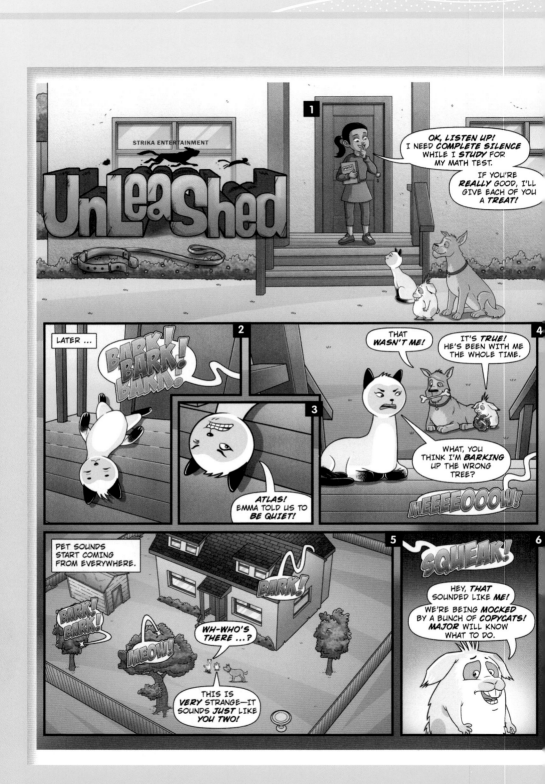

Camels at the Pushkar Camel Fair in Rajasthan, India

Say What?

Caimans are better suited for swimming than walking. They use their powerful tails to propel themselves through water.

NAME Bunsen

FAVORITE ACTIVITY
Hiding under the periodic table

FAVORITE TOY
Safety glasses

PET PEEVE
Overreactions

I have all the solutions!

I have a lot in common with my computer. We both have mega-bites!

I enjoy chemistry jokes periodically.

Solid, liquid, gas ... they all matter.

Never trust atoms—they make up everything.

FUNNY  BITES

"I'VE HEARD OF SAILFISH BEFORE, BUT THIS IS THE FIRST SALE FISH I'VE SEEN."

"I GUESS IT'S TIME FOR ME TO HEAD BACK TO THE STABLE."

"MY FAVORITE SANDWICH IS PEANUT BUTTER AND JELLYFISH."

"SOME PREDATORS DON'T LIKE CLOWNFISH. THEY THINK WE TASTE FUNNY."

"HERE COMES THE BIRTHDAY GIRL NOW."

153

RIDDLE ME THIS

What has a **mouth** but **can't talk,** a **head** but **can't think,** a **bed** but **doesn't sleep,** and can **run** but **never walk?**

A river.

I don't speak unless **spoken to.** Many have **heard** me, but none have **seen me.** **What am I?**

An echo.

What's **harder** to **catch** the **more** that you **run?**

Your breath.

You can **enter,** but you **can't come in.** I can **give you space,** but no room. I have **keys,** but **no lock.** **What am I?**

A computer keyboard.

At what **school** do you have to **drop out** in order to **graduate?**

Skydiving school.

Two fathers and **two sons** go fishing, but there are only **three people** in the boat. **How is this possible?**

It was a grandfather, a father, and a son on the fishing trip.

What **runs around** a **haunted house** but **doesn't move?**

A fence.

The **more** that it **appeared,** the **less Zeus** could see. **What was it?**

Darkness.

154

TONGUE TWISTERS
SAY THESE FAST THREE TIMES

Mad bunny, bad money.

Shelley sells shades.

Bamboo baboon.

Six slim sycamore saplings.

Hordes of Nords stormed the fjords.

Sheep should sleep in a shed.

Sneaker speakers.

Feathered finches flinch while flying forward fast.

JUST JOKING
COMICAL CATS

Q Why wouldn't you want to **play** against a team of **big cats?**

A They might be cheetahs.

Q What action movie stars a cat as a secret agent?

A Mission Im-paws-ible.

Q Which cat performs on a trapeze?

A An acro-cat.

Q When Cinderella went to the ball, who fed her cat?

A Her furry godmother.

KNOCK, KNOCK.

Who's there?
Howard.
Howard who?
Howard I ever resist your garden's catnip?

Q How is a cat like a coin?

A Each has a head on one side and a tail on the other.

JUST JOKING
RIDICULOUS DOGS

KNOCK, KNOCK.

Who's there?
Collie.
Collie who?
Collie you when it's time to take the dogs for a walk.

Q Why do Labradors like to wear hats?

A Because they look quite fetching.

STEPHEN: Are you going to teach your dog to play soccer?

ANNA: Of course not, he's a boxer!

POLICE OFFICER: We caught your dog chasing people on bikes.
DOG OWNER: That's impossible, my dog doesn't even own a bike.

Q Who do **dogs** hire to **design doghouses**?

A A bark-itect.

Q **What** do you **get** if you **cross** a **magician** and a **dog?**

A A Labracadabrador.

Q **What do you call a dog standing in the snow?**

A A chili dog.

157

FUNNY BITES

"THE VET SAYS I HAVE HAY FEVER."

"HE'S A KNIGHT OWL."

"I COULDN'T FIND A LONGER PAPER STRAW."

"IT'S NOT TOO BAD, PLUS I GET ALL KINDS OF TV CHANNELS."

RIDDLE ME THIS

A man rode into the **Grand Canyon** for a camping tour on **Friday,** stayed for two nights, and **left** on **Friday.** How is this possible?

His mule's name was Friday.

What happens **once** in a minute, **twice** in a moment, but **never** in a **thousand years?**

The letter m.

What has a **head,** a **tail,** no legs, and is **brown?**

A penny.

Three men were hunting **Bigfoot** when it started to **rain.** Only **two** of them got their **hair wet. How is that possible?**

The third man was bald.

What has **armor,** but **doesn't fight** and is **always home** when **on the move?**

A turtle.

I dig tiny holes and **fill them** with **silver or gold.** I also can build **bridges of silver** and **crowns of gold.** Sooner or later **everyone** sees me, but most are afraid of me. **Who am I?**

The dentist.

What starts out **tall,** but the **longer** it stands, **the shorter** it **grows?**

A candle.

What **instrument** can be **played** and **heard** but **never seen?**

Your voice.

159

JUST JOKING
FUNNY FOOD

Q Why are **potatoes** so popular on **social media?**

A Because of all the hashtags.

Q Who did Darth Vader summon when craving ice cream?

A Storm Scoopers.

STOP! I CAN'T TAKE ANY S'MORE!

Did you know that the **largest s'more** ever made weighed 267 pounds (121 kg)?

That's one-and-a-half times the weight of the **average adult** human.

Q What did the maple syrup say after the all-you-can-eat brunch?

A "I feel waffle."

CHARLOTTE: Which vegetables have the worst attitude?
GEORGE: I'm not sure, which do?
CHARLOTTE: Rude-abagas.

Q Why did the girl agree to go strawberry picking with her friends?

A She hoped to find berried treasure.

Q Why did the corn cancel at the last minute?

A Something popped up.

FUNNY BITES

"I HATE IT WHEN HE DOES THAT."

"HE LIKES TO GO FAST."

"WHY DIDN'T I THINK OF THIS BEFORE?"

"GOOD NIGHT KIDS … SEE YOU IN THE MORNING."

"I'M ON VACATION."

"OH, BOY! I CAN'T WAIT TO SEE WHAT IT IS!"

TONGUE TWISTERS
SAY THESE FAST THREE TIMES

Rough rafting rapids.

Mr. Meminger's editor's sweater.

Miss Mix picks chicks.

Six sharp smart sharks.

Real rural walrus.

Thin sticks, thick bricks.

Llamas lying lazily aloft a little log.

It's a **LONG** story ...

A FATHER AND SON *BRACHIOSAURUS*
were eating dinner one day and the son asked, "Dad, are we herbivores?"

"Yes, son. Now eat your dinner," his father replied.

"But if we are herbivores, that means we don't eat bugs, right?" the son asked.

The father sighed, "Yes, son, we don't eat bugs—only plants. Now stop asking questions and eat your dinner."

"But, Dad, are you SURE we don't eat bugs? Are there any kinds of bugs we DO eat?" he asked again.

"Listen!" the father yelled. "I've told you already, we don't eat any kind of bug. We can talk about this after we finish our leaves."

After dinner, the father dino asked, "Now, what did you want to ask me about eating bugs?"

"OH, NEVER MIND," the younger dino said. "There was a large beetle on your leaves but it's gone now."

JUST JOKING
WACKY WORLD

Q Why doesn't anyone want to be friends with **Big Ben?**

A Because all it does is tock, tock, tock.

Q Why can't you trust the **Atlantic Ocean?**

A Because there is something fishy about it.

Q How do the statues on the Notre-Dame Cathedral cure their sore throats?

A By gargoyling.

Q Why can't you make a **reservation** at the **Library** of **Congress?**

A Because it's completely booked.

Q Why should you **never** play **hide-and-seek** with **Mount Everest?**

A Because it always peaks.

I'M SURE THE EIFFEL TOWER IS AROUND HERE SOMEWHERE! I WISH I HAD A MAP.

Did you know that some **pigeons** were **war heroes?** Messenger pigeons carried notes and intelligence from behind enemy lines during **World War I** and **World War II.**

Pigeons can be found on every continent except Antarctica.

FUNNY BITES

"I DON'T HEAR ANYTHING!"

"DEAR DIARY, I LEARNED A NEW LANGUAGE TODAY."

"BE SURE TO WAKE ME AT HALF PAST SPRING. I DON'T WANT TO MISS ANYTHING."

CULTURE CONNECTION

A woman cooks noodle soup from her boat
in a floating market in Bangkok, Thailand.

CELEBRATIONS

LUNAR NEW YEAR
February 10

Also called Chinese New Year, this holiday marks the new year according to the lunar calendar. Families celebrate with parades, feasts, and fireworks. Young people may receive gifts of money in red envelopes.

ZHONGHE FESTIVAL
March 11

In China, this day honors the start of spring—specifically, the Blue Dragon, a deity said to bring rain. Holiday traditions include cleaning the house and getting a haircut for good luck, and eating "dragon's ears" (dumplings) and "dragon's beards" (noodles).

EASTER
March 31†

A Christian holiday that celebrates the resurrection of Jesus Christ, Easter is celebrated by giving baskets filled with gifts, decorated eggs, or candy to children.

INTI RAYMI
June 24**

Started as a way to honor the sun god Inti during the Inca Empire, Peruvians throw parties and parades on this colorful holiday, which honors the winter solstice—and the anticipation of longer days ahead.

LAMMAS
August 1

Commonly known as Loaf Mass Day, this holiday is celebrated in England, Scotland, Wales, and Ireland and marks the first wheat harvest. It's common for people to bake loaves of bread to eat—and offer to the church.

HERITAGE DAY
September 24

South Africans show their patriotic pride on this holiday, which celebrates the diverse cultures throughout the country. It's tradition for families and friends to gather around a wood fire—an event known as a *braai*—to cook and then feast on barbecued meats.

Around the World

ROSH HASHANAH
October 2*- 4

A Jewish holiday marking the beginning of a new year on the Hebrew calendar. Celebrations include prayer, ritual foods, and a day of rest.

DIWALI
October 31**

To symbolize the inner light that protects against spiritual darkness, people light their homes with clay lamps for India's largest and most important holiday.

HANUKKAH
December 25*– January 2

This Jewish holiday is eight days long. It commemorates the rededication of the Temple in Jerusalem. Hanukkah celebrations include the lighting of menorah candles for eight days and the exchange of gifts.

CHRISTMAS DAY
December 25

A Christian holiday marking the birth of Jesus Christ, Christmas is usually celebrated by decorating trees, exchanging presents, and having festive gatherings.

*Begins at sundown.
**Dates may vary slightly by location.
†Orthodox Easter is May 5.

2024 CALENDAR

JANUARY
S	M	T	W	T	F	S
	1	2	3	4	5	6
7	8	9	10	11	12	13
14	15	16	17	18	19	20
21	22	23	24	25	26	27
28	29	30	31			

FEBRUARY
S	M	T	W	T	F	S
				1	2	3
4	5	6	7	8	9	10
11	12	13	14	15	16	17
18	19	20	21	22	23	24
25	26	27	28	29		

MARCH
S	M	T	W	T	F	S
					1	2
3	4	5	6	7	8	9
10	11	12	13	14	15	16
17	18	19	20	21	22	23
24	25	26	27	28	29	30
31						

APRIL
S	M	T	W	T	F	S
	1	2	3	4	5	6
7	8	9	10	11	12	13
14	15	16	17	18	19	20
21	22	23	24	25	26	27
28	29	30				

MAY
S	M	T	W	T	F	S
			1	2	3	4
5	6	7	8	9	10	11
12	13	14	15	16	17	18
19	20	21	22	23	24	25
26	27	28	29	30	31	

JUNE
S	M	T	W	T	F	S
						1
2	3	4	5	6	7	8
9	10	11	12	13	14	15
16	17	18	19	20	21	22
23	24	25	26	27	28	29
30						

JULY
S	M	T	W	T	F	S
	1	2	3	4	5	6
7	8	9	10	11	12	13
14	15	16	17	18	19	20
21	22	23	24	25	26	27
28	29	30	31			

AUGUST
S	M	T	W	T	F	S
				1	2	3
4	5	6	7	8	9	10
11	12	13	14	15	16	17
18	19	20	21	22	23	24
25	26	27	28	29	30	31

SEPTEMBER
S	M	T	W	T	F	S
1	2	3	4	5	6	7
8	9	10	11	12	13	14
15	16	17	18	19	20	21
22	23	24	25	26	27	28
29	30					

OCTOBER
S	M	T	W	T	F	S
		1	2	3	4	5
6	7	8	9	10	11	12
13	14	15	16	17	18	19
20	21	22	23	24	25	26
27	28	29	30	31		

NOVEMBER
S	M	T	W	T	F	S
					1	2
3	4	5	6	7	8	9
10	11	12	13	14	15	16
17	18	19	20	21	22	23
24	25	26	27	28	29	30

DECEMBER
S	M	T	W	T	F	S
1	2	3	4	5	6	7
8	9	10	11	12	13	14
15	16	17	18	19	20	21
22	23	24	25	26	27	28
29	30	31				

awes8me

THESE EIGHT SUPER SPECTACLES WILL PUT YOU IN A PARTY MOOD.

1 NIGHT-LIGHTS

Boca Ciega Bay in St. Petersburg, Florida, U.S.A., comes alive with lighted boats during a floating celebration of the winter holidays. Participants in the annual St. Pete Beach holiday boat parade also donate toys to kids in need. Sounds like a perfect parade!

Festive Parades

2 FLOWER POWER

For more than a century, fantastic flower-covered floats and marching bands have dazzled crowds at the annual Rose Parade in Pasadena, California, U.S.A., on New Year's Day. Not a fan of flowers? Stick around for the college football game that follows the parade.

3 BLAZING BOAT

The Up Helly Aa festival in Lerwick, Scotland, ends every January in a blaze. Harking back to a Viking ritual, hundreds of torchbearers march through the town's streets before setting a 30-foot (9-m)-long galley—a type of ship—on fire.

4 COLORFUL RITUAL

Millions of people of the Hindu faith come together to take a ritual dip in one of four sacred rivers in India as part of the Kumbh Mela festival. The religious procession can include elephants and camels, and festival organizers often provide music and dance performances.

5 BALLOON BONANZA

More than three million people lined the streets of New York City to watch the debut of this Hello Kitty balloon in the Macy's Thanksgiving Day Parade. The parade has been held on the morning of Thanksgiving almost every year since 1924.

6 DANCE PARTY

With fancy headdresses and costumes, dancers perform the samba, an Afro-Brazilian group dance, in front of a crowd at the Carnival parade in Rio de Janeiro, Brazil. Carnival, a festival of merrymaking and feasting, allows people to let loose.

7 FLOATING FESTIVAL

People in Venice, Italy, take their parades to the water. That's because this city is built in a lagoon with canals for streets. Revelers float down the Grand Canal in decorated gondolas, like this giant mouse gondola, and other boats during the annual Carnival festival.

8 CLOWN REVELRY

Giant jesters parade through the streets of the historic French Quarter in New Orleans, Louisiana, U.S.A. During the annual Mardi Gras celebration, nearly a hundred krewes—or festive groups—toss goodies, including toys, stuffed animals, and Mardi Gras beads, to the people who come to watch.

What's Your Chinese Horoscope?
Locate your birth year to find out.

In Chinese astrology, the zodiac runs on a 12-year cycle, based on the lunar calendar. Each year corresponds to one of 12 animals, each representing one of 12 personality types. Read on to find out which animal year you were born in and what that might say about you.

RAT
1972, '84, '96, 2008, '20
Say cheese! You're attractive, charming, and creative. When you get mad, you can have really sharp teeth!

HORSE
1966, '78, '90, 2002, '14
Being happy is your *mane* goal. And though you're smart and hardworking, your teacher may ride you for talking too much.

OX
1973, '85, '97, 2009, '21
You're smart, patient, and as strong as an ... well, you know. Though you're a leader, you never brag.

SHEEP
1967, '79, '91, 2003, '15
Gentle as a lamb, you're also artistic, compassionate, and wise. You're often shy.

TIGER
1974, '86, '98, 2010, '22
You may be a nice person, but no one should ever enter your room without asking—you might attack!

MONKEY
1968, '80, '92, 2004, '16
No "monkey see, monkey do" for you. You're a clever problem-solver with an excellent memory.

RABBIT
1975, '87, '99, 2011, '23
Your ambition and talent make you jump at opportunity. You also keep your ears open for gossip.

ROOSTER
1969, '81, '93, 2005, '17
You crow about your adventures, but inside you're really shy. You're thoughtful, capable, brave, and talented.

DRAGON
1988, 2000, '12, '24
You're on fire! Health, energy, honesty, and bravery make you a living legend.

DOG
1970, '82, '94, 2006, '18
Often the leader of the pack, you're loyal and honest. You can also keep a secret.

SNAKE
1977, '89, 2001, '13
You may not speak often, but you're very smart. You always seem to have a stash of cash.

PIG
1971, '83, '95, 2007, '19
Even though you're courageous, honest, and kind, you never hog all the attention.

HOLIDAY HOOPLA

Every day is a party when you celebrate these wacky holidays!
Sure, they might not be the most popular holidays, but why let that stop you?
Get out your calendar and save these special dates for a party of your own!

MARCH 14

PI DAY
Math lovers, rejoice! Pi Day, founded in **1988**, is celebrated on the 14th day of the third month of the year. It aligns with the Greek symbol pi (π), a mathematical sign for an infinite number that begins with the digits 3.14. To celebrate, who wants pie?

FIRST FRIDAY IN JUNE

NATIONAL DOUGHNUT DAY
No wonder doughnuts have their own day: More than **10 BILLION** doughnuts are made (and eaten!) in America every year! This holiday has been celebrated in the United States since **1938**.

SEPTEMBER 19

TALK LIKE A PIRATE DAY
Shiver me timbers! Celebrated across the seven seas since 2002, this day is *arrr*-guably the most fun holiday ever. Put on an eye patch, grab your sword, and tell all your mateys "Ahoy!"

THIRD SATURDAY IN OCTOBER

SWEETEST DAY
Created in the 1920s by a candy company worker in Cleveland, Ohio, U.S.A., it's like Valentine's Day in October. Another excuse to enjoy some chocolate? Bring it on!

TOWER POWER

Behind the scenes of this amazing landmark

The Eiffel Tower in Paris, France, has serious celeb status. Completed in March 1889, it's one of the most recognizable monuments in the world. And the site, which is also known as the Iron Lady, receives nearly seven million tourists a year. But despite its fame, the tower has some monumental secrets. Get the lowdown on this Parisian highlight.

Hidden Apartment

If you were in charge of constructing the Eiffel Tower, where else would you live but ... the Eiffel Tower? Gustave Eiffel, who designed the landmark, built himself a small apartment on the top level of the structure. The sky-high hideaway had plush rugs, oil paintings, and even a grand piano. Only a few VIPs were allowed to visit, such as superstar scientist Thomas Edison. Unused since the 1920s after Eiffel's death, few knew about the 950-foot (290-m)-high pad until 2016 when it opened for public viewing.

Green Scene

Maybe this landmark should be renamed the Eco Tower. Workers recently gave the Iron Lady an environmentally friendly makeover by installing two wind turbines on the second level of the structure. These devices convert wind into electricity for the tower's shops and restaurants. A system was also set up to collect and funnel rainwater into the tower's toilets.

120 ANTENNAS

When the Eiffel Tower opened in the 19th century, it was the world's tallest building.

3 VIEWING PLATFORMS

1,665 STEPS

NEARLY **50** MILES (80 KM) OF ELECTRIC CABLES COVER THE STRUCTURE.

THE TOWER IS MADE OF **18,000** IRON PIECES BOLTED TOGETHER.

FAIR FRENZY

The Eiffel Tower was officially opened at the 1889 world's fair. First held in London, England, in 1851, world's fairs showcase cutting-edge inventions, architecture, and art from around the globe. The events have revealed many "futuristic" inventions, including the Ferris wheel, the television, x-ray machines, and ice-cream cones.

Spy High

The Eiffel Tower doubled as a secret agent! During World War I—a worldwide conflict that lasted from 1914 to 1918—the French military used the tower's radio and telegraph center to communicate with ground troops and battleships. It also intercepted enemy messages. In 1916, the tower picked up a message about a female spy known as Mata Hari. Using the captured information, the French military tracked down and arrested the agent.

SKATER

20,000 LIGHTBULBS ILLUMINATE THE LANDMARK EVERY NIGHT.

Calling All Daredevils

Some people visit the Eiffel Tower for the view. Others come for more daring thrills. In 1889, a man walked up 704 of the tower's steps ... on stilts. In 1952, three trapeze artists swung 400 feet (122 m) above ground from ropes without a net. And in 2010, a man roller-skated off a platform set up under the tower's first level down a 90-foot (27-m)-tall ramp to the ground.

UNITED KINGDOM
NETHERLANDS
BELGIUM
GERMANY
LUXEMBOURG
Paris ★ Eiffel Tower
ATLANTIC OCEAN
FRANCE
SWITZERLAND
ITALY
SPAIN
ANDORRA
Mediterranean Sea

PAINTERS

True Colors

The Eiffel Tower has had a colorful history—literally. The original structure was dark red. In 1899, it was painted yellow. About 50 years ago, the tower was coated with bronze paint. Today the Eiffel Tower, which gets a paint job every seven years, is covered in almost 16,000 gallons (60,567 L) of paint.

10 FACTS ABOUT GLOBAL GRUB

DEEP-FRIED TARANTULAS are a popular snack in Cambodia.

On New Year's Eve, it's a tradition for many Germans to eat a marzipan pig **TO BRING GOOD LUCK.**

In southern Africa, PEOPLE CATCH, SQUISH, DRY, AND EAT **GIANT CATERPILLARS** called mopane worms.

In Greenland, it's a Christmas custom for Inuit to eat MUKTUK—RAW WHALE SKIN and BLUBBER.

GELATO flavored with ricotta cheese and lemon is a **TASTY TREAT** in Italy.

FRENCH FRY-FLAVORED SODA is sold in Japan.

BRITISH ROYALS once served SWAN AT SPECIAL BANQUETS.

In Singapore, you can buy FROZEN NORWEGIAN SALMON out of a VENDING MACHINE.

PUSH

PEOPLE IN NORTHERN IRELAND AND SOME OTHER NORTH ATLANTIC COUNTRIES LIKE TO EAT DULSE, DRIED RED SEAWEED.

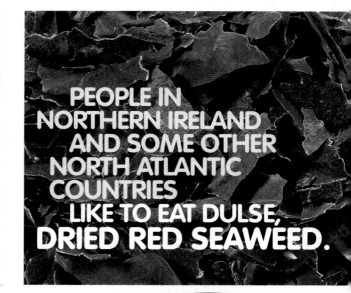

SANNAKJI, a traditional Korean dish, FEATURES PIECES OF FRESHLY CUT OCTOPUS SERVED WHILE THE TENTACLES ARE STILL WIGGLING.

177

THE SECRET HISTORY OF

These facts will make you say *cha-ching!*

You'd never try to pay for sneakers with a handful of bat droppings. But that's what some ancient civilizations once used as a form of money.

We usually think of money as bills and coins, but anything people agree is valuable enough to trade for goods or services can be considered as cash. That's why bat droppings, silk, bottle caps, and other items have been used throughout history to pay for stuff. Check out this timeline to discover a wealth of facts about money.

They should've called it *moo*-ney instead.

Historians don't always know the exact date of long-ago events. That's why you'll see "ca" next to some of the years listed here. It stands for "circa," meaning "around."

1 **ca 9000–6000 B.C.**

In early history, humans bartered, or traded, items or services without using a system of money that people agreed on. For example, ancient Egyptians swapped linen for ivory, or grain for cedar wood. The first and oldest form of money was cattle, including cows, camels, and goats. Cows are still used as money in certain parts of the world today.

2 **ca 1200 B.C.**

The Chinese begin using mollusk shells called cowries as money. Found in the Pacific and Indian Oceans, the cowrie is the most widely used form of money in history—more people have likely used cowrie shells as money than any other item.

3 **1000–45 B.C.**

The earliest bronze and copper coins are made by the Chinese. Silver coins first appear in Lydia, or modern-day Türkiye (Turkey), and the Greek and Roman Empires start using them. It's around this time that coins become stamped with faces of people like Roman politician and general Julius Caesar.

MONEY

Different nicknames for money used around the world include bacon, moolah, cheddar, and dough.

4 118 B.C.

People in China use square pieces of white deerskin as money—the first banknotes. The first paper banknotes appear there some 900 years later, in A.D. 806.

5 LATE 13th CENTURY A.D.

After returning from China, Italian merchant and explorer Marco Polo introduces the concept of paper money to Europeans. A variety of different paper banknotes are handmade and used throughout the continent over the next several centuries. It's not until 1661 that Sweden becomes the first European country to print paper banknotes.

6 1535

Native Americans in North America use wampum, strings of white and purple beads made from clam shells, as money. Some Native Americans and European colonists try to make counterfeit, or fake, money by dyeing the beads and pretending they're rarer, more valuable blue-black clam shells.

Cash is so 2004!

ICE CREAM

7 1871

Western Union, a telegraph company, allows money transfers via telegram, meaning people can quickly send money to other people.

In some countries, it's a crime to burn or destroy money.

AN EARLY CREDIT CARD

American Express Company
CREDIT CARD
EXPIRES APRIL 30, 1959
JOHN SMITH
123 MAIN STREET
CENTERVILLE USA
John Smith

9 2005

Smartphone technology provides contactless scan-and-pay options. Today, only about 8 percent of the world's currency exists as cash. The rest is electronic.

8 THE 1950s

The first universal credit card that could be used in many different places of business is invented. Now people can buy things without paper money or coins.

MONEY AROUND THE WORLD!

In 2022, the U.S. Mint began issuing quarters with **American women** on one side. The first two were poet **MAYA ANGELOU** and astronaut **SALLY RIDE,** the first American woman in space.

IN THE 1600s, SWEDEN ISSUED A plate-size COIN that weighed nearly **44 pounds** (20 kg).

IN FEBRUARY 2015, SCUBA DIVERS OFF ISRAEL FOUND MORE THAN 2,600 GOLD COINS DATING BACK AS FAR AS THE NINTH CENTURY.

A **JANITOR** at a **GERMAN LIBRARY** found and turned in a **BOX OF RARE COINS** thought to be worth **HUNDREDS OF THOUSANDS OF DOLLARS.**

A FRILLED LIZARD appeared on Australia's two-cent coin.

**PANAMA'S
CURRENCY,
THE
BALBOA,**
is named for the 16th century
SPANISH EXPLORER
Vasco Núñez de Balboa.

In 2019,
a **GIRAFFE
APPEARED**
on **GOLD
AND SILVER
COINS** for the
**DEMOCRATIC
REPUBLIC OF
THE CONGO—**
the first
in a series
celebrating the
world's wildlife.

Archaeologists have
dug up fourth-century clay
molds used by Roman coin
COUNTERFEITERS.

**KING TUT
APPEARS
ON THE
EGYPTIAN
ONE-POUND
COIN.**

An
**UNFLATTERING
PORTRAIT** of
Holy Roman Emperor
LEOPOLD I on a 1670 coin supposedly
led to the nickname
"LEOPOLD THE HOGMOUTH."

**A BRITISH
ARTIST**
MADE A DRESS
OUT OF USED
BANKNOTES
FROM AROUND THE
WORLD.

MONEY TIP!
CLIP COUPONS FOR
YOUR PARENTS.
Ask if they'll put the
money they save into
your piggy bank.

181

SAVING
Languages at Risk

Today, there are more than 7,000 languages spoken on Earth. But by 2100, more than half of these may disappear. In fact, some experts say one language dies every two weeks as a result of the increasing dominance of languages such as English, Spanish, and Mandarin.

So what can be done to keep dialects from disappearing altogether? To start, several National Geographic Explorers have embarked on various projects around the planet. Together, they are part of the race to save some of the world's most threatened languages, as well as to protect and preserve the cultures they belong to. Here are some of the Explorers' stories.

The Explorer: Tam Thi Ton
The Language: Bahnar

The Work: By gathering folklore like riddles and comics, Ton is creating bilingual learning materials for elementary students to teach them Bahnar, the language of an ethnic group living in Vietnam's Central Highlands.

TON IN A BAHNAR CLASSROOM

The Explorer: Sandhya Narayanan
The Languages: Quechua and Aymara

NARAYANAN SHARES STORIES FROM THE FIELD AT NATIONAL GEOGRAPHIC'S HEADQUARTERS IN WASHINGTON, D.C., U.S.A.

The Work: By immersing herself in the Indigenous languages of the Andean region along the Peru–Bolivia border, Narayanan aims to understand how interactions among Indigenous groups affect language over time.

HARRISON DOING AN INTERVIEW

The Explorer: K. David Harrison
The Language: Koro-Aka

The Work: Harrison led an expedition to India that identified Koro-Aka, a language that was completely new to science. He is also vice president of the Living Tongues Institute for Endangered Languages, dedicated to raising awareness and revitalizing little-documented languages.

The Explorer: Susan Barfield
The Language: Mapudungun

The Work: Barfield shines a light on the language of the Mapuche people of southern Chile with her trilingual children's book, *El Copihue*. The book is based on a Mapuche folktale and is illustrated by Mapuche students.

BARFIELD PRESENTS AN OFFERING DURING A BOOK BLESSING CEREMONY.

PERLIN INTERVIEWS A VILLAGE LEADER.

The Explorer: Ross Perlin
The Language: Seke

The Work: In an effort to preserve the Seke language of northern Nepal, Perlin has been working closely with speakers both in their villages and in New York, where many now live, including young speakers determined to document their own language.

The Explorer: Lal Rapacha
The Language: Kiranti-Kõits

The Work: As the founder and director of the Research Institute for Kiratology in Kathmandu, Nepal, Rapacha carries out research on the lesser known languages of Indigenous Himalayan people, including Kiranti-Kõits, his endangered mother tongue.

RAPACHA WORKING IN THE FIELD IN NEPAL

MYTHOLOGY

GREEK

EGYPTIAN

The ancient Greeks believed that many gods and goddesses ruled the universe. According to this mythology, the Olympians lived high atop Greece's Mount Olympus. Each of these 12 principal gods and goddesses had a unique personality that corresponded to particular aspects of life, such as love or death.

Egyptian mythology is based on a creation myth that tells of an egg that appeared on the ocean. When the egg hatched, out came Ra, the sun god. As a result, ancient Egyptians became worshippers of the sun and of the nine original deities, most of whom were the children and grandchildren of Ra.

THE OLYMPIANS

Aphrodite was the goddess of love and beauty.

Apollo, Zeus's son, was the god of the sun, music, and healing. Artemis was his twin.

Ares, Zeus's son, was the god of war.

Artemis, Zeus's daughter and Apollo's twin, was the goddess of the hunt and of childbirth.

Athena, born from the forehead of Zeus, was the goddess of wisdom and crafts.

Demeter was the goddess of fertility and nature.

Hades, Zeus's brother, was the god of the underworld and the dead.

Hephaestus, the son of Hera and Zeus, was the god of fire.

Hera, the wife and older sister of Zeus, was the goddess of women and marriage.

Hermes, Zeus's son, was the messenger of the gods.

Poseidon, the brother of Zeus, was the god of the seas and earthquakes.

Zeus was the most powerful of the gods and the top Olympian. He wielded a thunderbolt and was the god of the sky and thunder.

THE NINE DEITIES

Geb, son of Shu and Tefnut, was the god of the earth.

Isis (Ast), daughter of Geb and Nut, was the goddess of fertility and motherhood.

Nephthys (Nebet-Hut), daughter of Geb and Nut, was protector of the dead.

Nut, daughter of Shu and Tefnut, was the goddess of the sky.

Osiris (Usir), son of Geb and Nut, was the god of the afterlife.

Ra (Re), the sun god, is generally viewed as the creator. He represents life and health.

Seth (Set), son of Geb and Nut, was the god of the desert and chaos.

Shu, son of Ra, was the god of air.

Tefnut, daughter of Ra, was the goddess of rain.

All cultures around the world have unique legends and traditions that have been passed down over generations. Many myths refer to gods or supernatural heroes who are responsible for occurrences in the world. For example, Norse mythology tells of the red-bearded Thor, the god of thunder, who is responsible for creating lightning and thunderstorms. And many creation myths, especially those from some of North America's Native cultures, tell of an earth-diver represented as an animal that brings a piece of sand or mud up from the deep sea. From this tiny piece of earth, the entire world takes shape.

NORSE

ROMAN

Norse mythology originated in Scandinavia, in northern Europe. It was complete with gods and goddesses who lived in a heavenly place called Asgard that could be reached only by crossing a rainbow bridge.

Although Norse mythology is lesser known, we use it every day. Most days of the week are named after Norse gods, including some of these major deities.

NORSE GODS

Balder was the god of light and beauty.

Freya was the goddess of love, beauty, and fertility.

Frigg, for whom Friday was named, was the queen of Asgard. She was the goddess of marriage, motherhood, and the home.

Heimdall was the watchman of the rainbow bridge and the guardian of the gods.

Hel, the daughter of Loki, was the goddess of death.

Loki, a shape-shifter, was a trickster who helped the gods—and caused them problems.

Skadi was the goddess of winter and of the hunt. She is often represented as the "Snow Queen."

Thor, for whom Thursday was named, was the god of thunder and lightning.

Tyr, for whom Tuesday was named, was the god of the sky and war.

Wodan, for whom Wednesday was named, was the god of war, wisdom, death, and magic.

Much of Roman mythology was adopted from Greek mythology, but the Romans also developed a lot of original myths as well. The gods of Roman mythology lived everywhere, and each had a role to play. There were thousands of Roman gods, but here are a few of the stars of Roman myths.

ANCIENT ROMAN GODS

Ceres was the goddess of the harvest and motherly love.

Diana, daughter of Jupiter, was the goddess of hunting and the moon.

Juno, Jupiter's wife, was the goddess of women and fertility.

Jupiter, the patron of Rome and master of the gods, was the god of the sky.

Mars, the son of Jupiter and Juno, was the god of war.

Mercury, the son of Jupiter, was the messenger of the gods and the god of travelers.

Minerva was the goddess of wisdom, learning, and the arts and crafts.

Neptune, the brother of Jupiter, was the god of the sea.

Venus was the goddess of love and beauty.

Vesta was the goddess of fire and the hearth. She was one of the most important Roman deities.

World Religions

Around the world, religion takes many forms. Some belief systems, such as Christianity, Islam, and Judaism, are monotheistic, meaning that followers believe in just one supreme being. Others, like Hinduism, Shintoism, and most Native belief systems, are polytheistic, meaning that their followers believe in multiple gods.

All of the major religions have their origins in Asia, but they have spread around the world. Christianity, with the largest number of followers, has three divisions—Roman Catholic, Eastern Orthodox, and Protestant. Islam, with about one-quarter of all believers, has two main divisions—Sunni and Shiite. Hinduism and Buddhism account for about another one-fifth of believers. Judaism, dating back some 4,000 years, has some 15 million followers, less than one percent of all believers.

CHRISTIANITY

Based on the teachings of Jesus Christ, who was born some 2,000 years ago in the area of modern-day Israel, Christianity has spread worldwide and actively seeks converts. Followers in Switzerland (above) participate in an Easter season procession with lanterns and crosses.

BUDDHISM

Founded about 2,400 years ago in northern India by the Hindu prince Gautama Buddha, Buddhism spread throughout East and Southeast Asia. Buddhist temples have statues, such as the Mihintale Buddha (above) in Sri Lanka.

HINDUISM

Dating back more than 4,000 years, Hinduism is practiced mainly in India. Hindus follow sacred texts known as the Vedas and believe in reincarnation. During the festival of Navratri, which honors the goddess Durga, the Garba dance is performed (above).

Breaking the Fast

Eid al-Fitr marks the end of weeks of fasting from sunrise to sunset for Ramadan, the Muslim holy month. Families gather to attend mosque, followed by a celebration of feasting and fun with games, gift-exchanging, and time together.

ISLAM

Muslims believe that the Quran, Islam's sacred book, records the words of Allah (God) as revealed to the Prophet Muhammad beginning around A.D. 610. Believers (above) circle the Kaaba in the Grand Mosque in Mecca, Saudi Arabia, the spiritual center of the faith.

JUDAISM

The traditions, laws, and beliefs of Judaism date back to Abraham (the patriarch) and the Torah (the first five books of the Old Testament). Followers pray before the Western Wall (above), which stands below Islam's Dome of the Rock in Jerusalem.

QUIZ WHIZ

How vast is your knowledge about the world around you? Quiz yourself!

Write your answers on a piece of paper. Then check them below.

1 In Chinese astrology, the year 2024 is represented by which animal?
a. rabbit   **c.** dragon
b. rooster   **d.** dog

2 Which country uses the balboa, a coin named after a 16th-century Spanish explorer?
a. Argentina
b. Belize
c. Colombia
d. Panama

3 How many lightbulbs illuminate France's Eiffel Tower at night?
a. 200
b. 5,000
c. 20,000
d. 500,000

4 Squished and dried mopane worms are a snack eaten in _____ .
a. northern Europe   **c.** southern Africa
b. eastern Asia   **d.** western Australia

5 **True or false?** Italian merchant and explorer Marco Polo introduced the concept of paper money to Europeans.

Not **STUMPED** yet? Check out the *NATIONAL GEOGRAPHIC KIDS QUIZ WHIZ* collection for more crazy **CULTURE** questions!

ANSWERS: 1. c; 2. d; 3. c; 4. c; 5. True

Explore a New Culture

YOU'RE A STUDENT, but you're also a citizen of the world. Writing a report on another country or your own country is a great way to better understand and appreciate how different people live. Pick the country of your ancestors, one that's been in the news, or one that you'd like to visit someday.

STAMPS OF BRAZIL

CURRENCY AND COINS OF BRAZIL

FLAG OF BRAZIL

Passport to Success

A country report follows the format of an expository essay because you're "exposing" information about the country you choose.

The following step-by-step tips will help you with this international task.

1 **RESEARCH.** Gathering information is the most important step in writing a good country report. Look to internet sources, encyclopedias, books, magazine and newspaper articles, and other sources to find important and interesting details about your subject.

2 **ORGANIZE YOUR NOTES.** Put the information you gather into a rough outline. For example, sort everything you found about the country's system of government, climate, etc.

3 **WRITE IT UP.** Follow the basic structure of good writing: introduction, body, and conclusion. Remember that each paragraph should have a topic sentence that is then supported by facts and details. Incorporate the information from your notes, but make sure it's in your own words. And make your writing flow with good transitions and descriptive language.

4 **ADD VISUALS.** Include maps, diagrams, photos, and other visual aids.

5 **PROOFREAD AND REVISE.** Correct any mistakes, and polish your language. Do your best!

6 **CITE YOUR SOURCES.** Be sure to keep a record of your sources.

A robot sprays fertilizer on plants growing in a greenhouse.

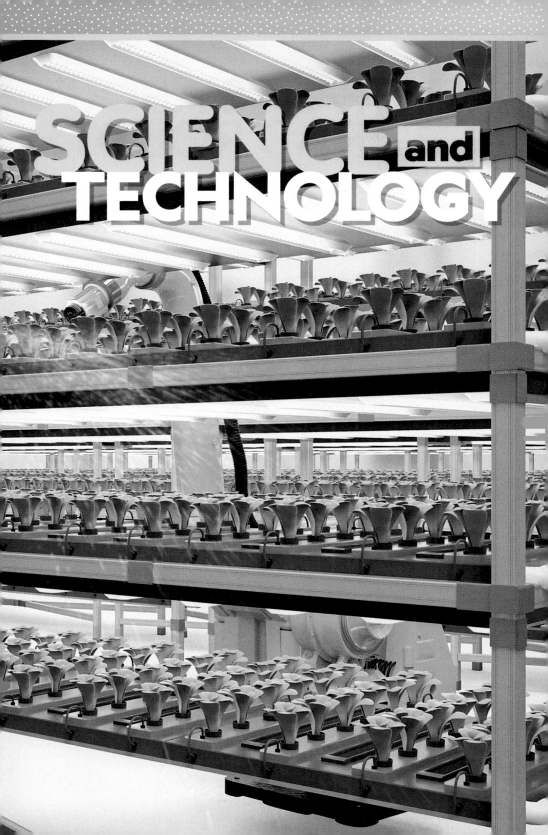

SCIENCE and TECHNOLOGY

10 FACTS ABOUT RAD ROBOTS

Developed in the 1960s, Shakey—the first ever artificial intelligence (AI) robot—could move, follow a route, and navigate around obstacles on its own.

In 2019, a full-size, interactive replica of *Star Wars'* DROID R2-D2 was released for $25,000.

In 350 B.C., an ancient Greek philosopher is said to have **created the world's first robot:** a **WOODEN BIRD** that flapped its wings and flew for 656 feet (200 m).

A four-legged **robot named Spot** was built to wander the ruins of ancient Pompeii in Italy, **looking for structural and safety issues.**

A Japanese billionaire designed a pet-size robot meant to respond to a human's emotions and be a constant companion.

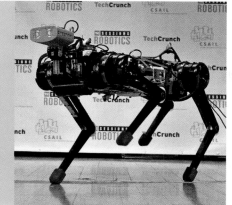

Cheetah 3, a quadruped **robot, can jump 31 inches** (79 cm) **off the ground.**

Nano robots— about a hundredth the width of a human hair—**may be used one day to deliver medicine to hard-to-treat cancerous tumors.**

Scientists at the University of Tokyo have **taught robots how to peel bananas** without smushing them.

In 2017, **a humanoid robot named Sophia was given citizenship** of Saudi Arabia.

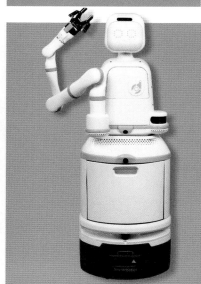

A four-foot (1.2-m)-tall robot named Moxi carries medication, supplies, lab samples, and personal items from room to room in a hospital in Virginia, U.S.A.

6 COOL INVENTIONS

SUPERSMART GADGETS AND ACCESSORIES THAT COULD CHANGE YOUR LIFE

1 ROBOT KITTY

If you're allergic to cats but still think they're adorable, you might want to "adopt" **MarsCat,** a bionic animal companion. Just like a real cat, MarsCat **reacts to your touch and voice,** wiggling when you pet it and even **meowing back** if you talk to it. Each MarsCat has a unique body shape and personality, and it will respond differently depending on how you play with it. The bot will also obey commands—sometimes. (Just like most real cats!) The best part? No **stinky litter boxes** to clean.

2 DIGITAL GAMES

Family game night sounds fun ... until you discover that you're missing game tokens or directions. Never again with the **Infinity Game Table, a touch-screen table surface.** Just turn on the device and choose from **dozens of board games,** like Monopoly and Connect 4. Up to six people can play at the same time. **Game on!**

③ FOAM PARTY

Love bubble baths? Bring that **foamy feeling** outside by turning your backyard into a knee-deep bubble party with **FOAMO Foam Machine.** This projector-like device sprays **tiny bubbles** onto the ground, creating mountains of foam. Just mix the soapy solution with water, pour it into the machine, then mold all the resulting bubbles into **fluffy castles or sudsy hats.** When you're done, wash away the foam with water. Now that's **good, clean fun.**

④ MUSICAL CLOTHING

With **SoundShirt,** you can literally *feel* the music. Made of stretchy fabric with tiny components that move, this shirt can either **capture sound waves from the air** or connect to a phone app. Then it translates the music into pulses and vibrations that the wearer can feel: You might sense the strumming of a **violin on your arms** while the **drumbeat rolls across your shoulders.** The inventors hope the device will be especially useful for people who are hard of hearing or deaf. **That rocks!**

⑤ VIRTUAL KEYBOARD

Tap out an **email right on** your **kitchen table,** or type up a report on your bedroom floor. With the **Magic Cube,** you can turn any flat, opaque surface into a **keyboard.** Connect the small, cube-shaped device to a smartphone, tablet, or computer. The cube uses a laser beam to **project a keyboard** onto the surface. A **sensor** inside the cube **tracks** where your fingers are tapping and then translates the movements into letters and numbers. The cube even plays **tapping sounds** while you type, just in case you miss the **clickety-clack** of your old-fashioned keyboard.

⑥ SMART RING

When the lights are too low for you to read on your couch, just tap your thumb to your ring finger three times. And while you're at it, **make a call,** too—all without ever touching your phone. That's what a smart ring called **ORII** can do. Simply slide the ring onto your finger, and a **Bluetooth chip** in the ring will control your smart devices wirelessly. **Sync it to your smart gadget,** then call a friend or **shoot off a text** just by speaking into a pair of microphones on the inside of the device. This ring's not quite the same as having a personal assistant— but it's the **next best thing.**

WHAT IS LIFE?

This seems like such an easy question to answer. Everybody knows that singing birds are alive and rocks are not. But when we start studying bacteria and other microscopic creatures, things get more complicated.

SO WHAT EXACTLY IS LIFE?

Most scientists agree that something is alive if it can reproduce, grow in size to become more complex in structure, take in nutrients to survive, give off waste products, and respond to external stimuli, such as increased sunlight or changes in temperature.

KINDS OF LIFE

Biologists classify living organisms by how they get their energy. Organisms such as algae, green plants, and some bacteria use sunlight as an energy source. Animals (like humans), fungi, and some single-celled microscopic organisms called Archaea use chemicals to provide energy. When we eat food, chemical reactions within our digestive system turn our food into fuel.

Living things inhabit land, sea, and air. In fact, life thrives deep beneath the oceans, embedded in rocks miles below Earth's crust, in ice, and in other extreme environments. The life-forms that thrive in these challenging environments are called extremophiles. Some of these draw directly upon the chemicals surrounding them for energy. Because these are very different forms of life than what we're used to, we may not think of them as alive, but they are.

HOW IT ALL WORKS

To understand how a living organism works, it helps to look at one example of its simplest form—the single-celled bacterium called *Streptococcus*. There are many kinds of these tiny organisms, and some are responsible for human illnesses. What makes us sick or uncomfortable are the toxins the bacteria give off in our bodies.

A single *Streptococcus* bacterium is so small that at least 500 of them could fit on the dot above this letter *i*. These bacteria are some of the simplest forms of life we know. They have no moving parts, no lungs, no brain, no heart, no liver, and no leaves or fruit. Yet this life-form reproduces. It grows in size by producing long-chain structures, takes in nutrients, and gives off waste products. This tiny life-form is alive, just as you are alive.

What makes something alive is a question scientists grapple with when they study viruses, such as the ones that cause the common cold and COVID-19. They can grow and reproduce within host cells, such as those that make up your body. Because viruses lack cells and cannot metabolize nutrients for energy or reproduce without a host, scientists ask if they are indeed alive. And don't go looking for them without a strong microscope— viruses are a hundred times smaller than bacteria.

Scientists think life began on Earth more than four billion years ago, but no fossils exist from that time. The earliest fossils ever found are from the primitive life that existed 3.5 billion years ago. Other life-forms, some of which are shown below, soon followed. Scientists continue to study how life evolved on Earth and whether it is possible that life exists on other planets.

MICROSCOPIC ORGANISMS

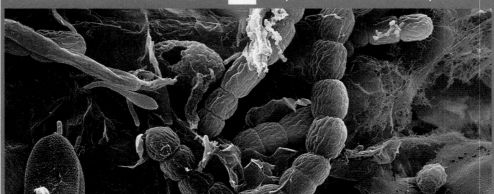

The Three Domains of Life

Biologists divide all living organisms into three domains, or groups: Bacteria, Archaea, and Eukarya. Archaea and Bacteria cells do not have nuclei—cellular parts that are essential to reproduction and other cell functions—but they are different from each other in many ways. Because human cells have a nucleus, we belong to the Eukarya domain.

1 BACTERIA

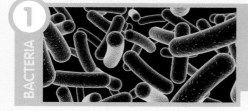

DOMAIN BACTERIA: These single-celled microorganisms are found almost everywhere in the world. Bacteria are small and do not have nuclei. They can be shaped like rods, spirals, or spheres. Some of them are helpful to humans, and some are harmful.

2 ARCHAEA

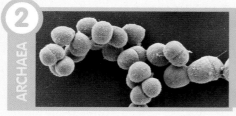

DOMAIN ARCHAEA: These single-celled microorganisms are often found in extremely hostile environments. Like Bacteria, Archaea do not have nuclei, but they have some genes in common with Eukarya. For this reason, scientists think the Archaea living today most closely resemble the earliest forms of life on Earth.

3 EUKARYA

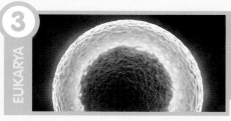

DOMAIN EUKARYA: This diverse group of life-forms is more complicated than Bacteria and Archaea, as Eukarya have one or more cells with nuclei. These are the tiny cells that make up your whole body. Eukarya are divided into four groups: fungi, protists, plants, and animals.

FYI

WHAT IS A DOMAIN? Scientifically speaking, a domain is a major taxonomic division into which natural objects are classified (see page 44 for "What Is Taxonomy?").

FUNGI

KINGDOM FUNGI Mainly multicellular organisms, fungi cannot make their own food. Mushrooms and yeast are fungi.

PLANTS

KINGDOM PLANTAE Plants are multicellular, and many can make their own food using photosynthesis.

PROTISTS

PROTISTS Once considered a kingdom, this group is a "grab bag" that includes unicellular and multicellular organisms of great variety.

ANIMALS

KINGDOM ANIMALIA Most animals, which are multicellular, have their own organ systems. Animals do not make their own food.

Sneaky Plants

Think all plants are just gentle growers? Then you'll be shocked by these sneaky sprouts that eat bugs, send secret messages, and more.

MEAT EATER Most plants live on nutrients from the soil, but the Venus flytrap lives only in low-nutrient dirt near the coasts of North and South Carolina, U.S.A. So to lure dinner (like flies and crickets), it oozes nectar inside its leaves. Attracted to the sweetness, an unsuspecting bug that bumps against the plant's alarm hairs will trigger jawlike leaves to slam shut. As the prey struggles, the plant releases digestive juices so it can eat. After about a week, the trap opens, and the plant is ready to strike again.

GROSS GROWER What's that smell? If you're on the island of Sumatra in Southeast Asia, it might be the titan arum plant, also called the corpse flower. Like its name suggests, the plant stinks like rotten meat, which attracts flies and beetles that lay their eggs on dead animals. Growing up to 12 feet (3.7 m) tall, it heats up to about 98°F (37°C) and releases its odor. The bugs visit multiple flowers, spreading pollen to help them reproduce.

Ugh, these squirrels are driving me NUTS.

Tell them to make like a tree and leaf.

I'm trying to shake them off, but they know my moves.

. . .

TRUNKY TALKER The forest might seem quiet, but that doesn't mean the trees and plants aren't "talking." Sometimes they're sending each other messages underground through a system of roots and fungi. For instance, if a tree is under attack from leaf-eating insects, it can send chemical and electrical signals to nearby trees, telling them to produce a type of acid that makes bugs sick. Or a healthy tree might send nutrients to a struggling neighbor. Even better: The trees don't even need to be the same species to communicate.

Green Scene

How to Compost

Grow a healthy garden and reduce waste by using leftovers to make your own compost, which is organic material that adds nutrients to the soil.

Recycle the Natural Way

By composting, you reduce the need for chemical fertilizers in your yard and send less waste to landfills. Yard trimmings and food scraps make up about 30 percent of the trash from cities and towns in the United States. So put that banana peel to good use. Turn it—and a lot of other things in your trash can—into environmentally helpful compost. By making natural fertilizer, you'll help the environment and have a great excuse to play with your food!

HOW TO MAKE COMPOST

COMPOST THESE

"BROWN" MATERIALS
- Dead leaves
- Eggshells
- Twigs
- Shredded newspaper
- Nutshells

"GREEN" MATERIALS
- Grass clippings
- Coffee grounds
- Vegetable and fruit scraps
- Tea bags

COMPOST NO-NOS

DON'T ADD THESE TO YOUR COMPOST!
- Meat and fish scraps
- Dairy products
- Fats, grease, or oils
- Kitty litter
- Nonorganic materials

1 Choose a dry, shady spot to create your compost pile.

2 Use a bin with a tight-fitting lid and plenty of air holes to hold your compost ingredients. In the bin, start with a six-inch (15-cm) layer of dry "brown" material. (See examples in the list above.) Break down large pieces before you place them in the bin.

3 Add a three-inch (7.6-cm) layer of "green" materials. (See list.) Add a little soil to this layer.

4 Mix the brown and green layers.

5 Finish with another three-inch (7.6-cm) layer of brown materials.

6 Add water until the contents are moist, like a wrung-out sponge. If you accidentally add too much water, just add more brown materials to the bin. Mix your compost pile every week or two.

7 After one to four months, the compost will be almost ready. When it's dark brown and moist and you can't identify the original ingredients, wait two more weeks. Then add your finished compost to your garden.

Your Amazing Body!

RED MARROW— a tissue in your bones—produces **EIGHT MILLION NEW BLOOD CELLS** a second.

The human body is a complicated mass of systems—nine systems, to be exact. Each has a unique and critical purpose in the body, and we wouldn't be able to survive without all of them.

The **NERVOUS** system controls the body.

The **MUSCULAR** system makes movement possible.

The **SKELETAL** system supports the body.

The **CIRCULATORY** system moves blood throughout the body.

The **RESPIRATORY** system provides the body with oxygen.

The **DIGESTIVE** system breaks down food into nutrients and gets rid of waste.

The **IMMUNE** system protects the body against disease and infection.

The **ENDOCRINE** system regulates the body's functions.

The **REPRODUCTIVE** system enables people to produce offspring.

Weird but true!

HUMAN TEETH ARE JUST AS **HARD** AS **SHARK TEETH.**

ROLLER-COASTER RIDES CAN CAUSE YOUR INTERNAL ORGANS TO MOVE AROUND IN YOUR BODY.

FOOD MUST BE **MIXED** WITH **SALIVA** OR **WATER** TO HAVE PROPER **TASTE.**

FINGERPRINT FACTS

Take a look at your fingers. See anything special?
It's your fingerprint! This unique set of ridges and swirls
is yours—and yours alone. Grab on to these fascinating
fingerprint facts.

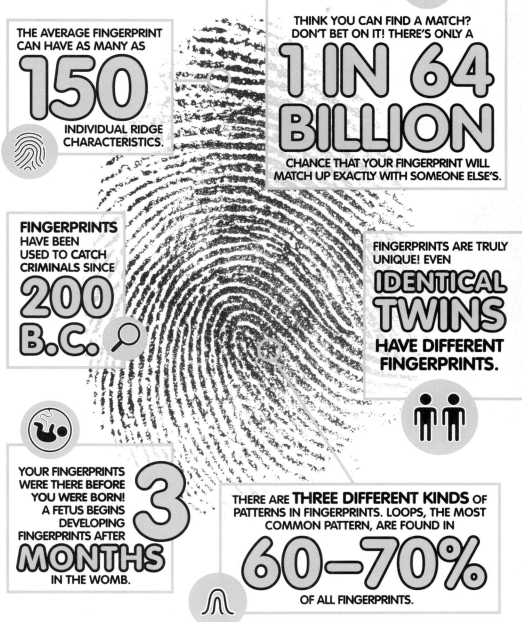

THE AVERAGE FINGERPRINT
CAN HAVE AS MANY AS

150

INDIVIDUAL RIDGE
CHARACTERISTICS.

THINK YOU CAN FIND A MATCH?
DON'T BET ON IT! THERE'S ONLY A

1 IN 64 BILLION

CHANCE THAT YOUR FINGERPRINT WILL
MATCH UP EXACTLY WITH SOMEONE ELSE'S.

FINGERPRINTS
HAVE BEEN
USED TO CATCH
CRIMINALS SINCE

200 B.C.

FINGERPRINTS ARE TRULY
UNIQUE! EVEN

IDENTICAL TWINS

HAVE DIFFERENT
FINGERPRINTS.

YOUR FINGERPRINTS
WERE THERE BEFORE
YOU WERE BORN!
A FETUS BEGINS
DEVELOPING
FINGERPRINTS AFTER

3 MONTHS

IN THE WOMB.

THERE ARE **THREE DIFFERENT KINDS** OF
PATTERNS IN FINGERPRINTS. LOOPS, THE MOST
COMMON PATTERN, ARE FOUND IN

60–70%

OF ALL FINGERPRINTS.

201

Why does my heart beat faster
when I'm nervous?

FOUR FUNCTIONS OF THE HEART

Your heart has some important jobs to do! Here are four of them.

1 Your heart beats more than 100,000 times every day. With each beat, it sends blood around your body, providing your cells with oxygen and nutrients.

2 It carries away waste, such as carbon dioxide, from other parts of the body.

3 The right side of the heart receives blood from the body and pumps it to the lungs to pick up more oxygen.

4 The left side of the heart receives blood from the lungs and pumps it out to the body—all in less than a minute!

NIX THOSE NERVES!

Feeling anxious about something? Here are three ways to breathe easier.

1 Practice, practice, practice. Whether it's practicing your recital song or shooting hoops, the more you do something, the more prepared you'll be—and the less nervous you'll be at go-time.

2 Relax your mind and body. Whether it's a few long, slow breaths or visualizing yourself making the game-winning goal, try to shift your mindset to a calmer place.

3 Know that you'll be fine, no matter what. Take the pressure off yourself. If you slip up and make a mistake? No biggie! Learn from your missteps, and you'll be better the next time.

PICTURE THIS: You're about to go on stage for your piano recital when suddenly your heart starts beating so fast, it feels like it's going to pop right out of your chest. What's going on?

Believe it or not, this is a normal reaction to stressful events. When you're nervous, your brain fires off hormones that jump-start your "fight or flight" response, which is the body's natural reaction to a scary situation. Sometimes it happens when you're faced with a serious threat, such as a hungry bear approaching your campsite. But it can also happen when you're safe. This results in a quicker heart rate, tense muscles, and rapid breathing—all of which usually go away soon after they start. And humans aren't the only ones to experience this: Experts have observed similar fight-or-flight responses in many other animals, including dogs and cats.

WHY can't I USE
my left hand as well as my right one
(or the other way around)?

About nine out of 10 of you reading this book will turn its pages with your right hand— the same hand you use to write a note or chuck a fastball. About 90 percent of humans are right-handed, meaning their right hand is their dominant hand. The other 10 percent are left-handed. Activities that feel natural with the dominant hand are awkward or difficult with the other one. Ever try to sign your name with your nondominant hand? Not so easy!

Cave paintings going back more than 5,000 years show humans favoring their right or left hand according to the same nine-to-one ratio we see today. And the same goes for the stone tools our evolutionary ancestors used 1.5 million years ago: Studies show a similar dominance of the right hand long before the human species, *Homo sapiens*, appeared in the fossil record.

ARE YOU A "mixed-hander"?

What about people who can use their nondominant hand almost as well as their dominant? They're called mixed-handers. (Scientists don't like using the term "ambidextrous," which implies neither hand is dominant.) About one percent of people are elite lefties/righties. Are you? Grab a piece of scratch paper and find out!

So why is one hand dominant?

Scientists have discovered a sequence of genes linked to hand dominance, making it a trait that's passed along to children just like hair color or dimples. These traits determine how our brains are wired. How? The brain is split into two symmetrical halves known as hemispheres. In about 90 percent of people, the left side of the brain processes language skills. These people are typically right-handed. People born with genes for left-handedness—about 10 percent of the population—typically have brains that process speech on the right side.

So whichever side of the brain controls speech usually corresponds with a dominant hand on the opposite side. Because the left side of the brain controls the right side of the body and vice versa, scientists suspect that the evolution of our dominant hand is somehow connected to the development of our language capabilities. Humans can have a dominant eye, foot, and ear, too—but scientists aren't quite sure why. That's just one of many reasons the human brain is considered the most complex object in the universe.

203

How Viruses spread

IMAGINE YOU'RE AT BASKETBALL PRACTICE when your teammate coughs. He covers his mouth, but tiny droplets—hardly visible to the naked eye—escape. You don't notice, and you keep playing. The next day, your teammate stays home from school. A few days later, you have a fever and a sore throat. Did you get sick from your teammate?

It's hard to pinpoint the source of a virus. Some germs spread through the air, while others can be picked up from surfaces, such as doorknobs, light switches, and desks. If you're around someone who's carrying a virus and that person coughs, sneezes, or even talks near you, you could be in the virus's direct line of fire. Once you're exposed to infectious particles, your immune system will do its best to protect you from getting sick.

But if the virus muscles its way past your body's line of defense, it then has to find a host to stay alive. If it does, the virus invades the host cells in your body and begins to replicate, or make copies of itself. This causes a disease (such as the flu or COVID-19) that usually makes you feel sick. Meanwhile, your immune system continues to work hard against the virus. For example, you might get a fever, which is a sign that your body's fighting off those germs.

What can you do? It's best to rest, hydrate, and lay low while your body rids itself of the virus. Then hopefully within a few days, both you and your teammate will be back on the basketball court!

Germy Terms!

BACTERIA: Microorganisms that can cause sicknesses like ear infections or strep throat. But some are good for your health, like the kind that break down food in your gut.

EPIDEMIC: A sudden increase in the number of people in a certain area—like a town, city, or state—with the same disease.

PANDEMIC: A worldwide outbreak of a disease. This happens when a virus spreads easily and infects a lot of people.

VIRUS: Tiny organisms found all around— in dirt, water, and the air—that need a host's energy to grow and survive. Once inside a host, a virus can multiply and attack cells.

WHAT'S YOUR TYPE?

Everyone's blood is made of the same basic elements, but not all blood is alike. There are four main blood types. If a person needs to use donated blood, the donated blood can react with their body's immune system if it's not the right type. This diagram shows which types of blood are compatible with each other.

GROUP O can donate red blood cells to anybody. It's the universal donor.

GROUP A can donate red blood cells to A's and AB's.

GROUP B can donate red blood cells to B's and AB's.

GROUP AB can donate to other AB's, but can receive from all others.

O+ is the most common blood type:

38%

of people in the U.S. have this type.

Blood types can be positive or negative. Only **18%** of people in the U.S. have a negative blood type.

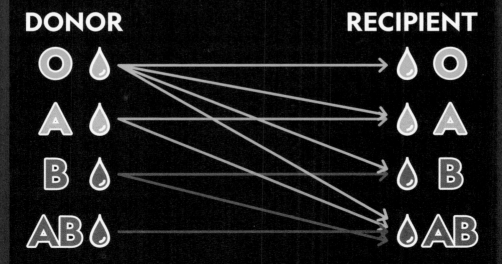

DONOR

RECIPIENT

O

A

B

AB

O

A

B

AB

THE SCIENCE OF
SPOOKY

HOW THESE CREEPY THINGS AFFECT YOUR BRAIN

What's that strange noise in the night? Is it the wind? Or something else?

"When you encounter something scary, your brain releases chemicals," psychologist Martin Antony says. "These chemicals make our hearts race, so we breathe faster and sweat. Your nervous system is preparing your body to either fight a threat or run away from it." Scientists call this the "fight-or-flight" response.

So which so-called spookiness makes us feel this way—and why? Discover what puts the *eek!* in these five freaky things.

THE FEAR: SPIDERS

SCIENTIFIC NAME: Arachnophobia

SPOOKY SCIENCE: Humans have been afraid of spiders since our ancient human ancestors thought they carried deadly diseases. "Today, we know that's not true," psychologist Kyle Rexer says. "But a lot of people still have incorrect ideas about how dangerous spiders are." Although some spiders *can* be deadly, most are not. In fact, humans actually benefit from the existence of spiders. By eating disease-carrying critters such as mosquitoes and cockroaches, these arachnids act as a form of pest control. Plus, scientists are currently studying spider venom in the hope that it can one day be used in medicines to manage pain or cure illnesses.

THE FEAR: CLOWNS

SCIENTIFIC NAME: Coulrophobia

SPOOKY SCIENCE: One way we decide if a person is friend or foe is by evaluating their facial expressions. Clowns—with their makeup, wigs, and fake noses—are hard to read, which is what makes them scary to some people. "It's hard to tell how a clown is feeling," psychology professor Frank McAndrew says. "So we think, If clowns can hide their emotions, what else might they be hiding?"

FIGHT THE FRIGHT

It's natural to avoid things that scare us. "But to get over your fears—whether you're afraid of spiders, clowns, the dark, or, well, anything—you have to *focus* on them instead of avoid them," Rexer says. He shares some useful tips to help you manage your fears.

THE FEAR: HEIGHTS
SCIENTIFIC NAME: Acrophobia
SPOOKY SCIENCE: When you're standing on solid ground, your eyes work with your inner ears to help you stay balanced. But if you're standing, say, at the edge of a cliff, your sense of balance can get out of whack. "Your inner ear is saying you're surrounded by solid ground, but your eyes are saying, 'Nope,'" inner-ear specialist Dennis Fitzgerald says. Your brain is getting mixed signals, which can cause vertigo, or dizziness that makes heights feel scary.

THE FEAR: DARKNESS
SCIENTIFIC NAME: Nyctophobia
SPOOKY SCIENCE: As with other phobias, humans developed a fear of the dark to avoid danger. Our ancestors had to be extra cautious at night to protect themselves against things like animal predators and human invaders. (This was before electric lighting!) "Many people still have that fear of the dark today," Antony says. "It's a fear of the unknown."

THE FEAR: SMALL SPACES
SCIENTIFIC NAME: Claustrophobia
SPOOKY SCIENCE: Maybe you've been stuck in an elevator before and thought it was no big deal. For some people, though, just the fear of being stuck can cause them to take the stairs. "Small spaces might cause some people to worry about running out of oxygen, or never being able to get out—no matter how unlikely that is," Antony says. "To increase our chances of survival, people have evolved to avoid being trapped. For some, that could be anywhere."

- Expose yourself to things that you're afraid of in a way that you feel safe. For example, if you fear public speaking, try practicing in front of a mirror first, and then give the speech to a small group of trusted friends.

- If you feel anxious, place one or both of your hands on your stomach and focus on breathing slowly and deeply. Regulating your breathing will help you feel calmer and can lessen your sense of panic.

- Don't be too hard on yourself! Everyone's afraid of *something*. Just make sure it doesn't stop you from living your life. Talk to an adult if it feels like too much to handle on your own.

FUTURE WORLD:

The year is 2070, and it's time to get dressed for school. You step in front of a large video mirror that projects different clothes on you. After you decide on your favorite T-shirt, a robot fetches your outfit. No time is lost trying to find matching socks! Chores? What chores? Get ready for a whole new home life.

STAY CONNECTED

Whether your future home is an urban skyscraper or an underwater pod, all buildings may one day be connected via a central communications hub. Want to check out a *T. rex* skeleton at a faraway museum? You can virtually connect to it as though you were checking it out in person. But you're not just seeing something miles away. Connect to a beach house's balcony and smell the salty air and feel the breeze. Buildings might also share information about incoming weather and emergencies to keep you safe.

CUSTOM COMFORT

Soon, your house may give you a personal welcome home. No need for keys—sensors will scan your body and open the door. Walk into the living room, and the lighting adjusts to your preferred setting. Thirsty? A glass of water pops up on the counter. Before bed, you enter the bathroom and say, "Shower, please." The water starts flowing at exactly the temperature you want.

ON LOCATION

Your room has a spectacular view of the ocean ... because your house is suspended above it. New technologies may allow us to build our homes in unusual spots. In the future, "floating" structures elevated by supporting poles above water or other hard-to-access spots (think mountain peaks) could be more common as cities become more crowded. And this likely won't be limited to dry land on Earth. That means that one day your family could even live in space!

Homes

No one really knows what the future holds. These predictions are just for fun!

ON THE GO

Homes of the future might always be on the move. Walls could be capable of expanding and contracting, and houses may rotate with the sun's movements to conserve energy. Buildings could also be capable of changing size depending on who's inside. Grandparents could even "move in" by attaching a modular section to the front, back, or top of the house.

BRING ON THE BOTS

Imagine this: While you were outside playing with your friends, your house robot did the laundry, vacuumed, and cleaned the bathroom. Meanwhile, a drone just delivered groceries for the home-bot to put away. Minutes later, lunch is ready. The service is great ... but how will you earn your allowance? Instead of taking out the garbage or setting the table, you could earn money by helping clean and maintain the robots.

FUTURE WORLD:

A few decades from now, how will you get to the store? Maybe you'll take a drone to go shopping—or, if it's raining, you might go for a ride in a driverless cube car.

"The sky's no longer the limit in terms of where transportation is headed," says Tom Kurfess, a mechanical engineering professor at the Georgia Institute of Technology. Take a peek at these possible wild rides of the future.

GOING UP ... WAY UP!

The space elevator doors open—welcome to the space station lobby. It's possible that people will one day ride a space elevator from Earth to a space station that orbits our planet from 22,370 miles (36,000 km) above. The elevator could carry passengers and cargo into space without burning huge amounts of fuel, unlike today's rockets. Aboard the station, travelers might stay in a hotel room with a truly out-of-this-world view. Then those heading to, say, Mars can transfer to a spaceship to continue their journey.

NO DRIVER NEEDED

Picture this: You exit your high-rise apartment balcony into your own private glass elevator, take a seat, and say your destination. The elevator car descends 205 floors to street level before detaching from the building and moving to the street. It's now a cube-shaped car. Another cube carrying your friends is nearby; the vehicles connect while in motion, transforming into one bigger car. The cube drops you off at school and parks itself. According to Tommaso Gecchelin, founder of NEXT Future Transportation, driverless cars will work together to end traffic jams and improve safety.

Transportation

No one really knows what the future holds. These predictions are just for fun!

POWER PLANE

Passenger planes will still be around in the future—they'll just likely travel *much* faster. Today, flying 6,850 miles (11,025 km) from New York City to Beijing, China, takes about 14 hours. But thanks to future technological advancements such as sleeker, more lightweight aircraft, a passenger plane could make the same trip in just under two hours.

FLOWN BY DRONE

"One day soon drones and robots will deliver our meals," Gecchelin says. But further into the future, helicopter-size drones could also deliver *people*. Some experts even think that cargo drones will be able to lift small houses from a city and carry them to scenic vacation spots.

PIZZA

TOTALLY TUBULAR

Say your friend invites you to her birthday party. It's today—and across the country. No prob. In the future, you could tube it from the West Coast to the East Coast in a couple of hours. You sit in a capsule that looks like a train without rails. Whoosh! The capsule's sucked into a vacuum tube. Like a bullet train, the capsule uses magnets to fly forward in the tube without friction, or resistance. The result: a smooth, fast ride that never slows from 750 miles an hour (1,200 km/h).

QUIZ WHIZ

Test your science and technology smarts by taking this quiz!

Write your answers on a piece of paper. Then check them below.

1 The earliest fossils ever found are from the primitive life that existed _____ years ago.

a. 1.5 billion   **c.** 3.5 billion
b. 2.5 billion   **d.** 4.5 billion

2 **True or false?** Your heart beats more than 100,000 times every day.

3 A sudden increase in the number of people in a certain area with the same disease is called a(n) _____ .

a. bacteria
b. epidemic
c. pandemic
d. virus

4 What substance does the Venus flytrap ooze inside its leaves to attract insects?

a. venom   **c.** nectar
b. milk   **d.** honey

CHAMP 2021

5 Moxi, a four-foot (1.2-m)-tall robot, carries items between rooms inside a _____ in Virginia, U.S.A.

a. hospital
b. school
c. bank
d. restaurant

Not **STUMPED** yet? Check out the *NATIONAL GEOGRAPHIC KIDS QUIZ WHIZ* collection for more crazy **SCIENCE AND TECHNOLOGY** questions!

This Is How It's Done!

Sometimes, the most complicated problems are solved with step-by-step directions. These "how-to" instructions are also known as a process analysis essay. Although scientists and engineers use this tool to program robots and write computer code, you also use process analysis every day, from following a recipe to putting together a new toy or gadget. Here's how to write a basic process analysis essay.

Step 1: Choose Your Topic Sentence

Pick a clear and concise topic sentence that describes what you're writing about. Be sure to explain to the readers why the task is important—and how many steps there are to complete it.

Step 2: List Materials

Do you need specific ingredients or equipment to complete your process? Mention these right away so the readers will have all they need to do the activity.

Step 3: Write Your Directions

Your directions should be clear and easy to follow. Assume that you are explaining the process for the first time, and define any unfamiliar terms. List your steps in the exact order the readers will need to follow to complete the activity. Try to keep your essay limited to no more than six steps.

Step 4: Restate Your Main Idea

Your closing idea should revisit your topic sentence, drawing a conclusion relating to the importance of the subject.

EXAMPLE OF A PROCESS ANALYSIS ESSAY

Downloading an app is a simple way to enhance your tablet. Today, I'd like to show you how to search for and add an app to your tablet. First, you will need a tablet with the ability to access the internet. You'll also want to ask a parent for permission before you download anything onto your tablet. Next, select the specific app you want by going to the app store on your tablet and entering the app's name into the search bar. Once you find the app you're seeking, select "download" and wait for the app to load. When you see that the app has fully loaded, tap on the icon and you will be able to access it. Now you can enjoy your app and have more fun with your tablet.

Lake Abraham in Alberta, Canada, is known for its frozen methane bubbles. When plants and animals die, they sink to the bottom of the lake and decompose. This releases methane gas, which then rises to the surface in bubbles.

Biomes

A BIOME, OFTEN CALLED A MAJOR LIFE ZONE, is one of the natural world's major communities where plants and animals adapt to their specific surroundings. Biomes are classified depending on the predominant vegetation, climate, and geography of a region. They can be divided into six major types: forest, freshwater, marine, desert, grassland, and tundra. Each biome consists of many ecosystems.

Biomes are extremely important. Balanced ecological relationships among biomes help to maintain the environment and life on Earth as we know it. For example, an increase in one species of plant, such as an invasive one, can cause a ripple effect throughout a whole biome.

FOREST

Forests occupy about one-third of Earth's land area. There are three major types of forests: tropical, temperate, and boreal (taiga). Forests are home to a diversity of plants, some of which may hold medicinal qualities for humans, as well as thousands of animal species, some still undiscovered. Forests can also absorb carbon dioxide, a greenhouse gas, and give off oxygen.

More than half of the world's animal species live in rainforests.

FRESHWATER

Most water on Earth is salty, but freshwater ecosystems—including lakes, ponds, wetlands, rivers, and streams—usually contain water with less than one percent salt concentration. The countless animal and plant species that live in freshwater biomes vary from continent to continent, but they include algae, frogs, turtles, fish, and the larvae of many insects.

Icebergs—mostly made of freshwater—are formed from glaciers on land and drift out to sea.

MARINE

The marine biome covers almost three-fourths of Earth's surface, making it the largest habitat on our planet. Oceans make up the majority of the saltwater marine biome. Coral reefs are considered to be the most biodiverse of any of the biome habitats. The marine biome is home to more than one million plant and animal species.

The world ocean contains about 320 million cubic miles (1.3 billion cubic km) of water.

DESERT

Covering about one-fifth of Earth's surface, deserts are places where precipitation is less than 10 inches (25 cm) a year. Although most deserts are hot, there are other kinds as well. The four major kinds of deserts are hot, semiarid, coastal, and cold. Far from being barren wastelands, deserts are biologically rich habitats.

The average rainfall in South America's Atacama Desert is just .04 inch (1 mm) a year.

GRASSLAND

Biomes called grasslands are characterized by having grasses instead of large shrubs or trees. Grasslands generally have precipitation for only about half to three-fourths of the year. If it were more, they would become forests. Grasslands can be divided into two types: tropical (savannas) and temperate. Some of the world's largest land animals, such as elephants, live there.

Much of central North America is grassland, where animals such as the American bison—almost hunted to extinction in the 1800s—graze in herds.

TUNDRA

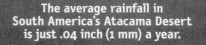

The coldest of all biomes, a tundra is characterized by an extremely cold climate, simple vegetation, little precipitation, poor nutrients, and a short growing season. There are two types of tundra: Arctic and alpine. A tundra is home to few kinds of vegetation. Surprisingly, though, quite a few animal species can survive the tundra's extremes, such as wolves and caribou, and even mosquitoes.

Native to the Arctic tundra, arctic foxes are the only member of the dog family that have fully furred footpads that work like built-in snow boots.

The Awesome AMAZON

It's midnight in the Amazon rainforest. And while much of the rest of the world is sound asleep, thousands of species residing in this lush swath of land are just waking up. Under a sky sparkling with thousands of stars, snakes slither along the forest floor while bright green frogs hop from plant to plant. A sleek, spotted jaguar skulks through tall grasses, stalking its next meal. And owl monkeys—appropriately nicknamed night monkeys—screech at one another from high in the treetops.

AN AMAZING ECOSYSTEM

These critters of the night—also known as nocturnal animals—are just some of the thousands of species that call the Amazon rainforest home. The world's largest tropical rainforest, the Amazon covers more than 2.1 million square miles (5.5 million sq km) spread across parts of Brazil, Bolivia, Peru, Ecuador, Colombia, Venezuela, Guyana, Suriname, and French Guiana in South America. All told, the Amazon's ecosystem is made up of some 40,000 plant species, nearly 1,300 bird species, more than 400 amphibians, 427 types of mammals, and more than two million different kinds of insects.

NORTH AMERICA

ATLANTIC OCEAN

VENEZUELA
SURINAME
COLOMBIA
GUYANA
French Guiana (France)
ECUADOR
Amazon River
PERU
BRAZIL
SOUTH AMERICA
BOLIVIA
PACIFIC OCEAN

SOUTH AMERICA
ATLANTIC OCEAN
PACIFIC OCEAN

■ Amazon Rainforest
— Amazon River

A TREETOP VIEW OF THE AMAZON RAINFOREST

ONE WILD RIVER

And that's just what you may see on land. There are another 3,000 types of fish swimming in the Amazon River, which ribbons through the rainforest for more than 4,150 miles (6,679 km), making it the world's second longest river. River dolphins, piranhas, electric eels, and the pirarucu (also known as the arapaima) live in the Amazon River. The pirarucu, a huge fish, can grow up to 15 feet (4.5 m) long and has teeth on the roof of its mouth and tongue!

PROTECTING THE AMAZON

With so much biodiversity and even more that has yet to be discovered, it is super important to protect the Amazon from threats like deforestation and climate change. Over the last 50 years, some 20 percent of the forest cover has been lost due to human impact, and some 10,000 plant and animal species are at risk of extinction. But many people are working hard to minimize further damage and protect this magical place. Law officers are in place to monitor protected areas, and farmers are replanting parts of forest that have been cut down. Together, people can help keep the Amazon buzzing from day to night for many years to come.

The Amazon River winds through the Amazon rainforest.

Giant arapaima fish

Jaguar

Night monkeys

RAINFOREST LAYERS

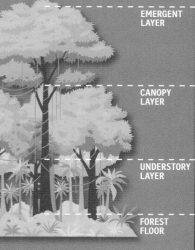

EMERGENT LAYER

CANOPY LAYER

UNDERSTORY LAYER

FOREST FLOOR

EMERGENT: Here, soaring trees grow far apart and tall, their branches reaching above the canopy.

UPPER CANOPY: A dense, deep layer of vegetation roughly 20 feet (6 m) thick, it hosts most of the rainforest's animal species.

UNDERSTORY: This low-light layer is made up of shorter plants with broad leaves, like palm trees.

FOREST FLOOR: On the ground is a dark area where few plants are able to grow. Here, decaying matter from the upper layers feeds the roots of the trees.

THE OCEANS

PACIFIC OCEAN

STATS

Surface area

65,100,000 sq mi (168,600,000 sq km)

Percentage of all oceans

46 percent

Surface temperatures

**Summer high:
90°F (32°C)
Winter low: 28°F (-2°C)**

Tides

**Highest: 30 ft (9 m)
near Korean Peninsula
Lowest: 1 ft (0.3 m) near Midway Islands**

Cool creatures **giant Pacific octopus,
bottlenose whale, clownfish, great
white shark**

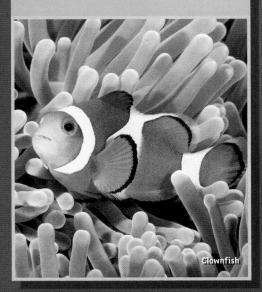

Clownfish

ATLANTIC OCEAN

STATS

Surface area

33,100,000 sq mi (85,600,000 sq km)

Percentage of all oceans

24 percent

Surface temperatures

**Summer high: 90°F (32°C)
Winter low: 28°F (-2°C)**

Tides

**Highest: 52 ft (16 m)
Bay of Fundy, Canada
Lowest: 1.5 ft (0.5 m)
Gulf of Mexico and Mediterranean Sea**

Cool creatures **blue whale, Atlantic
spotted dolphin, sea turtle, bottlenose
dolphin**

Bottlenose dolphin

INDIAN OCEAN

STATS

Surface area

27,500,000 sq mi (71,200,000 sq km)

Percentage of all oceans

20 percent

Surface temperatures

**Summer high: 93°F (34°C)
Winter low: 28°F (-2°C)**

Tides

**Highest: 36 ft (11 m)
Lowest: 2 ft (0.6 m)
Both along Australia's west coast**

Cool creatures: **humpback whale,
Portuguese man-of-war, dugong
(sea cow), leatherback turtle**

Leatherback turtle

ARCTIC OCEAN

STATS

Surface area

6,100,000 sq mi (15,700,000 sq km)

Percentage of all oceans

4 percent

Surface temperatures

**Summer high:
41°F (5°C)
Winter low: 28°F (-2°C)**

Tides

**Less than 1 ft (0.3 m)
variation throughout the ocean**

Cool creatures:

**beluga whale, orca,
harp seal, narwhal**

Narwhal

SOUTHERN OCEAN

STATS

Surface area

8,500,000 sq mi (21,900,000 sq km)

Percentage of all oceans

6 percent

Tides

**Less than 2 ft (0.6 m)
variation throughout the ocean**

Surface temperatures

**Summer high: 50°F (10°C)
Winter low: 28°F (-2°C)**

Cool creatures: **emperor
penguin, colossal squid, mackerel
icefish, Antarctic toothfish**

Emperor penguin

To see the major oceans and bays in relation to landmasses, look at the map on pages 272 and 273.

THE DEEP BLUE SEA

Oceans cover 71 percent of our planet's surface. Some areas in them are so deep that they'd cover the tallest mountains on Earth! Dive in and discover the deepest parts of our oceans.

PACIFIC OCEAN
CHALLENGER DEEP

36,037 FEET
(10,984 M)

INDIAN OCEAN
JAVA TRENCH

23,376 FEET
(7,125 M)

The average ocean depth is **12,100 FEET** (3,688 m).

ARCTIC OCEAN
MOLLOY DEEP

18,599 FEET
(5,669 M)

ATLANTIC OCEAN
PUERTO RICO TRENCH

28,232 FEET
(8,605 M)

SOUTHERN OCEAN
SOUTH SANDWICH TRENCH

24,390 FEET
(7,434 M)

WATER CYCLE

Precipitation falls

Water storage in ice and snow

Water vapor condenses in clouds

Water filters into the ground

Meltwater and surface runoff

Evaporation

Freshwater storage

Groundwater discharge

Water storage in ocean

The amount of water on Earth is more or less constant— only the form changes. As the sun warms Earth's surface, liquid water is changed into water vapor in a process called **evaporation.** Water on the surface of plants' leaves turns into water vapor in a process called **transpiration.** As water vapor rises into the air, it cools and changes form again. This time, it becomes clouds in a process called **condensation.** Water droplets fall from the clouds as **precipitation,** which then travels as groundwater or runoff back to the lakes, rivers, and oceans, where the cycle (shown above) starts all over again.

To a meteorologist— a person who studies the weather—a "light rain" is less than 1/48 inch (0.5 mm). A "heavy rain" is more than 1/6 inch (4 mm).

You drink the same water as the dinosaurs! Earth has been recycling water for more than four billion years.

223

Weather and Climate

Weather is the condition of the atmosphere—temperature, wind, humidity, and precipitation—at a given place at a given time. Climate, however, is the average weather for a particular place over a long period of time. Different places on Earth have different climates, but climate is not a random occurrence.

It is a pattern that is controlled by factors such as latitude, elevation, prevailing winds, the temperature of ocean currents, and location on land relative to water. Climate is generally constant, but evidence indicates that human activity is causing a change in its patterns —a long-term shift called climate change.

WEATHER EXTREMES

LONGEST-LASTING TYPHOON: Typhoon John lasted 31 days between August and September 1994 as it traveled from the eastern to the western Pacific.

HOTTEST MONTH: July 2018 in Death Valley, California, U.S.A., when the average daily temperature reached 108.1°F (42.3°C)

LONGEST LIGHTNING FLASH: 477 miles (767 km), stretching across Texas, Louisiana, and Mississippi, U.S.A., in 2022

GLOBAL CLIMATE ZONES

Climatologists, people who study climate, have created different systems for classifying climates. One that is often used is called the Köppen system, which classifies climate zones according to precipitation, temperature, and vegetation. It has five major categories—tropical, dry, temperate, cold, and polar—with a sixth category for locations where high elevations override other factors.

ARCTIC OCEAN
ARCTIC CIRCLE
TROPIC OF CANCER
ATLANTIC OCEAN
EQUATOR
PACIFIC OCEAN
TROPIC OF CAPRICORN
PACIFIC OCEAN
INDIAN OCEAN
ANTARCTIC CIRCLE
SOUTHERN OCEAN

Climate
Tropical Dry Temperate Cold Polar

Climate CHANGE

A POLAR BEAR ON A PIECE OF MELTING ICEBERG

SCIENTISTS ARE CONCERNED THAT GREENLAND'S ICE SHEET HAS BEGUN TO MELT IN SUMMER. BIRTHDAY CANYON, SHOWN HERE, WAS CARVED BY MELTWATER.

Rising Temperatures, Explained

Fact: The world is getting warmer. Earth's surface temperature has been increasing. In the past 50 years, our planet has warmed twice as fast as in the 50 years before that. This is the direct effect of climate change, which refers not only to the increase in Earth's average temperature (known as global warming), but also to its long-term effects on winds, rain, and ocean currents. Global warming is the reason glaciers and polar ice sheets are melting—resulting in rising sea levels and shrinking habitats. This makes survival for some animals a big challenge. Warming also means more flooding along coasts and drought for inland areas.

Why are temperatures climbing?

While some of the recent climate changes can be tied to natural causes—such as changes in the sun's intensity, the unusually warm ocean currents of El Niño, and volcanic activity— human activities are the greatest contributor.

Everyday activities that require burning fossil fuels, such as driving gasoline-powered cars, contribute to global warming. These activities produce greenhouse gases, which enter the atmosphere and trap heat. At the current rate, Earth's global average temperature is projected to rise some 5°F (3°C) or more since 1900, and it will get even warmer after that. And as the climate continues to warm, it will unfortunately continue to affect the environment and our society in many ways.

225

THE SKY IS FALLING

"PRECIPITATION" IS A FANCY WORD
FOR THE WET STUFF THAT FALLS FROM THE SKY.

Precipitation is rain, freezing rain, sleet, snow, or hail. It forms when water vapor in the air condenses into clouds, gets heavier, and drops to the ground. Precipitation can ruin a picnic, but life on Earth couldn't exist without it.

Develops when ice crystals fall toward the ground, partly melt, and then refreeze. This happens mainly in winter when air near the ground is below freezing temperatures.

SLEET

RAIN

Formed when ice crystals in high, cold clouds get heavy and fall. Even in summer, falling ice crystals could remain frozen, but warm air near the ground melts them into raindrops.

FREEZING RAIN

Falls during winter, when rain freezes immediately as it hits a surface. Freezing rain creates layers of ice on roads and causes dangerous driving conditions.

Produced when ice crystals in clouds get heavy enough to fall. The air has to be cold enough all the way down for the crystals to stay frozen.

SNOW

HAIL

Formed inside thunderstorms when ice crystals covered in water pass through patches of freezing air in the tops of cumulonimbus clouds. The water on the ice crystals freezes. The crystals become heavy and fall to the ground.

Types of Clouds

If you want a clue about the weather, look up at the clouds. They'll tell a lot about the condition of the air and what weather might be on the way. Clouds are made of both air and water. On fair days, warm air currents rise and push against the water in clouds, keeping it from falling. But as the raindrops in a cloud get bigger, it's time to set them free. The bigger raindrops become too heavy for the air currents to hold up, and they fall to the ground.

How Much Does a Cloud Weigh?

A light, fluffy cumulus cloud typically weighs about 216,000 pounds (98,000 kg). That's about the weight of 18 elephants. A rain-soaked cumulonimbus cloud typically weighs 105.8 million pounds (48 million kg), or about the same as 9,000 elephants.

1 STRATUS These clouds make the sky look like a bowl of thick gray porridge. They hang low in the sky, blanketing the day in dreary darkness. Stratus clouds form when cold, moist air close to the ground moves over a region.

2 CIRRUS These wispy tufts of clouds are thin and hang high up in the atmosphere where the air is extremely cold. Cirrus clouds are made of tiny ice crystals.

3 CUMULUS These white, fluffy clouds make people sing, "Oh, what a beautiful morning!" They form low in the atmosphere and look like marshmallows. They often mix with large patches of blue sky. Formed when hot air rises, cumulus clouds usually disappear when the air cools at night.

4 CUMULONIMBUS These are the monster clouds. Rising air currents force fluffy cumulus clouds to swell and shoot upward, as much as 70,000 feet (21,000 m). When these clouds bump against the top of the troposphere, known as the tropopause, they flatten out on top like tabletops.

10 FACTS ABOUT WACKY WEATHER

The Empire State Building in New York City is **HIT BY LIGHTNING** an average of **25 times a year.**

FROGS and fish can "RAIN" FROM THE SKY——the animals are carried into the sky by strong winds and then fall, making it look like they are "raining" down.

Layers of moisture inside clouds freeze to form hailstones, **CREATING BALLS OF ICE THAT LOOK LIKE FROZEN ONIONS.**

ASTRAPHOBIA is the fear of **thunder and lightning.**

A "ZOMBIE FIRE"— an underground blaze sparked by wildfire—can smolder under the snowpack in cold parts of the world, such as Siberia.

A storm in New Mexico, U.S.A., once produced **hail glaciers,** accumulations of hail, measuring **16 feet** (5 m) tall.

The uncommon phenomenon known as **thundersnow** occurs when it is thundering and snowing at the same time.

Research shows that **tornadoes are most common** in the late afternoon and early evening.

RED SPRITES are reddish lightning bolts above thunderstorms that look like **fireworks or giant jellyfish.**

A **HABOOB** is a SUPERSTRONG SANDSTORM that creates walls of dust some **3,300 feet** (1 km) **high.**

HURRICANE
HAPPENINGS

A storm is brewing—but is this a tropical cyclone, a hurricane, or a typhoon? These weather events go by different names depending on where they form, how fast their winds get, or both. Strong tropical cyclones are called hurricanes in the Atlantic and parts of the Pacific Ocean; in the western Pacific, they are called typhoons. But any way you look at it, these storms pack a punch. And they all form when warm moist air rises from the ocean, causing air from surrounding areas to be "sucked" in. That air then becomes warm and moist and rises, too, beginning a cycle that forms clouds, which rotate with the spin of Earth. If there is enough warm water to feed the storm, it will result in a hurricane. And the warmer the water, and the more moisture in the air, the more powerful the hurricane.

HURRICANE NAMES FOR 2024

Atlantic hurricane names come from six official international lists. The names alternate between male and female. When a storm becomes a hurricane, a name from the list is used, in alphabetical order. (If the hurricane season is especially active and the list runs out, the World Meteorological Organization will provide extra names to draw from.) Each list is reused every six years. A name is "retired" if that hurricane caused a lot of damage or many deaths.

Alberto	Francine	Joyce	Nadine	Sara
Beryl	Gordon	Kirk	Oscar	Tony
Chris	Helene	Leslie	Patty	Valerie
Debby	Isaac	Milton	Rafael	William
Ernesto				

SCALE OF HURRICANE INTENSITY

CATEGORY	ONE	TWO	THREE	FOUR	FIVE
DAMAGE	Minimal	Moderate	Extensive	Extreme	Catastrophic
WINDS	74–95 mph (119–153 km/h)	96–110 mph (154–177 km/h)	111–129 mph (178–208 km/h)	130–156 mph (209–251 km/h)	157 mph or higher (252+ km/h)
(DAMAGE refers to wind and water damage combined.)					

What Is a Tornado?

THE ENHANCED FUJITA SCALE

The Enhanced Fujita (EF) Scale, named after tornado expert T. Theodore Fujita, classifies tornadoes based on wind speed and the intensity of damage that they cause.

EF0
65–85 mph winds
(105–137 km/h)
Slight damage

EF1
86–110 mph winds
(138–177 km/h)
Moderate damage

EF2
111–135 mph winds
(178–217 km/h)
Substantial damage

EF3
136–165 mph winds
(218–266 km/h)
Severe damage

EF4
166–200 mph winds
(267–322 km/h)
Massive damage

EF5
More than 200 mph winds
(322+ km/h)
Catastrophic damage

TORNADOES, ALSO KNOWN AS TWISTERS, are funnels of rapidly rotating air that are created during thunderstorms. With wind speeds that can exceed 300 miles an hour (483 km/h), tornadoes have the power to pick up and destroy everything in their path.

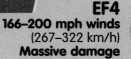

THIS ROTATING FUNNEL OF AIR, formed in a cumulus or cumulonimbus cloud, became a tornado when it touched the ground.

TORNADOES HAVE OCCURRED IN ALL 50 U.S. STATES AND ON EVERY CONTINENT EXCEPT ANTARCTICA.

BEACHFRONT BUILDINGS ON TONGATAPU, TONGA'S MAIN ISLAND, WERE DESTROYED BY AN UNDERWATER VOLCANO.

Tsunami

When the Hunga Tonga–Hunga Ha'apai volcano erupted in the South Pacific on an evening in January 2022, people as far as 400 miles (644 km) away heard a loud boom and felt the earth shake. It wasn't clear what had caused the disturbance at first. But people soon found out. The violent eruption triggered a tsunami, giant waves caused by a disturbance (like an earthquake) below the sea. The tsunami swept over much of Tonga, a remote country of 106,000 people in the Pacific Ocean that consists of about 170 islands stretching over an area roughly the size of Texas, U.S.A.

While the tsunami came fast and ferociously, locals were told of the incoming surge by an early warning system. Others picked up on telltale signs of the massive wave just before it hit: Dogs barking nonstop, and the ocean's tide moving in an unfamiliar way, receding unusually rapidly as the water level rose. While residents ran for higher ground, huge waves, some almost 50 feet (15 m) high, washed over some of the islands, destroying homes and buildings and impacting the entire population of Tonga.

Cicada Invasion!

Like a scene plucked straight from a science fiction movie, millions of bugs with bulging red eyes slowly clawed their way from deep underground burrows throughout parts of the eastern United States during the late spring and early summer of 2021. But this was no setup for the camera—this was Brood X, a massive emergence of cicadas that occurs just once every 17 years.

While annual cicadas—those that appear every year— are not an uncommon sight in the summertime, Brood X made a big scene in many states because of the bugs' huge numbers and their loud, distinctive song. Described by many as an ear-splitting buzz, the collective high-pitched hum of millions of male cicadas (the females are silent) could be heard from miles away.

Thankfully for humans, the Brood X invasion didn't last long. After spending 17 years developing underground, the insects die only about a month after emerging, leaving behind nothing but their brown exoskeletons, a hard outer covering—but not before they mate and the females lay some 500 eggs in the trees. When the nymphs—or baby bugs—hatch, they drop to the ground, where they burrow and grow for the next 17 years. In 2038, Brood X will be back again!

BLACK BEAR WILDFIRE RESCUE

Excellent swimmers, black bears can paddle more than a mile (1.6 km) in freshwater.

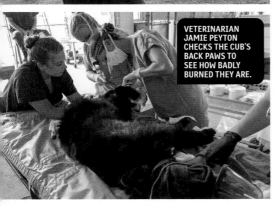

WILDLIFE PROGRAM MANAGER JEFF STODDARD CARRIES THE TRANQUILIZED BEAR SO SHE DOESN'T HAVE TO WALK ON HER BURNED PAWS.

VETERINARIAN JAMIE PEYTON CHECKS THE CUB'S BACK PAWS TO SEE HOW BADLY BURNED THEY ARE.

A one-and-a-half-year-old bear sits next to a mountainside creek beneath a red sky clouded by smoke. Unable to walk, she tries to soothe her burned paws by licking them. The bear is just one of thousands of animals left injured or displaced after the Carr Fire burned through some 230,000 acres (93,078 ha) throughout Northern California, U.S.A.

Wearing smoke masks and protective clothing, an electrical crew enters the forest to repair utility poles and restore power to the area. At first, they see only charred trees. Then they spot the bear. Realizing she's injured, the crew calls the California Department of Fish and Wildlife office in Rancho Cordova, nearly 200 miles (322 km) away. Program manager Jeff Stoddard decides the bear can't be left alone. He gathers a team and arrives at the scene in just a few hours.

"When we arrived, her paws were so burned, they were crispy," wildlife officer Peter Blake says. The scared bear is also dehydrated. Senior environmental scientist Eric Haney tranquilizes the animal with a dart so the team can safely transport her to a wildlife lab for treatment.

GETTING FISHY

Veterinarians Deana Clifford and Jamie Peyton are shocked by how badly burned the bear's paws are. They give the bear a new type of treatment to heal its wounds: fish skin. By wrapping the bear's paws in bandages made from tilapia (a type of fish) skin, they can protect the paws from getting infected; plus, the collagen—a kind of protein—found in the tilapia might help the wounds heal faster.

The bear doesn't struggle when they wrap her paws, and she seems to be in less pain with the bandages on. As the days pass, the bandages remain on, but the animal doesn't want to interact with people or take her medicine. This is a good sign—it means she's not becoming too tame to return to the wild, and she's getting stronger.

After six weeks, doctors remove the bandages. The treatment worked even better than they had hoped. The bear's paws have completely healed, and it's time for her to go home.

Black bears also come in shades of blue and cinnamon, depending on their habitat.

BACK TO THE WOODS

Finding the right spot to release the bear cub is tricky. "We didn't want to put her back in the same burn area," Haney says. "But we wanted to keep her relatively close to where we found her." With help from a team from the Bureau of Land Management, rescuers find an area that has plenty of prey and water and is surrounded by cleared brush to hopefully help prevent new fires from spreading.

Haney stands on top of the large metal cage containing the bear cub and slowly pulls the door open. The bear cautiously peeks out before she sprints toward the woods. "This fire was caused by people," Stoddard says. "So it's our responsibility to help the animals we hurt."

QUIZ WHIZ

Quiz yourself to find out if you're a natural when it comes to nature knowledge!

Write your answers on a piece of paper. Then check them below.

1 **True or false?** Black bears can paddle more than a mile (1.6 km) in freshwater.

2 **Which of the following animals does NOT swim in the Amazon River?**
a. piranha
b. river dolphin
c. hippopotamus
d. electric eel

3 Superstrong sandstorms called haboobs create walls of dust that can be _____ high.
a. 3.3 feet (1 m)　　　c. 330 feet (100 m)
b. 33 feet (10 m)　　　d. 3,300 feet (1 km)

4 **True or false?** The Southern Ocean—home to cool creatures like the emperor penguin—makes up 60 percent of all oceans.

5 Deserts cover how much of Earth's surface?
a. one-fifth　　　c. one-third
b. one-fourth　　　d. one-half

Not **STUMPED** yet? Check out the
NATIONAL GEOGRAPHIC KIDS QUIZ WHIZ collection
for more crazy **NATURE** questions!

ANSWERS: 1. True; 2. c; 3. d; 4. False: It's 6 percent; 5. a

Oral Reports Made Easy

Does the thought of public speaking start your stomach churning like a tornado? Would you rather get caught in an avalanche than give a speech?

Giving an oral report does not have to be a natural disaster. The basic format is very similar to that of a written essay. There are two main elements that make up a good oral report—the writing and the presentation. As you write your oral report, remember that your audience will be hearing the information as opposed to reading it. Follow the guidelines below, and there will be clear skies ahead.

Writing Your Material

Follow the steps in the "How to Write a Perfect Essay" section on page 129, but prepare your report to be spoken rather than written.

Try to keep your sentences short and simple. Long, complex sentences are harder to follow. Limit yourself to just a few key points. You don't want to overwhelm your audience with too much information. To be most effective, hit your key points in the introduction, elaborate on them in the body, and then repeat them once again in your conclusion.

AN ORAL REPORT HAS THREE BASIC PARTS:

- **Introduction**—This is your chance to engage your audience and really capture their interest in the subject you are presenting. Use a funny personal experience or a dramatic story, or start with an intriguing question.

- **Body**—This is the longest part of your report. Here you elaborate on the facts and ideas you want to convey. Give information that supports your main idea, and expand on it with specific examples or details. In other words, structure your oral report in the same way you would a written essay, so that your thoughts are presented in a clear and organized manner.

- **Conclusion**—This is the time to summarize the information and emphasize your most important points to the audience one last time.

Preparing Your Delivery

1 Practice makes perfect. Practice! Practice! Practice! Confidence, enthusiasm, and energy are key to delivering an effective oral report, and they can best be achieved through rehearsal. Ask family and friends to be your practice audience and give you feedback when you're done. Were they able to follow your ideas? Did you seem knowledgeable and confident? Did you speak too slowly or too fast, too softly or too loudly? The more times you practice giving your report, the more you'll master the material. Then you won't have to rely so heavily on your notes or papers, and you will be able to give your report in a relaxed and confident manner.

2 Present with everything you've got. Be as creative as you can. Incorporate videos, sound clips, slide presentations, charts, diagrams, and photos. Visual aids help stimulate your audience's senses and keep them intrigued and engaged. They can also help to reinforce your key points. And remember that when you're giving an oral report, you're a performer. Take charge of the spotlight and be as animated and entertaining as you can. Have fun with it.

3 Keep your nerves under control. Everyone gets a little nervous when speaking in front of a group. That's normal. But the more preparation you've done— meaning plenty of researching, organizing, and rehearsing—the more confident you'll be. Preparation is the key. And if you make a mistake or stumble over your words, just regroup and keep going. Nobody's perfect, and nobody expects you to be.

HISTORY HAPPENS

New meets old at the Basilica of Our Lady of Guadalupe in Mexico City, Mexico. The Old Basilica was built in 1709 and the New Basilica was built in 1976.

10 AWESOME ARCHAEOLOGICAL DISCOVERIES

The remains of the ancient city of Pompeii, Italy, were not excavated until roughly 1,800 years after the **VOLCANIC ERUPTION** that destroyed it.

A team of researchers in **TIBET** found **FIVE HANDPRINTS** and **FIVE FOOTPRINTS** preserved in limestone, thought to be **169,000 to 226,000 years old.**

Found underwater in Lake Huron, U.S.A., **human-built stone structures spanning THE SIZE OF A FOOTBALL FIELD** have revealed clues to how early humans worked together to find meat.

Some 450 decorated, sealed coffins containing **MUMMIES** dating back as far as 2,500 years have been discovered near Cairo, Egypt.

Ruins thought to come from Cleopatra's palace— as well as coins and sphinxes— **WERE FOUND UNDER THE MEDITERRANEAN SEA** off Alexandria, Egypt, in the 1990s.

Buildings from the only known **VIKING SETTLEMENT** in **North America were unearthed at L'Anse aux Meadows, Canada.**

SILVER AND GOLD TUBES unearthed in an ancient tomb in Russia are thought to be **the earliest known drinking straws, used by** people **5,000 YEARS AGO.**

SOME SCIENTISTS THINK **teeth and bones** ROUGHLY **9,500 years old** were found among the ruins of an ancient city underwater in the GULF OF KHAMBHAT, INDIA.

THE DISCOVERY OF A GRAVE SITE IN SPAIN revealed the **3,700-year-old** remains of a woman wearing a crown, bracelets, and necklaces.

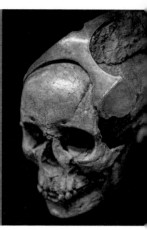

In 2010, construction workers found a **200-year-old ship** underneath the former site of the World Trade Center in New York City.

SECRETS OF STONEHENGE

Could a new discovery help solve this ancient puzzle?

Ancient stones form a circle on a grassy plain. Some of the rocks stand 20 feet (6 m) tall, while others lie on the ground. Thousands of years ago, people erected this monument to align perfectly with the sun: On the longest day of the year, the sun rose between the tallest arch; on the shortest, it set on the opposite side. Why did people build this monument, called Stonehenge? It's still one of the world's biggest mysteries.

MYTHS AND LEGENDS

For hundreds of years, people have wondered who built this massive stone structure on England's Salisbury Plain. Some have suggested the Romans, the Vikings, an ancient group of people called the Celts, and even aliens. (It's definitely not the last one!) Now experts are taking a closer look at a magical myth about Stonehenge to discover the truth.

A tale from the 12th century says that giants placed the monument on a hill to the west of where Stonehenge is today, in what's now Wales. Then a wizard named Merlin magically moved the stone circle to England.

While experts know that a spell didn't move the stones, they wondered if maybe Stonehenge had indeed been moved from somewhere else and reconstructed on this spot. Taking a hint from the myth, archaeologists started looking for the remains of stone circles west of the monument.

STONEHENGE: THE PREQUEL

The first part of Stonehenge—a raised circle of dirt surrounding 56 wooden posts—was created around 3000 B.C. (This makes it much older than the theories about the Romans, Vikings, or Celts.)

About 500 years after first digging the circular mound, people replaced the wooden poles with a circle of bluestones, named for their slightly blue tint when broken or wet.

But after studying these 6,000-pound (2,722-kg) stones, scientists discovered that they came from a quarry about 140 miles (225 km) west of Stonehenge, in what's now Wales— nowhere near the current site in England. And according to new research, these rocks were once part of an older stone circle in Wales that had the same diameter and alignment with the sun.

This means that another ancient monument similar to Stonehenge had been built perhaps 500 years before. Then those ancient people pulled, dragged, or maybe even floated the stones to the spot where they rest today.

Why would ancient people—who hadn't yet invented the wheel—drag these rocks all that way? Experts think that the bluestones must have represented something very important— like their ancestors.

Thirty upright sandstone rocks called sarsen stones made up the outer ring of Stonehenge.

Up to 80 bluestone rocks were the first large stones to be placed at Stonehenge, around 2600 B.C.

ATLANTIC OCEAN

North Sea

SCOTLAND

UNITED KINGDOM

NORTHERN IRELAND

IRELAND

WALES

ENGLAND

Stonehenge

NORTH AMERICA

ATLANTIC OCEAN

EUROPE

AFRICA

CALENDAR, TEMPLE, OR PARTY SPOT?

A few hundred years after placing the bluestones in the current location, ancient people added heavier sandstone blocks called sarsen stones, which were quarried nearby. These 50,000-pound (22,680-kg) stones make up the widest part of the circle, plus the inner horseshoe shape.

But experts still don't know for sure *why* ancient people built the monument. Could it have been a giant calendar, helping to mark the summer and winter solstices as the sun rose and set? Or perhaps a place to worship the dead, since archaeologists have found cremated remains nearby? They've also found pig remains from livestock that came from all over Britain, so maybe Stonehenge was actually a gathering place for huge celebrations.

For now, the story isn't written in stone.

RAISING THE ROCKS

Here's what Stonehenge looked like about 4,200 years ago.

On the solstices, the sunlight came through the opening in the largest arch, called the Great Trilithon.

Experts think these bluestones in a horseshoe formation were moved around a few times.

MOAI MYSTERY

A tiny island in the middle of the South Pacific Ocean is home to nearly 900 mysterious stone figures. Scattered across the coast of Easter Island (Rapa Nui), the giant statues have fascinated visitors for centuries. Who built them—and how? Read on to find out more.

NUMBER OF STATUES ON EASTER ISLAND:

887

TIME TO CARVE EACH STATUE:

2 YEARS

AVERAGE HEIGHT:

13 FEET (4 m)

AVERAGE WEIGHT:

14 TONS (12.7 t)

DATE CARVED:

A.D. 1100–1680

Q: HOW DID THE ANCIENT RAPA NUI PEOPLE MOVE THESE GIANT STATUES AROUND THE ISLAND, UP TO 11 MILES (18 KM) AT A TIME?

A: ROPES! RESEARCHERS WERE ABLE TO MOVE A FIVE-TON (4,536-KG) MOAI REPLICA MORE THAN 200 YARDS (183 M) BY ROCKING IT BACK AND FORTH.

Brainy Questions

HEY, SMARTY-PANTS!

GOT BIG, WEIRD QUESTIONS?

WE'VE GOT ANSWERS!

Why are ancient statues and buildings always white?

The paint has come off! Ancient Greeks and Romans painted their statues and temples in many different colors, but over the past few thousand years, the paint has worn away. Ancient artists mixed colorful minerals—like crushed-up malachite for green or azurite for blue—with beeswax or egg yolks to create paint. Today, archaeologists are using ultraviolet and infrared lamps, along with chemical analysis, to discover the traces of colors and patterns left behind on the statues. We know ancient people would approve: A line in one Greek play implies that wiping color off a statue would make it uglier.

What's inside the Great Pyramid of Giza?

Not much, anymore! The Great Pyramid was built about 4,570 years ago as the final resting place of Khufu, an Egyptian pharaoh. It also stored all the stuff he'd need in the afterlife, like bread, fruit, furniture, clothes, and jewelry. The 481-foot (147-m)-tall stone structure was Khufu's way of telling people that he was super important. But it also screamed, "Hey, stuff to steal inside!" Today, you can walk through a passageway deep into the center of the pyramid until you reach the King's Chamber, which has a granite sarcophagus—but nothing else.

PHARAOHS RULE!

Meet four mighty royals from ancient Egypt.

Pharaohs, who ruled ancient Egypt from ca 3100 to 30 B.C., weren't just old-timey government officials. Ancient Egyptians believed that pharaohs were gods on Earth who controlled nature, owned all the land, and had a direct connection to all the other deities. Fabulously wealthy, these rulers instructed their people to build the pyramids, temples, and tombs that we can still visit today. Read on to meet a few of these famous pharaohs.

Historians don't always know the exact dates of events from ancient times. That's why you'll see "ca" next to some of the years listed. It stands for "circa," meaning "around."

HATSHEPSUT

Reign: ca 1479-1458 B.C.

Claim to Fame The daughter of a pharaoh, Hatshepsut (pronounced hat-SHEP-sut) became queen when she married another pharaoh. After her husband died, she was allowed to rule Egypt temporarily until her toddler-age stepson became old enough to rule. But as the boy grew older, Hatshepsut held on to power and eventually declared *herself* pharaoh. Since almost all Egyptian rulers were male, she began calling herself king and often instructed her royal sculptors and artists to depict her with a traditional pharaoh's beard and a man's body. And she was good at her job: In 21 years on the throne, Hatshepsut organized a trading expedition to faraway lands, constructed a temple called Djeser Djeseru (dedicated to herself, of course!) that still stands today, and kept Egypt peaceful and wealthy.

PYRAMID POWER

Most people think of ancient Egyptian pharaohs and their treasures being entombed forever in pyramids. But the earliest rulers were simply buried in the ground. Check out how the pyramid shape developed over time.

ca 3100 B.C.

Rulers are buried underneath **mastabas,** which are flat, rectangular structures made of mud bricks. (*Mastaba* means "bench" in the Arabic language.)

ca 2780 B.C.

Pharaoh Djoser commissions a **step pyramid** for his tomb— basically six mastabas stacked on top of each other.

HISTORY HAPPENS

RAMSES II
Reign: 1279–1213 B.C.

Claim to Fame If you believe the murals that Ramses II had created, you'd think he single-handedly defeated an invading army accompanied by a pet lion named Slayer of His Foes. In reality, the battles lasted 16 years, and Ramses eventually signed a peace treaty to end the war. But this ruler understood the importance of telling a good story—about how great *he* was. Ramses II built more monuments to himself than any other pharaoh. One temple at the southern edge of the Egyptian Empire, named Abu Simbel, includes four 66-foot (20-m)-tall statues of Ramses, plus much smaller statues of his family. But he didn't need to exaggerate much: Ramses II reigned for an incredible 66 years, had more than a hundred children, and was considered "Ramses the Great" by the Egyptians who came after him.

TAHARQA
Reign: 690–664 B.C.

Claim to Fame Taharqa (TUH-har-kuh) belonged to a dynasty (or family) of rulers from the kingdom of Kush, which today is in Sudan, a country in Africa just south of Egypt. Kush was a separate state from Egypt, but its rulers believed in the same gods and had similar traditions. At the time, many rulers throughout Egypt were fighting to claim the throne. That's when Taharqa's father, the Kush king, marched north with his army to defeat the warring kings and lead Egypt himself. For nearly a hundred years, this dynasty ruled over the ancient Egyptians and the people of Kush, and Taharqa was the most powerful and wealthy of them all. He started a massive project to repair crumbling temples and build new ones; he even began building pyramids again for the first time in about 800 years.

CLEOPATRA VII
Reign: 51–30 B.C.

Claim to Fame Cleopatra was like the smartest kid in your class: She loved to learn, and experts think she spoke multiple languages. In fact, she was the only pharaoh in her family line who could speak the Egyptian language. (Her ancestors were from Macedonia—now part of Greece—and had conquered ancient Egypt more than 200 years earlier.) While Cleopatra was alive, the Roman Empire was gaining power. At the start of her reign, she convinced Roman general Julius Caesar to support her instead of her younger brother. But later, she lost a war with another Roman ruler. Egypt became part of the Roman Empire, and it never had another pharaoh.

We don't know for sure what the pharaohs really looked like, so these portraits are just for fun!

ca 2600 B.C.

Pharaoh Snefru needs three attempts to build a smooth-sided pyramid. The second—now called the **Bent Pyramid**—had to be changed halfway through!

ca 2550 B.C.

Snefru's son Khufu constructs the **Great Pyramid,** Egypt's largest tomb structure. Khufu's son and grandson build the two other Giza pyramids nearby.

ca 690 B.C.

About 800 years after the last pharaoh was buried in a pyramid, pharaohs from Kush begin building smaller and steeper **sandstone pyramids** in what's now Sudan.

245

TO HONOR A QUEEN

The Taj Mahal might be the world's grandest tomb.

The Taj Mahal in India might look like a fancy home for important kings and queens. After all, it was likely the inspiration for the palace in *Aladdin*. But no one ever lived here: It's actually a tomb. Who's buried inside? Read on to find out!

PORTRAITS OF MUMTAZ MAHAL (LEFT) AND SHAH JAHAN

MEET THE MAKER

For more than 200 years, the Mughal Empire ruled over parts of what is today India, Pakistan, Afghanistan, and Nepal. To become emperor, a royal male had to prove himself to be the best choice before being named as heir—but the family could still change its mind.

That's what happened to Shah Jahan, a third-born son who had been named heir but later fell from favor. After his father died, he returned home in 1628 to reclaim the throne. And just in case, he put his rivals—including his brother and a few nephews—to death.

The new emperor loved architecture and art, and he adored his second wife, Mumtaz Mahal. (Shah Jahan had three wives; emperors at this time usually had many spouses to gain power through their families.) Mumtaz Mahal traveled with him everywhere, even on military campaigns. "They had a true partnership and a true love," Mughal art historian Mehreen Chida-Razvi says. The couple was married for nearly 20 years before Mumtaz Mahal died in 1631.

Legend says that after his wife's death, Shah Jahan's black hair turned white from grief. He decided her tomb would be a grand monument to his lost love. "Nothing had ever been built like this to honor a queen before," Chida-Razvi says.

BEST BUILDING

About 20,000 craftsmen baked bricks made of mud to form the building's structure. They then

Mumtaz Mahal means "chosen one of the palace."

In the Persian language, Shah Jahan means "king of the world."

Shah Jahan sat on a throne called the Peacock Throne, which was studded with gems from his treasury.

ASIA

INDIAN OCEAN

PAKISTAN

New Dehli

CHINA

BHUTAN

NEPAL

Agra

INDIA

MYANMAR (BURMA)

BANGLADESH

Arabian Sea

Bay of Bengal

WORKERS CLEAN THE TAJ MAHAL WITH CLAY, AND THEN WASH IT OFF WITH DISTILLED WATER.

Solving a Mystery

Every few years, the Taj Mahal gets a mud bath to remove mysterious yellow-brown stains from the white marble. Environmental scientist Mike Bergin thought that if he could find the cause of the stains, people could better protect the tomb.

In 2012, he placed marble tiles on the monument for two months, then used a special high-powered microscope to look at the stained tiles. He found tiny particles of pollution from cars and the burning of wood, trash, and dung. The pollution absorbed light instead of reflecting it, which created the stains. As a result, the Indian government restricted burning trash and driving cars near the monument to help decrease the staining pollution.

"Once you know the problem," Bergin says, "you can make policies to fix it."

covered them in white marble for the tomb or red sandstone for nearby buildings. Artisans covered the tomb with designs made from more than 40 types of semiprecious gems. And calligraphers hand-carved poems and scripture all over walls and columns.

What looks like Mumtaz Mahal's sarcophagus was placed in the central room. But it's actually a cenotaph, a false tomb that allows visitors to pay their respects without disturbing her actual remains. Those were laid in a crypt directly underneath.

Nearly 20 years later, the massive, 42-acre (17-ha) complex was complete.

INLAID PIECES OF JADE AND CORAL CREATE ART THROUGHOUT THE TAJ MAHAL.

TOMB TRUTH

Shah Jahan likely would have built his own tomb nearby, Chida-Razvi says. But in 1657, he fell gravely ill. Seizing the chance to become ruler—just like Shah Jahan had done 30 years before—one of his sons imprisoned him in a fort. His only comfort: that he could see the Taj Mahal from a window.

The ex-emperor died eight years later, but his son didn't honor him with a majestic tomb. Instead, his body was brought to the Taj Mahal at night. His sarcophagus was plopped beside his wife's, even though the tomb was to honor Mumtaz Mahal—and no one else.

More than 350 years later, people still marvel at the Taj Mahal. Shah Jahan would probably be happy that people continue to honor his beloved wife.

PiRATES!

MEET THREE OF HISTORY'S MOST FEARSOME HIGH-SEAS BADDIES.

Yo-ho, yo-ho—*uh-oh!* A mysterious ship on the horizon flying a skull-and-crossbones flag wasn't a welcome sight to sailors in the 18th and 19th centuries. That flag meant one thing: pirates. Faced with faster, cannon-crammed vessels typically crewed by pirates, a ship captain was left with two choices: lower the sails and surrender—or turn and fight.

Life wasn't one big swashbuckling adventure for the pirates, however. Lousy food, cramped quarters, stinky crewmates, and hurricanes were all part of the job. Still, a handful of pirates managed to enjoy success at sea ... and inspire fear in those who were unfortunate enough to meet them face-to-face. Check out some of history's most famous pirates.

RACHEL WALL

REIGN OF TERROR **New England coast, U.S.A., late 1700s**

Rachel Wall and her husband, George, worked together as pirates, targeting small islands off the coast of present-day Maine in the Atlantic Ocean. After storms, they'd stop their sailboat and raise a distress flag. When passersby responded to Rachel's screams for help, they were robbed—or worse—for their trouble. After just two summers of piracy, Rachel and George had killed at least 24 men and raked in about $6,000, plus an unknown amount of valuable goods. They later sold their loot, pretending they'd found it washed up on a beach.

CRIME DOESN'T PAY Eventually, the law caught up with Rachel Wall. In 1789, she made history when she was the last woman to be hanged in the state of Massachusetts.

CHENG I SAO

REIGN OF TERROR South China Sea, 1801–1810

Cheng I Sao ruled a pirate fleet of nearly 2,000 ships. Sometimes called Madame Cheng, she turned to crime after she married a famous pirate. More than 80,000 buccaneers—men, women, and even children—reported to Madame Cheng. They seized loot in all sorts of ways: selling "protection" from pirate attacks, raiding ships, and kidnapping for ransom. Madame Cheng was best known for paying her pirates cash for each head they brought back from their assaults. (Yikes!)

CRIME DOESN'T PAY—USUALLY Every government attempt to stop Madame Cheng was a failure. Rumor has it that after she retired from piracy, she started a second career as a smuggler. She died peacefully at age 69.

BLACKBEARD

REIGN OF TERROR North America's East Coast and the Caribbean, 1713–1718

Nobody knows Blackbeard's real name—historians think it might've been Edward Teach—but he's arguably history's most famous pirate. He began his career as a privateer, or a kind of legal pirate, who was hired by the British government to attack enemy fleets and steal their goods.

Blackbeard abandoned privateering in 1713 and went full-pirate when he sailed to the Caribbean on a French ship that was gifted to him by another pirate, adding cannons to the vessel and renaming it *Queen Anne's Revenge*. He terrified his enemies by strapping pistols and knives across his chest and sticking smoking cannon fuses in his beard. According to legend, Blackbeard hid a treasure somewhere ... but it's never been found.

CRIME DOESN'T PAY A few years into Blackbeard's time as a pirate, he was nabbed by the British Navy. He was executed, and his head stuck on the front of a ship as a way to warn wannabe pirates to stay away from seafaring crime.

GOING TO WAR

Since the beginning of time, different countries, territories, and cultures have feuded with each other over land, power, and politics. Major military conflicts include the following wars:

1095-1291 THE CRUSADES
Starting late in the 11th century, these wars over religion were fought in the Middle East for nearly 200 years.

1337-1453 HUNDRED YEARS' WAR
France and England battled over rights to land for more than a century before the French eventually drove the English out in 1453.

1754-1763 FRENCH AND INDIAN WAR (part of Europe's Seven Years' War)
A nine-year war between the British and French for control of North America.

1775-1783 AMERICAN REVOLUTION
Thirteen British colonies in America united to reject the rule of the British government and to form the United States of America.

1861-1865 AMERICAN CIVIL WAR
This war occurred when the northern states (the Union) went to war with the southern states, which had seceded, or withdrawn, to form the Confederate States of America. Slavery was one of the key issues in the Civil War.

1910-1920 MEXICAN REVOLUTION
The people of Mexico revolted against the rule of dictator President Porfirio Díaz, leading to his eventual defeat and to a democratic government.

1914-1918 WORLD WAR I
The assassination of Austria's Archduke Ferdinand by a Serbian nationalist sparked this wide-spreading war. The U.S. entered after Germany sank the British ship Lusitania, killing more than 120 Americans.

1918-1920 RUSSIAN CIVIL WAR
Following the 1917 Russian Revolution, this conflict pitted the Communist Red Army against the foreign-backed White Army. The Red Army won, leading to the establishment of the Union of Soviet Socialist Republics (U.S.S.R.) in 1922.

1936-1939 SPANISH CIVIL WAR
Aid from Italy and Germany helped Spain's Nationalists gain victory over the Communist-supported Republicans. The war resulted in the loss of more than 300,000 lives and increased tension in Europe leading up to World War II.

1939-1945 WORLD WAR II
This massive conflict in Europe, Asia, and North Africa involved many countries that aligned with the two sides: the Allies and the Axis. After the bombing of Pearl Harbor in Hawaii in 1941, the U.S. entered the war on the side of the Allies. More than 50 million people died during the war.

1946–1949 CHINESE CIVIL WAR

Also known as the "War of Liberation," this war pitted the Communist and Nationalist Parties in China against each other. The Communists won.

1950–1953 KOREAN WAR

Kicked off when the Communist forces of North Korea, with backing from the Soviet Union, invaded their democratic neighbor to the south. A coalition of 16 countries from the United Nations stepped in to support South Korea. An armistice, or temporary truce, ended active fighting in 1953.

1950s–1975 VIETNAM WAR

This war was fought between the Communist North, supported by allies including China, and the government of South Vietnam, supported by the United States and other anticommunist nations.

1967 SIX-DAY WAR

This was a battle for land between Israel and the states of Egypt, Jordan, and Syria. The outcome resulted in Israel's gaining control of coveted territory, including the Gaza Strip and the West Bank.

1991–PRESENT SOMALI CIVIL WAR

The war began when Somalia's last president, a dictator named Mohamed Siad Barre, was overthrown. This has led to years of fighting and anarchy.

2001–2014 WAR IN AFGHANISTAN

After attacks in the U.S. by the terrorist group al Qaeda, a coalition that eventually included more than 40 countries invaded Afghanistan to find Osama bin Laden and other al Qaeda members and to dismantle the Taliban. Bin Laden was killed in a U.S. covert operation in 2011. The North Atlantic Treaty Organization (NATO) took control of the coalition's combat mission in 2003. That combat mission officially ended in 2014. The United States completed its withdrawal of troops in 2021.

2003–2011 WAR IN IRAQ

A coalition led by the U.S., and including Britain, Australia, and Spain, invaded Iraq over suspicions that Iraq had weapons of mass destruction.

2022–PRESENT RUSSIA-UKRAINE WAR

Military forces led by Russian president Vladimir Putin crossed the border into Ukraine, seeking to take control of the country. Russia launched attacks on major cities across the country, including the capital city of Kyiv.

WARTIME INVENTIONS

It's said that necessity is the mother of invention. And in wartime, necessity—or at least the need for making life easier—is especially key. So it's not too surprising that some of the more useful things in our world today were created during times of conflict—in particular, during World War I, when industrialization led to innovations across the board.

Take, for example, Kleenex tissues. What we use today to blow our noses was born out of what was first meant to be a thin, cottony liner used in a gas mask. In 1924, the company Kimberly-Clark started selling the same tissue liners as a disposable makeup remover for women. But when an employee with hay fever started blowing his nose in the wipes, Kimberly-Clark saw an opportunity—and sold the Kleenex as an alternative to cloth handkerchiefs.

Then there are zippers: Originally known as "hookless fasteners," they first widely appeared on the flying suits of aviators during World War I. Before then, buttons were the fashionable way to fasten shirts, pants, and boots, but the new invention was much more, well, zippy. In 1923, the B.F. Goodrich Company coined the term zipper, and the name stuck.

And whenever you check the time on your wristwatch, you can thank World War I soldiers for making this type of timepiece trendy. At the time of the war, wristwatches were popular with women, while men mostly kept the time on pocket watches, which they'd have tucked away on a chain. But during the war, male soldiers switched to wristwatches for easier access to the time (and to keep both hands free in the trenches). After the war, the wristwatch became a common look for all genders—and remains so today.

THE CONSTITUTION & THE BILL OF RIGHTS

The United States Constitution was written in 1787 by a group of political leaders from the 13 states that made up the United States at the time. Thirty-nine men, including Benjamin Franklin and James Madison, signed the document to create a national government. While some feared the creation of a strong federal government, all 13 states eventually ratified, or approved, the Constitution, making it the law of the land. The Constitution has three major parts: the preamble, the articles, and the amendments.

Here's a summary of what topics are covered in each part of the Constitution.
The Constitution can be found online or at your local library for the full text.

THE PREAMBLE outlines the basic purposes of the government: *We the People of the United States, in order to form a more perfect Union, establish justice, insure domestic tranquility, provide for the common defense, promote the general welfare, and secure the blessings of liberty to ourselves and our posterity, do ordain and establish this Constitution for the United States of America.*

SEVEN ARTICLES outline the powers of Congress, the president, and the court system:

Article I outlines the legislative branch—the Senate and the House of Representatives—and its powers and responsibilities.

Article II outlines the executive branch—the presidency—and its powers and responsibilities.

Article III outlines the judicial branch—the court system—and its powers and responsibilities.

Article IV describes the individual states' rights and powers.

Article V outlines the amendment process.

Article VI establishes the Constitution as the law of the land.

Article VII gives the requirements for the Constitution to be approved.

THE AMENDMENTS, or additions to the Constitution, were put in later as needed. In 1791, the first 10 amendments, known as the Bill of Rights, were added. Since then, another 17 amendments have been added. This is the Bill of Rights:

1st Amendment: guarantees freedom of religion, speech, and the press, and the right to assemble and petition. The U.S. may not have a national religion.

2nd Amendment: discusses the militia and the right of people to bear arms

3rd Amendment: prohibits the military or troops from using private homes without consent

4th Amendment: protects people and their homes from search, arrest, or seizure without probable cause or a warrant

5th Amendment: grants people the right to have a trial and prevents punishment before prosecution; protects private property from being taken without compensation

6th Amendment: guarantees the right to a speedy and public trial

7th Amendment: guarantees a trial by jury in certain cases

8th Amendment: forbids "cruel and unusual punishments"

9th Amendment: states that the Constitution is not all-encompassing and does not deny people other, unspecified rights

10th Amendment: grants the powers not covered by the Constitution to the states and the people

Ask an adult to help you read the full text version online at the National Constitution Center.

White House

BRANCHES OF GOVERNMENT

The **UNITED STATES GOVERNMENT** is divided into three branches: executive, legislative, and judicial. The system of checks and balances is a way to control power and to make sure one branch can't take the reins of government. For example, most of the president's actions require the approval of Congress. Likewise, the laws passed in Congress must be signed by the president before they can take effect.

Executive Branch

The Constitution lists the central powers of the president: to serve as commander in chief of the armed forces; make treaties with other nations; grant pardons; inform Congress on the state of the union; and appoint ambassadors, officials, and judges. The executive branch includes the president and the 15 governmental departments.

Legislative Branch

This branch is made up of Congress—the Senate and the House of Representatives. The Constitution grants Congress the power to make laws. Congress is made up of elected representatives from each state. Each state has two representatives in the Senate, while the number of representatives in the House is determined by the size of the state's population. Washington, D.C., and the territories elect nonvoting representatives to the House of Representatives. The Founding Fathers set up this system as a compromise between big states—which wanted representation based on population—and small states—which wanted all states to have equal representation rights.

The U.S. Capitol in Washington, D.C.

Judicial Branch

The judicial branch is composed of the federal court system—the U.S. Supreme Court, the courts of appeals, and the district courts. The Supreme Court is the most powerful court. Its motto is "Equal Justice Under Law." This influential court is responsible for interpreting the Constitution and applying it to the cases that it hears. The decisions of the Supreme Court are absolute—they are the final word on any legal question.

The U.S. Supreme Court Building in Washington, D.C.

There are nine justices on the Supreme Court. They are appointed by the president of the United States and confirmed by the Senate.

The Native American Experience

Native Americans are Indigenous

to North and South America—they are the people who were here before Columbus and other European explorers came to these lands. They live in nations, tribes, and bands across both continents. For decades following the arrival of Europeans in 1492, Native Americans clashed with the newcomers who had ruptured the Indigenous people's ways of living.

Tribal Land

During the 19th century, both United States legislation and military action restricted the movement of Native Americans, forcing them to live on reservations and attempting to dismantle tribal structures. For centuries, Native Americans were displaced or killed. In 1924, the Indian Citizenship Act granted citizenship to all Native Americans. Unfortunately, this was not enough to end the social discrimination and mistreatment that many Indigenous people have faced. Today, Native Americans living in the United States still face many challenges.

Healing the Past

Many members of the 570-plus recognized tribes in the United States live primarily on reservations. Some tribes have more than one reservation, while others have none. Together these reservations make up less than 3 percent of the nation's land area. The tribal governments on reservations have the right to form their own governments and to enforce laws, similar to individual states. Many feel that this sovereignty is still not enough to right the wrongs of the past: They hope for a change in the U.S. government's relationship with Native Americans.

An annual powwow in New Mexico features more than 3,000 dancers from more than 500 North American tribes.

Navajo is the most commonly spoken Native American language in the United States.

Top: A Navajo teenager holds her pet lamb.

Middle: A Monacan girl dances in a traditional jingle dress.

Bottom: Navajo siblings ride their horses.

The president of the United States is the chief of the executive branch, the commander in chief of the U.S. armed forces, and head of the federal government. Elected every four years, the president is the highest policy-maker in the nation. The 22nd Amendment (1951) says that no person may be elected to the office of president more than twice. There have been 46 presidencies and 45 presidents.

JAMES MONROE
5th President of the United States ★ *1817–1825*
BORN April 28, 1758, in Westmoreland County, VA
POLITICAL PARTY Democratic-Republican
NO. OF TERMS two
VICE PRESIDENT Daniel D. Tompkins
DIED July 4, 1831, in New York, NY

GEORGE WASHINGTON
1st President of the United States ★ *1789–1797*
BORN Feb. 22, 1732, in Pope's Creek, Westmoreland County, VA
POLITICAL PARTY Federalist
NO. OF TERMS two
VICE PRESIDENT John Adams
DIED Dec. 14, 1799, at Mount Vernon, VA

JOHN QUINCY ADAMS
6th President of the United States ★ *1825–1829*
BORN July 11, 1767, in Braintree (now Quincy), MA
POLITICAL PARTY Democratic-Republican
NO. OF TERMS one
VICE PRESIDENT John Caldwell Calhoun
DIED Feb. 23, 1848, at the U.S. Capitol, Washington, D.C.

JOHN ADAMS
2nd President of the United States ★ *1797–1801*
BORN Oct. 30, 1735, in Braintree (now Quincy), MA
POLITICAL PARTY Federalist
NO. OF TERMS one
VICE PRESIDENT Thomas Jefferson
DIED July 4, 1826, in Quincy, MA

ANDREW JACKSON
7th President of the United States ★ *1829–1837*
BORN March 15, 1767, in the Waxhaw region, NC and SC
POLITICAL PARTY Democrat
NO. OF TERMS two
VICE PRESIDENTS 1st term: John Caldwell Calhoun
2nd term: Martin Van Buren
DIED June 8, 1845, in Nashville, TN

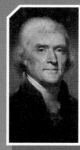

THOMAS JEFFERSON
3rd President of the United States ★ *1801–1809*
BORN April 13, 1743, at Shadwell, Goochland (now Albemarle) County, VA
POLITICAL PARTY Democratic-Republican
NO. OF TERMS two
VICE PRESIDENTS 1st term: Aaron Burr
2nd term: George Clinton
DIED July 4, 1826, at Monticello, Charlottesville, VA

MARTIN VAN BUREN
8th President of the United States ★ *1837–1841*
BORN Dec. 5, 1782, in Kinderhook, NY
POLITICAL PARTY Democrat
NO. OF TERMS one
VICE PRESIDENT Richard M. Johnson
DIED July 24, 1862, in Kinderhook, NY

JAMES MADISON
4th President of the United States ★ *1809–1817*
BORN March 16, 1751, at Belle Grove, Port Conway, VA
POLITICAL PARTY Democratic-Republican
NO. OF TERMS two
VICE PRESIDENTS 1st term: George Clinton
2nd term: Elbridge Gerry
DIED June 28, 1836, at Montpelier, Orange County, VA

JAMES MADISON appears on the very rare—but still in circulation—$5,000 BILL.

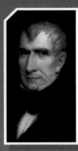

WILLIAM HENRY HARRISON

9th President of the United States ★ 1841

BORN Feb. 9, 1773, in Charles City County, VA
POLITICAL PARTY Whig
NO. OF TERMS one (died while in office)
VICE PRESIDENT John Tyler
DIED April 4, 1841, in the White House, Washington, D.C.

JOHN TYLER

10th President of the United States ★ 1841–1845

BORN March 29, 1790, in Charles City County, VA
POLITICAL PARTY Whig
NO. OF TERMS one (partial)
VICE PRESIDENT none
DIED Jan. 18, 1862, in Richmond, VA

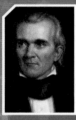

JAMES K. POLK

11th President of the United States ★ 1845–1849

BORN Nov. 2, 1795, near Pineville, Mecklenburg County, NC
POLITICAL PARTY Democrat
NO. OF TERMS one
VICE PRESIDENT George Mifflin Dallas
DIED June 15, 1849, in Nashville, TN

ZACHARY TAYLOR

12th President of the United States ★ 1849–1850

BORN Nov. 24, 1784, in Orange County, VA
POLITICAL PARTY Whig
NO. OF TERMS one (died while in office)
VICE PRESIDENT Millard Fillmore
DIED July 9, 1850, in the White House, Washington, D.C.

MILLARD FILLMORE

13th President of the United States ★ 1850–1853

BORN Jan. 7, 1800, in Cayuga County, NY
POLITICAL PARTY Whig
NO. OF TERMS one (partial)
VICE PRESIDENT none
DIED March 8, 1874, in Buffalo, NY

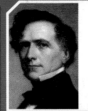

FRANKLIN PIERCE

14th President of the United States ★ 1853–1857

BORN Nov. 23, 1804, in Hillsborough (now Hillsboro), NH
POLITICAL PARTY Democrat
NO. OF TERMS one
VICE PRESIDENT William Rufus De Vane King
DIED Oct. 8, 1869, in Concord, NH

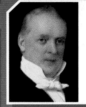

JAMES BUCHANAN

15th President of the United States ★ 1857–1861

BORN April 23, 1791, in Cove Gap, PA
POLITICAL PARTY Democrat
NO. OF TERMS one
VICE PRESIDENT John Cabell Breckinridge
DIED June 1, 1868, in Lancaster, PA

ABRAHAM LINCOLN

16th President of the United States ★ 1861–1865

BORN Feb. 12, 1809, near Hodgenville, KY
POLITICAL PARTY Republican (formerly Whig)
NO. OF TERMS two (assassinated)
VICE PRESIDENTS 1st term: Hannibal Hamlin
2nd term: Andrew Johnson
DIED April 15, 1865, in Washington, D.C.

ANDREW JOHNSON

17th President of the United States ★ 1865–1869

BORN Dec. 29, 1808, in Raleigh, NC
POLITICAL PARTY Democrat
NO. OF TERMS one (partial)
VICE PRESIDENT none
DIED July 31, 1875, in Carter's Station, TN

ULYSSES S. GRANT

18th President of the United States ★ 1869–1877

BORN April 27, 1822, in Point Pleasant, OH
POLITICAL PARTY Republican
NO. OF TERMS two
VICE PRESIDENTS 1st term: Schuyler Colfax
2nd term: Henry Wilson
DIED July 23, 1885, in Mount McGregor, NY

RUTHERFORD B. HAYES
19th President of the United States ★ 1877–1881

BORN Oct. 4, 1822,
in Delaware, OH

POLITICAL PARTY Republican

NO. OF TERMS one

VICE PRESIDENT William Almon Wheeler

DIED Jan. 17, 1893, in Fremont, OH

JAMES A. GARFIELD
20th President of the United States ★ 1881

BORN Nov. 19, 1831, near
Orange, OH

POLITICAL PARTY Republican

NO. OF TERMS one (assassinated)

VICE PRESIDENT Chester A. Arthur

DIED Sept. 19, 1881, in Elberon, NJ

CHESTER A. ARTHUR
21st President of the United States ★ 1881–1885

BORN Oct. 5, 1829, in Fairfield, VT

POLITICAL PARTY Republican

NO. OF TERMS one (partial)

VICE PRESIDENT none

DIED Nov. 18, 1886, in New York, NY

GROVER CLEVELAND
22nd and 24th President of the United States
1885–1889 ★ 1893–1897

BORN March 18, 1837, in Caldwell, NJ

POLITICAL PARTY Democrat

NO. OF TERMS two (nonconsecutive)

VICE PRESIDENTS 1st administration:
Thomas Andrews Hendricks
2nd administration:
Adlai Ewing Stevenson

DIED June 24, 1908, in Princeton, NJ

BENJAMIN HARRISON
23rd President of the United States ★ 1889–1893

BORN Aug. 20, 1833, in North Bend, OH

POLITICAL PARTY Republican

NO. OF TERMS one

VICE PRESIDENT Levi Parsons Morton

DIED March 13, 1901, in Indianapolis, IN

Check out
this book!

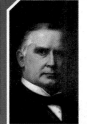

WILLIAM MCKINLEY
25th President of the United States ★ 1897–1901

BORN Jan. 29, 1843, in Niles, OH

POLITICAL PARTY Republican

NO. OF TERMS two (assassinated)

VICE PRESIDENTS 1st term:
Garret Augustus Hobart
2nd term:
Theodore Roosevelt

DIED Sept. 14, 1901, in Buffalo, NY

THEODORE ROOSEVELT
26th President of the United States ★ 1901–1909

BORN Oct. 27, 1858, in New York, NY

POLITICAL PARTY Republican

NO. OF TERMS one, plus balance of
McKinley's term

VICE PRESIDENTS 1st term: none
2nd term: Charles
Warren Fairbanks

DIED Jan. 6, 1919, in Oyster Bay, NY

While living in the
WHITE HOUSE,
THEODORE ROOSEVELT
enjoyed **SWIMMING**
IN THE POTOMAC RIVER.

WILLIAM HOWARD TAFT
27th President of the United States ★ 1909–1913

BORN Sept. 15, 1857, in Cincinnati, OH

POLITICAL PARTY Republican

NO. OF TERMS one

VICE PRESIDENT James Schoolcraft
Sherman

DIED March 8, 1930, in Washington, D.C.

WOODROW WILSON
28th President of the United States ★ 1913–1921

BORN Dec. 29, 1856, in Staunton, VA

POLITICAL PARTY Democrat

NO. OF TERMS two

VICE PRESIDENT Thomas Riley Marshall

DIED Feb. 3, 1924, in Washington, D.C.

OUR COUNTRY'S
PRESIDENTS

257

WARREN G. HARDING

29th President of the United States ★ 1921–1923

BORN Nov. 2, 1865, in Caledonia (now Blooming Grove), OH
POLITICAL PARTY Republican
NO. OF TERMS one (died while in office)
VICE PRESIDENT Calvin Coolidge
DIED Aug. 2, 1923, in San Francisco, CA

CALVIN COOLIDGE

30th President of the United States ★ 1923–1929

BORN July 4, 1872, in Plymouth, VT
POLITICAL PARTY Republican
NO. OF TERMS one, plus balance of Harding's term
VICE PRESIDENTS 1st term: none
2nd term: Charles Gates Dawes
DIED Jan. 5, 1933, in Northampton, MA

HERBERT HOOVER

31st President of the United States ★ 1929–1933

BORN Aug. 10, 1874, in West Branch, IA
POLITICAL PARTY Republican
NO. OF TERMS one
VICE PRESIDENT Charles Curtis
DIED Oct. 20, 1964, in New York, NY

HERBERT HOOVER SPOKE MANDARIN CHINESE.

FRANKLIN D. ROOSEVELT

32nd President of the United States ★ 1933–1945

BORN Jan. 30, 1882, in Hyde Park, NY
POLITICAL PARTY Democrat
NO. OF TERMS four (died while in office)
VICE PRESIDENTS 1st & 2nd terms: John Nance Garner; 3rd term: Henry Agard Wallace; 4th term: Harry S. Truman
DIED April 12, 1945, in Warm Springs, GA

HARRY S. TRUMAN

33rd President of the United States ★ 1945–1953

BORN May 8, 1884, in Lamar, MO
POLITICAL PARTY Democrat
NO. OF TERMS one, plus balance of Franklin D. Roosevelt's term
VICE PRESIDENTS 1st term: none
2nd term: Alben William Barkley
DIED Dec. 26, 1972, in Independence, MO

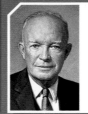

DWIGHT D. EISENHOWER

34th President of the United States ★ 1953–1961

BORN Oct. 14, 1890, in Denison, TX
POLITICAL PARTY Republican
NO. OF TERMS two
VICE PRESIDENT Richard Nixon
DIED March 28, 1969, in Washington, D.C.

JOHN F. KENNEDY

35th President of the United States ★ 1961–1963

BORN May 29, 1917, in Brookline, MA
POLITICAL PARTY Democrat
NO. OF TERMS one (assassinated)
VICE PRESIDENT Lyndon B. Johnson
DIED Nov. 22, 1963, in Dallas, TX

LYNDON B. JOHNSON

36th President of the United States ★ 1963–1969

BORN Aug. 27, 1908, near Stonewall, TX
POLITICAL PARTY Democrat
NO. OF TERMS one, plus balance of Kennedy's term
VICE PRESIDENTS 1st term: none
2nd term: Hubert Horatio Humphrey
DIED Jan. 22, 1973, near San Antonio, TX

RICHARD NIXON

37th President of the United States ★ 1969–1974

BORN Jan. 9, 1913, in Yorba Linda, CA
POLITICAL PARTY Republican
NO. OF TERMS two (resigned)
VICE PRESIDENTS 1st term & 2nd term (partial): Spiro Theodore Agnew; 2nd term (balance): Gerald R. Ford
DIED April 22, 1994, in New York, NY

GERALD R. FORD
38th President of the United States ★ 1974–1977
BORN July 14, 1913, in Omaha, NE
POLITICAL PARTY Republican
NO. OF TERMS one (partial)
VICE PRESIDENT Nelson Aldrich Rockefeller
DIED Dec. 26, 2006, in Rancho Mirage, CA

GEORGE W. BUSH
43rd President of the United States ★ 2001–2009
BORN July 6, 1946, in New Haven, CT
POLITICAL PARTY Republican
NO. OF TERMS two
VICE PRESIDENT Richard Bruce Cheney

JIMMY CARTER
39th President of the United States ★ 1977–1981
BORN Oct. 1, 1924, in Plains, GA
POLITICAL PARTY Democrat
NO. OF TERMS one
VICE PRESIDENT Walter Frederick (Fritz) Mondale

BARACK OBAMA
44th President of the United States ★ 2009–2017
BORN Aug. 4, 1961, in Honolulu, HI
POLITICAL PARTY Democrat
NO. OF TERMS two
VICE PRESIDENT Joe Biden

A MOVIE BUFF, JIMMY CARTER WATCHED MORE THAN 400 FILMS DURING HIS FOUR-YEAR TERM IN OFFICE.

DONALD TRUMP
45th President of the United States ★ 2017–2021
BORN June 14, 1946, in Queens, NY
POLITICAL PARTY Republican
NO. OF TERMS one
VICE PRESIDENT Mike Pence

RONALD REAGAN
40th President of the United States ★ 1981–1989
BORN Feb. 6, 1911, in Tampico, IL
POLITICAL PARTY Republican
NO. OF TERMS two
VICE PRESIDENT George H. W. Bush
DIED June 5, 2004, in Los Angeles, CA

JOE BIDEN
46th President of the United States ★ 2021–
BORN November 20, 1942, in Scranton, PA
POLITICAL PARTY Democrat
VICE PRESIDENT Kamala Harris

GEORGE H. W. BUSH
41st President of the United States ★ 1989–1993
BORN June 12, 1924, in Milton, MA
POLITICAL PARTY Republican
NO. OF TERMS one
VICE PRESIDENT James Danforth (Dan) Quayle III
DIED Nov. 30, 2018, in Houston, TX

AS A LAWYER IN DELAWARE, JOE BIDEN ONCE DEFENDED A FISHERMAN WHO STOLE A PRIZE-WINNING COW.

BILL CLINTON
42nd President of the United States ★ 1993–2001
BORN Aug. 19, 1946, in Hope, AR
POLITICAL PARTY Democrat
NO. OF TERMS two
VICE PRESIDENT Albert Arnold Gore, Jr.

THIS CAR IS CONFIDENTIAL

But we've got some secrets about the president's ride.

The president of the United States doesn't take the bus or fly coach. For long trips, the commander in chief boards the presidential plane, called Air Force One, or the official helicopter, Marine One. But once the leader lands, he or she climbs inside the Beast.

The Beast is the nickname of the official state vehicle that carries the president in comfort and safety using the latest in science and technology. It's based off a Cadillac CT6 (the model rolled out in 2018), but the Beast is more like an armored truck—President Barack Obama called it a "Cadillac on a tank frame." And like a tank, the 10-ton (9-t) Beast was designed to be nearly indestructible.

Many of the Beast's features are classified. But according to reports, it's loaded with James Bond–style tricks, including the ability to create a smoke screen or oil slick as well as launch tear gas. Check out these other sort-of-secret details about the president's ride.

HOW TO GO UNDERCOVER

The Beast is like an extremely large-and-in-charge bodyguard. But spies—who also help protect the country—are more secretive. Want to try out your spy skills? Check out these tricks for going undercover.

COVER STORY

Invent a boring backstory (aka your legend). Tell people you're a distant relative in your family or a student from far away. The legend should be believable but forgettable. Make it more convincing by highlighting specific phony experiences.

DRESS FOR SUCCESS

Look for outfits that won't seem out of place with the group or event you're trying to snoop on. (Wear a superhero T-shirt if you're going to a sci-fi convention, for instance.) Throw people off by borrowing duds from an older sibling or close buddy.

BEHIND THE WHEEL
The Beast's most impressive feature isn't any of its high-tech gadgets—it's the human driver, trained for making getaways and handling dangerous situations. The driver even has access to night-vision technology to keep on rolling if the headlights go out.

MORE THAN FREE WI-FI
The president has access to a state-of-the-art communications system that keeps him or her connected to the world. The leader can even place a call to a nuclear submarine on the other side of the world.

WINDOW TREATMENT
Up to seven people can ride inside the Beast. Several passengers are Secret Service agents, who protect the president in case of an attack. The Beast typically rides in a convoy that includes Secret Service vehicles, a backup Beast, and a communications truck.

AIR FORCED
The interior of the Beast can be sealed off and supplied with its own air in case of a chemical attack or if the vehicle crashes into water. It can basically turn into a submarine!

DOOR BUSTERS
The Beast's doors are rumored to be at least eight inches (20 cm) thick—about as thick as the doors of a commercial airplane. That's one reason you never see the president open their car door. It's too heavy!

BEASTLY HIDE
The Beast's skin is made of layers of aluminum, steel, and ceramic armors, designed to withstand any sort of attack—even from rockets!

FLAT CHANCE
The Beast's tires are called run-flat tires, meaning they're designed to keep rolling even if they're damaged.

FACING FACTS
Forget the fake beards and eye patches. Dark sunglasses are an easy way to disguise your eyes, one of your most recognizable features.

PLAY THE PART
Do your hair in a way that doesn't look like you. Part it a different way or slick it back. Make a bun. Braid it.

WALK THIS WAY
Keep people from recognizing you by walking in a new way. Try moving your arms more or taking longer steps. You can even put pebbles in your shoes.

CIVIL RIGHTS

A lthough the Constitution protects the civil rights of American citizens, it has not always been able to protect all Americans from persecution or discrimination. During the first half of the 20th century, many Americans, particularly Black Americans, were subjected to widespread discrimination and racism. By the mid-1950s, many people were eager to end the barriers caused by racism and bring freedom to all men and women.

The civil rights movement of the 1950s and 1960s sought to end racial discrimination against Black people, especially in the southern states. The movement wanted to give the fundamentals of economic and social equality to those who had been oppressed.

Woolworth Counter Sit-in

On February 1, 1960, four Black college students walked into a Woolworth's "five-and-dime" store in Greensboro, North Carolina. They planned to have lunch there, but were refused service as soon as they sat down at the counter. In a time of pervasive racism, the Woolworth's manager had a strict whites-only policy. But the students wouldn't take no for an answer. The men—later dubbed the "Greensboro Four"—stayed seated, peacefully and quietly, at the lunch counter until closing. The next day, they returned with 15 additional college students. The following day, even more. By February 5, some 300 students gathered at Woolworth's, forming one of the most famous sit-ins of the civil rights movement. The protest—which sparked similar sit-ins throughout the country—worked: Just six months later, restaurants across the South began to integrate.

Key Events in the Civil Rights Movement

1954	The Supreme Court case *Brown v. Board of Education* declares school segregation illegal.
1955	Rosa Parks refuses to give up her bus seat to a white passenger and spurs a bus boycott.
1957	The Little Rock Nine help to integrate schools.
1960	Four Black college students begin sit-ins at a restaurant in Greensboro, North Carolina.
1961	Freedom Rides to southern states begin as a way to protest segregation in transportation.
1963	Martin Luther King, Jr., leads the famous March on Washington.
1964	The Civil Rights Act, signed by President Lyndon B. Johnson, prohibits discrimination based on race, color, religion, sex, and national origin.
1967	Thurgood Marshall becomes the first Black American to be named to the Supreme Court.
1968	President Lyndon B. Johnson signs the Civil Rights Act of 1968, which prohibits discrimination in the sale, rental, and financing of housing.

STONE OF HOPE:
THE LEGACY OF MARTIN LUTHER KING, JR.

On April 4, 1968, Martin Luther King, Jr., was shot by James Earl Ray while standing on a hotel balcony in Memphis, Tennessee, U.S.A. The news of his death sent shock waves throughout the world: King, a Baptist minister and founder of the Southern Christian Leadership Conference, was the most prominent civil rights leader of his time. His nonviolent protests and marches against segregation, as well as his powerful speeches—including his famous "I Have a Dream" speech—motivated people to fight for justice for all.

More than 50 years after his death, King's dream lives on through a memorial on the National Mall in Washington, D.C. Built in 2011, the memorial features a 30-foot (9-m) statue of King carved into a granite boulder named the "Stone of Hope."

Today, King continues to inspire people around the world with his words and his vision for a peaceful world without racism. He will forever be remembered as one of the most prominent leaders of the civil rights movement.

"The time is always right to do what is right."

Martin Luther King, Jr., Memorial in Washington, D.C.

JOHN LEWIS: GETTING IN GOOD TROUBLE

John Lewis joins hands with President Barack Obama as they lead a commemorative march across the Edmund Pettus Bridge in Selma, Alabama, in 2015.

On March 7, 1965, a 25-year-old man linked arms with five other people, including Martin Luther King, Jr., as they led hundreds in a march across the Edmund Pettus Bridge in Selma, Alabama, U.S.A. It was a simple act, but it carried a very loud message: Those marching along the bridge were marching for racial justice and equality during a time when Black people were treated unjustly by many and were denied the same basic rights as white people, including the right to vote.

That young man was John Lewis. And, after crossing the bridge, Lewis was attacked by state troopers and beaten badly. The scene was so shocking that it made national news and created a public outcry. An act that prevented Black people from being denied the right to vote was passed just five months later. From then on, Lewis, who survived the attack, became a legend in the civil rights movement for his quiet yet powerful ability to create change. He called it getting in "good trouble": Standing up for what you believe is right and just, even if it means ruffling feathers along the way.

Lewis went on to serve in the U.S. House of Representatives for 33 years until his death in 2020. Before he passed, he was able to speak about the Black Lives Matter movement, once again encouraging people to fight for justice. "We must use our time and our space on this little planet that we call Earth to make a lasting contribution, to leave it a little better than we found it," said Lewis. "And now that need is greater than ever before."

WOMEN
FIGHTING FOR EQUALITY

Women in New York City cast their votes for the first time in November 1920.

Today, women make up about half of the workforce in the United States. But a little over a century ago, less than 20 percent worked outside the home. In fact, they didn't even have the right to vote!

That began to change in the mid-1800s when women, led by pioneers like Elizabeth Cady Stanton and Susan B. Anthony, started speaking up about inequality. They organized public demonstrations, gave speeches, published documents, and wrote newspaper articles to express their ideas. In 1848, about 300 people attended the Seneca Falls Convention in New York State to address the need for equal rights. By the late 1800s, the National American Woman Suffrage Association had made great strides toward giving women the freedom to vote. One by one, states began allowing women to vote. By 1920, the U.S. Constitution was amended, giving women across the country the ability to cast a vote during any election.

But the fight for equality did not end there. In the 1960s and 1970s, the women's rights movement experienced a rebirth, as feminists protested against injustices in areas such as the workplace and in education.

While these efforts enabled women to make great strides in our society, the efforts to even the playing field among men and women continue today.

New Zealand gave women the right to vote in 1893, becoming the world's first country to do so.

In 2020, Katie Sowers became the first female football coach in Super Bowl history.

KAMALA HARRIS IS SWORN IN AS VICE PRESIDENT ON JANUARY 20, 2021.

Key Events in U.S. Women's History

1848: **Elizabeth Cady Stanton** and **Lucretia Mott** organize the Seneca Falls Convention in New York. Attendees rally for equitable laws, equal educational and job opportunities, and the right to vote.

1920: The 19th Amendment, guaranteeing women the right to vote, is ratified.

1964: Title VII of the Civil Rights Act of 1964, which prohibits employment discrimination on the basis of sex, is successfully amended.

1971: Gloria Steinem heads up the National Women's Political Caucus, which encourages women to be active in government. She also launches *Ms.*, a magazine about women's issues.

1972: Congress approves **the Equal Rights Amendment** (ERA), proposing that women and men have equal rights under the law. It is ratified by 35 of the necessary 38 states, and is still not part of the U.S. Constitution.

1981: President Ronald Reagan appoints **Sandra Day O'Connor** as the first female Supreme Court justice.

2009: President Obama signs **the Lilly Ledbetter Fair Pay Act** to protect against pay discrimination among men and women.

2013: The **ban against women in military combat positions** is removed, overturning a 1994 Pentagon decision restricting women from combat roles.

2016: Democratic presidential nominee **Hillary Rodham Clinton** becomes the first woman to lead the ticket of a major U.S. party.

2021: Kamala Harris is sworn in as vice president of the United States, becoming the first woman to hold that office.

Ellen Ochoa
Lived: 1958–

WHY SHE'S MEMORABLE: The first Hispanic woman to travel to space, the California-born Ochoa began working at NASA in 1988 as a research engineer. She became an astronaut two years later and went on to fly to space on four different missions and log nearly 1,000 hours in orbit. Her history-making career continued in 2013 when she became the first person of Hispanic descent—and just the second woman—to land the job of director of the Johnson Space Center in Houston, Texas, U.S.A., a position she held until 2018. For her trailblazing efforts, Ochoa was recognized with NASA's highest award, the Distinguished Service Medal, among many other honors, including having at least six schools named for her. She continues to support Latinxs and minorities in the Science, Technology, Engineering, and Math (STEM) fields.

Shirley Chisholm
Lived: 1924–2005

WHY SHE'S MEMORABLE: The daughter of immigrants from Barbados and Guyana, Chisholm grew up in Brooklyn, New York, U.S.A., where she began working with local political organizations. In 1964, she won a seat on the New York state legislature, representing her childhood neighborhood. Four years later, she etched her name in the history books as the first Black woman elected to Congress, where she served seven terms, totaling 14 years. In 1972, she became the first Black woman from a major political party to run for president of the United States. Although she did not win, she is remembered for her bravery and commitment to fighting for equal rights for women, minorities, and the poor.

QUIZ WHIZ

Go back in time to seek the answers to this history quiz!

Write your answers on a piece of paper. Then check them below.

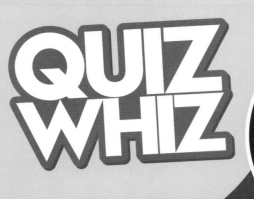

1 **True or false?** The only known Viking settlement in North America is found in Mexico.

2 At Stonehenge, the upright sandstone rocks making up the outer ring are called _____ stones.
a. sarsen
b. blarney
c. skipping
d. standing

3 How long did it take the ancient Rapa Nui people in the South Pacific to carve each Moai statue?
a. one month
b. two months
c. one year
d. two years

4 **True or false?** Hatshepsut instructed royal artists to depict her with a traditional pharaoh's beard.

5 What is the nickname for the official state vehicle that carries the president of the United States?
a. the Beetle
b. the Bear
c. the Monster
d. the Beast

Not **STUMPED** yet? Check out the *NATIONAL GEOGRAPHIC KIDS QUIZ WHIZ* collection for more crazy **HISTORY** questions!

ANSWERS: 1. False: It is in Canada; 2. a; 3. d; 4. True; 5. d

HOMEWORK HELP

Brilliant Biographies

A biography is the story of a person's life. It can be a brief summary or a long book. Biographers—those who write biographies—use many different sources to learn about their subjects. You can write your own biography of a famous person you find inspiring.

How to Get Started

Choose a subject you find interesting. If you think Cleopatra is cool, you have a good chance of getting your readers interested, too. If you're bored by ancient Egypt, your readers will be snoring after your first paragraph.

Your subject can be almost anyone: an author, an inventor, a celebrity, a politician, or a member of your family. To find someone to write about, ask yourself these simple questions:

1. Who do I want to know more about?
2. What did this person do that was special?
3. How did this person change the world?

Do Your Research

- Find out as much about your subject as possible. Read books, news articles, and encyclopedia entries. Watch video clips and movies. Conduct interviews, if possible.
- Take notes, writing down important facts and interesting stories about your subject.

Write the Biography

- Come up with a title. Include the person's name.
- Write an introduction. Consider asking a probing question about your subject.
- Include information about the person's childhood. When was this person born? Where did they grow up? Who did they admire?
- Highlight the person's talents, accomplishments, and personal attributes.
- Describe the specific events that helped to shape this person's life. Did this person ever have a problem and overcome it?
- Write a conclusion. Include your thoughts about why it is important to learn about this person.
- Once you have finished your first draft, revise and then proofread your work.

Malala Yousafzai

Here's a **SAMPLE BIOGRAPHY** of Malala Yousafzai, a human rights advocate and the youngest ever recipient of the Nobel Peace Prize. Of course, there is so much more for you to discover and write about on your own!

Malala Yousafzai

Malala Yousafzai was born in Pakistan on July 12, 1997. Malala's father, Ziauddin, a teacher, made it a priority for his daughter to receive a proper education. Malala loved school. She learned to speak three languages and even wrote a blog about her experiences as a student.

Around the time Malala turned 10, the Taliban—a group of strict Muslims who support terrorism and believe women should stay at home—took over the region where she lived. The Taliban did not approve of Malala's outspoken love of learning. One day, on her way home from school, Malala was shot in the head by a Taliban gunman. Very badly injured, she was sent to a hospital in England.

Not only did Malala survive the shooting—she thrived. She used her experience as a platform to fight for girls' education worldwide. She began speaking out about educational opportunities for all. Her efforts gained worldwide attention, and she was eventually awarded the Nobel Peace Prize in 2014 at the age of 17. She is the youngest person to earn the prestigious prize.

Each year on July 12, World Malala Day honors her heroic efforts to bring attention to human rights issues.

GEOGRAPHY
ROCKS

The sun sets over Joshua trees at Joshua Tree National Park in California, U.S.A.

ㅌPOLITICAL WORLD

Earth's land area is made up of seven continents, but people have divided much of the land into smaller political units called countries. Australia is a continent made up of a single country, and Antarctica is used for scientific research. But the other five continents include almost 200 independent countries. The political map shown here depicts boundaries—imaginary lines created by treaties—that separate countries. Some boundaries, such as the one between the United States and Canada, are very stable and have been recognized for many years.

ARCTIC

Chukchi Sea
Beaufort Sea
Queen Elizabeth Is.
Baffin Bay
Greenland
(Kalaallit Nunaat)
(Denmark)

RUSSIA

Alaska
(U.S.)

Bering Sea

60°

Gulf of Alaska

Great Bear Lake
Great Slave Lake

Hudson Bay

Labrador Sea

ARCTIC CIRCLE
ICELAND

C A N A D A

Lake Winnipeg

Great Lakes

UNITED KINGDOM

IRELAND
(ÉIRE)

FRANCE

Great Salt Lake

UNITED STATES

See Europe map for more detail.

PORT. **SPAIN**

30°

MOROCCO

TROPIC OF CANCER

Gulf of Mexico

WESTERN SAHARA
(Morocco)

Hawai'i
(U.S.)

THE BAHAMAS
DOMINCAN REP.
Puerto Rico (U.S.)
CUBA
ST. KITTS & NEVIS
CABO **MAURITANIA**
VERDE
MALI

BELIZE
HAITI
ANTIGUA & BARBUDA
Guadeloupe (France)
DOMINICA

JAMAICA
Caribbean Sea
ST. LUCIA
–*Martinique* (France)
–BARBADOS

BURKINA FASO

GUATEMALA HONDURAS
SENEGAL
EL SALVADOR NICARAGUA
GRENADA
ST. VINCENT & THE GRENADINES
TRINIDAD AND TOBAGO
THE GAMBIA
GUINEA-BISSAU

COSTA RICA
PANAMA
VENEZUELA
GUYANA
GUINEA

COLOMBIA
French Guiana
(France)
SIERRA LEONE

SURINAME
LIBERIA

EQUATOR
150°
120°
90°
30°
0°

CÔTE D'IVOIRE
(IVORY COAST)

KIRIBATI

Galápagos Islands
(Ecuador)
ECUADOR

EQ. GUINEA

OCEAN

Marquesas Islands
(France)

PERU

B R A Z I L

SAO TOME
AND
PRINCIPE

SAMOA
_American Samoa
(U.S.)

French Polynesia
(France)

BOLIVIA

ATLANTIC

TONGA

TROPIC OF CAPRICORN

PARAGUAY

OCEAN

30°

URUGUAY

CHILE **ARGENTINA**

0   miles   2000

0   kilometers   3000

Winkel Tripel Projection

*Falkland Islands
(Islas Malvinas)
(U.K.)*

Chatham Is.
(N.Z.)

Tierra del Fuego

Strait of Magellan

Drake Passage

SOUTHERN

60°

ANTARCTIC

Weddell Sea

Ross Sea

A   N   T

Prime Meridian

Other boundaries, such as the one between Sudan and South Sudan in northeast Africa, are relatively new and still disputed. Countries come in all shapes and sizes. Russia and Canada are giants; others, such as El Salvador and Qatar, are small. Some countries are long and skinny—look at Chile in South America! Still other countries—such as Indonesia and Japan in Asia—are made up of groups of islands. The political map is a clue to the diversity that makes Earth so fascinating.

TAIWAN
The People's Republic of China claims Taiwan as its 23rd province. Taiwan's government (Republic of China) maintains that there are two political entities.

271

THE PHYSICAL WORLD

Earth is dominated by large landmasses called continents—seven in all—and by an interconnected global ocean that is divided into five parts by the continents. More than 70 percent of Earth's surface is covered by oceans, and the rest is made up of land areas.

Different landforms give variety to the surface of the continents. The Rocky Mountains divide North America, the Andes mark the western edge of South America, and the Himalaya tower above South Asia. The Plateau of Tibet forms the rugged core of Asia,

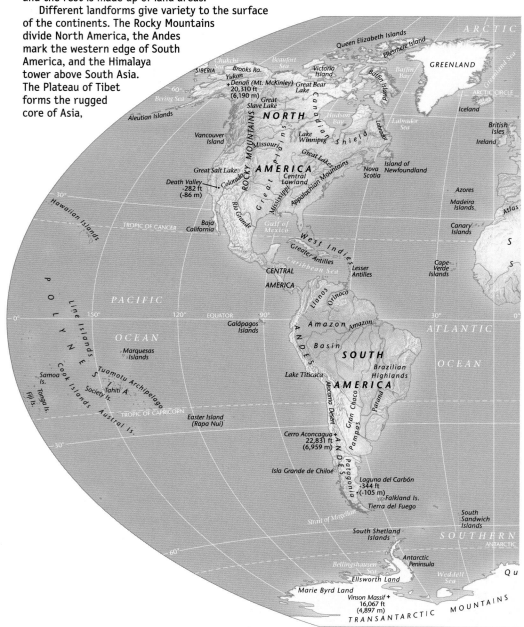

while the Northern European Plain extends from the North Sea to the Ural Mountains. Much of Africa is a plateau, and dry plains cover large areas of Australia. Mountains rise more than 16,000 feet (4,877 m) above Antarctica's massive ice sheets. Mountains and trenches make the ocean floors as varied as any continent. A mountain chain called the Mid-Atlantic Ridge runs the length of the Atlantic Ocean. In the western Pacific, trenches drop deep into the ocean floor.

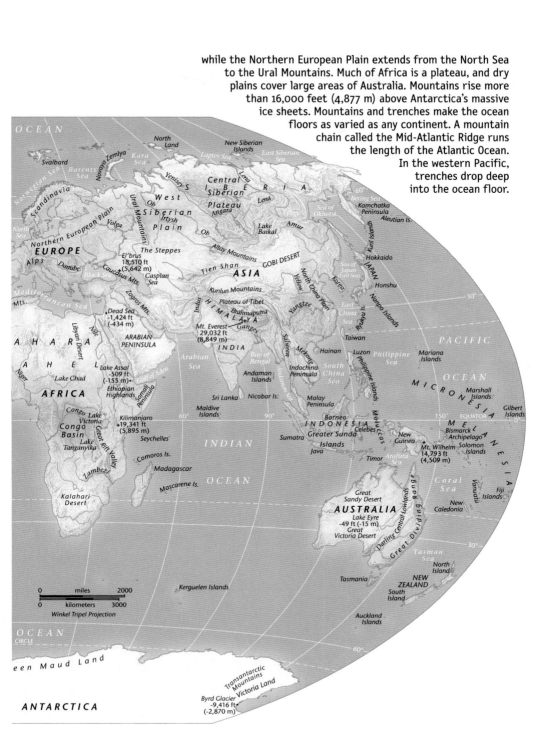

273

KINDS OF MAPS

Maps are special tools that geographers use to tell a story about Earth. Maps can be used to show just about anything related to places. Some maps show physical features, such as mountains or vegetation. Maps can also show climates or natural hazards and other things we cannot easily see. Other maps illustrate different features on Earth—political boundaries, urban centers, and economic systems.

AN IMPERFECT TOOL

Maps are not perfect. A globe is a scale model of Earth with accurate relative sizes and locations. Because maps are flat, they involve distortions of size, shape, and direction. Also, cartographers—people who create maps—make choices about what information to include. Because of this, it is important to study many different types of maps to learn the complete story of Earth. Three commonly found kinds of maps are shown on this page.

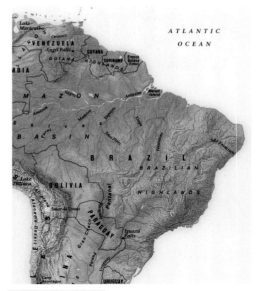

PHYSICAL MAPS. Earth's natural features—landforms, water bodies, and vegetation—are shown on physical maps. The map above uses color and shading to illustrate mountains, lakes, rivers, and deserts of central South America. Country names and borders are added for reference, but they are not natural features.

POLITICAL MAPS. These maps represent characteristics of the landscape created by humans, such as boundaries, cities, and place-names. Natural features are added only for reference. On the map above, capital cities are represented with a star inside a circle, while other cities are shown with black dots.

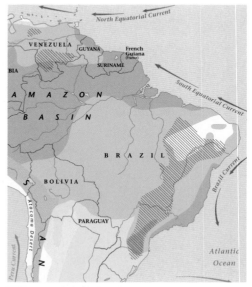

THEMATIC MAPS. Patterns related to a particular topic or theme, such as population distribution, appear on these maps. The map above displays the region's climate zones, which range from tropical wet (bright green) to tropical wet and dry (light green) to semiarid (dark yellow) to arid or desert (light yellow).

MAKING MAPS

Meet a Cartographer!

As a National Geographic cartographer, **Mike McNey** works with maps every day. Here, he shares more about his cool career.

National Geographic staff cartographers Mike McNey and Rosemary Wardley review a map of Africa for the *National Geographic Kids World Atlas.*

What exactly does a cartographer do?

I create maps specifically for books and atlases to help the text tell the story on the page. The maps need to fit into the size and the style of the book, with the final goal being that it's accurate and appealing for the reader.

What kinds of stories have you told with your maps?

Once, I created a map that showed the spread of the Burmese python population in Florida, U.S.A., around the Everglades National Park. I've also made maps that show data like farmland, food production, cattle density, and fish catch in a particular location, like the United States.

How do you rely on technology in your job?

All aspects of mapmaking are on the computer. This makes it much quicker to make a map. It also makes it easier to change anything on the map. If you want to change the color of the rivers on the map, you just click the mouse.

How do you create your maps?

I work with geographic information systems (GIS), a computer software that allows us to represent any data on a specific location of the world, or even the entire world. Data can be anything from endangered species, animal ranges, and population of a particular place. We also use remote systems, like satellites and aerial imagery, to analyze Earth's surface.

Satellites in orbit around Earth act as eyes in the sky, recording data about the planet's land and ocean areas. The data are converted to numbers transmitted back to computers that are specially programmed to interpret the data. They record the information in a form that cartographers can use to create maps.

What will maps of the future look like?

In the future, you'll see more and more data on maps. I also think more online maps are going to be made in a way that you can switch from a world view to a local view to see data at any scale.

What's the best part of your job?

I love the combination of science and design involved in it. It's also fun to make maps interesting for kids.

275

UNDERSTANDING
MAPS

MAKING A PROJECTION

Globes present a model of Earth as it is—a sphere—
but they are bulky and can be difficult to use and store.
Flat maps are much more convenient, but certain problems
can result from transferring Earth's curved surface to a
flat piece of paper, a process called projection. Imagine a
globe that has been cut in half, like the one to the right. If a
light is shined into it, the lines of latitude and longitude and the
shapes of the continent will cast shadows that can be "projected"
onto a piece of paper, as shown here. Depending on how the paper is
positioned, the shadows will be distorted in different ways.

KNOW THE CODE

Every map has a story to tell, but first you have to know how to read one. Maps represent
information by using a language of symbols. When you know how to read these symbols, you can
access a wide range of information. For example, look at the scale and compass rose or arrow to
understand distance and direction (see box below).

To find out what each symbol on a map means, you must use the key. It's your secret decoder—
identifying information by each symbol on the map.

There are three main types of map symbols: points, lines, and areas. Points, which can be either
dots or small icons, represent the location or the number of things, such as schools, cities, or
landmarks. Lines are used to show boundaries, roads, or rivers and can vary in color or thickness.
Area symbols use pattern or color to show regions, such as a sandy area or a neighborhood.

SCALE AND DIRECTION

The scale on a map can be shown as a fraction, as words, or as a line or bar. It relates
distance on the map to distance in the real world. Sometimes the scale identifies the
type of map projection. Maps may include an arrow to indicate north on the map or a
compass rose to show all principal directions.

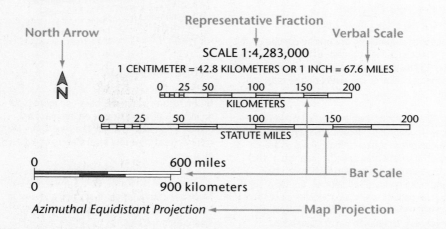

North Arrow

Representative Fraction

Verbal Scale

SCALE 1:4,283,000

1 CENTIMETER = 42.8 KILOMETERS OR 1 INCH = 67.6 MILES

N

0   25   50   100   150   200
KILOMETERS

0   25   50   100   150   200
STATUTE MILES

0   600 miles
0   900 kilometers

Bar Scale

Azimuthal Equidistant Projection ◄——————— Map Projection

GEOGRAPHIC FEATURES

From roaring rivers to parched deserts, from underwater canyons to jagged mountains, Earth is covered with beautiful and diverse environments. Here are examples of the most common types of geographic features found around the world.

WATERFALL

Waterfalls form when rivers reach an abrupt change in elevation. At left, the Iguazú waterfall system—on the border of Brazil and Argentina—is made up of 275 falls.

VALLEY

Valleys, cut by running water or moving ice, may be broad and flat or narrow and steep, such as the Indus River Valley (above) in Ladakh, India.

RIVER

As a river moves through flatlands, it twists and turns. Above, the Rio Los Amigos winds through a rainforest in Peru.

MOUNTAIN

Mountains are Earth's tallest landforms, and Mount Everest (above) rises highest of all, at 29,031.69 feet (8,848.86 m) above sea level.

GLACIER

Glaciers—"rivers" of ice—such as Hubbard Glacier (above) in Alaska, U.S.A., move slowly from mountains to the sea. Global warming is shrinking them.

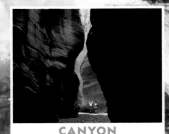

CANYON

Steep-sided valleys called canyons are created mainly by running water. Buckskin Gulch (above) in Utah, U.S.A., is the deepest "slot" canyon in the American Southwest.

DESERT

Deserts are land features created by climate, specifically by a lack of water. Here, a camel caravan crosses the Sahara in North Africa.

AFRICA

Snow sometimes falls on parts of the Sahara.

Leopards usually live alone and scratch trees to mark their territory.

A leopard in South Africa

The massive continent of Africa, where humankind began millions of years ago, is second only to Asia in size. Stretching nearly as far from west to east as it does from north to south, Africa is home to both the longest river in the world (the Nile) and the largest hot desert on Earth (the Sahara).

Luanda, Angola

NANO-CHAMELEON

Talk about a little lizard! What may be the world's smallest chameleon was recently discovered in the mountains of Madagascar. Male nano-chameleons are less than an inch long (25 mm), tiny enough to fit on the fingertip of an adult human.

COOL CANYON

Local legend says that Namibia's Fish River Canyon—the largest canyon in Africa—was carved by a giant serpent when it burrowed deep into the ground while hiding from hunters.

Great Pyramid, Great Numbers
How do the numbers for Earth's biggest pyramid stack up?

Due to erosion, the pyramid is **30 feet (9 m)** shorter than it was originally.

Weight of largest stone blocks: **15 tons (14 t)**

Number of stone blocks: **2.3 million**

Number of builders: **20,000**

Angle at which the sides rise: **51°52'**

Height: **451 feet (138 m)**

Average length of each side: **756 feet (230 m)**

REMARKABLE RIVER

Africa is home to one of the longest rivers in the world: the Nile. Flowing south to north along some 4,100 miles (6,600 km), the Nile runs through or along the border of 11 African countries. Throughout history, the Nile has been a key source of freshwater and food for both people and the animals that live nearby, including hippos, turtles, and crocodiles.

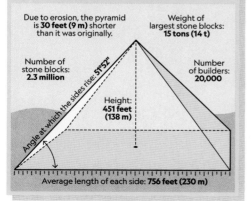

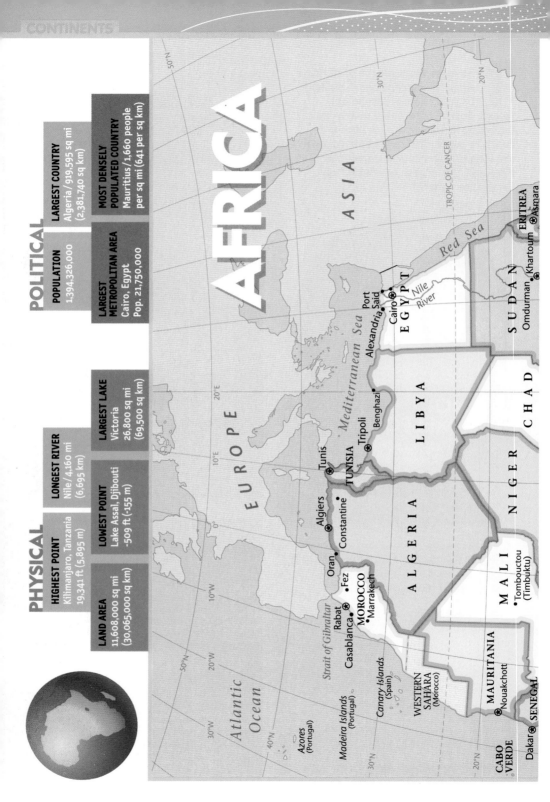

AFRICA

POLITICAL

POPULATION
1,394,326,000

LARGEST COUNTRY
Algeria / 919,595 sq mi
(2,381,740 sq km)

LARGEST METROPOLITAN AREA
Cairo, Egypt
Pop. 21,750,000

MOST DENSELY POPULATED COUNTRY
Mauritius / 1,660 people
per sq mi (641 per sq km)

PHYSICAL

LAND AREA
11,608,000 sq mi
(30,065,000 sq km)

HIGHEST POINT
Kilimanjaro, Tanzania
19,341 ft (5,895 m)

LOWEST POINT
Lake Assal, Djibouti
-509 ft (-155 m)

LONGEST RIVER
Nile / 4,160 mi
(6,695 km)

LARGEST LAKE
Victoria
26,800 sq mi
(69,500 sq km)

EUROPE

ASIA

Mediterranean Sea

Red Sea

Atlantic Ocean

Strait of Gibraltar

Azores
(Portugal)

Madeira Islands
(Portugal)

Canary Islands
(Spain)

TROPIC OF CANCER

Tunis ⊛

TUNISIA

Algiers ⊛
Constantine

Oran

Fez
Rabat
Casablanca
MOROCCO
Marrakech

WESTERN
SAHARA
(Morocco)

MAURITANIA
Nouakchott ⊛

CABO
VERDE

Dakar ⊛ SENEGAL

ALGERIA

LIBYA

Tripoli ⊛
Benghazi

Port
Said
Alexandria
Cairo ⊛
EGYPT

Nile
River

SUDAN
Omdurman Khartoum ⊛

ERITREA
Asmara ⊛

CHAD

NIGER

MALI
Tombouctou
(Timbuktu)

50°N

30°N

20°N

TROPIC OF CANCER

30°E

20°E

10°E

0°

10°W

20°W

30°W

40°W

50°N

40°N

30°N

20°N

SOMALIA

Gulf of Aden

SOMALILAND

DJIBOUTI Djibouti

Lake Assal
(-155 m) -509 ft▼

Addis
Ababa

ETHIOPIA

Mogadishu

SEYCHELLES

Victoria

COMOROS
Moroni

MADAGASCAR

Antananarivo

MAURITIUS
Port Louis
Réunion
(France)

Indian
Ocean

SOUTH
SUDAN

Juba

UGANDA

Kampala

DARFUR

CENTRAL
AFRICAN REPUBLIC

Bangui

N'Djamena

Lake
Victoria

KENYA

Nairobi

Kilimanjaro
19,341 ft▲
(5,895 m)

Mombasa

RWANDA
Kigali

BURUNDI
Bujumbura
Gitega

TANZANIA

Dodoma

Dar es Salaam

Mozambique Channel

DEMOCRATIC
REPUBLIC
OF THE CONGO

Kisangani

Kinshasa

Kananga

Mbuji-Mayi

Lubumbashi

MALAWI

Lilongwe

MOZAMBIQUE

Harare

ZIMBABWE

Kolwezi

Kitwe

ZAMBIA

Lusaka

Maputo

Lobamba

ESWATINI (SWAZILAND)

Mbabane

Maseru

LESOTHO

Durban

BOTSWANA

Pretoria
(Tshwane)

Johannesburg

Gaborone

Bloemfontein

SOUTH
AFRICA

Port
Elizabeth

CONGO

Brazzaville

Pointe-Noire

Cabinda
(Angola)

Luanda

ANGOLA

NAMIBIA

Windhoek

Cape Town

GABON

Libreville

CAMEROON

Yaoundé

Douala

EQUATORIAL GUINEA

Malabo

São Tomé

SAO TOME & PRINCIPE

NIGERIA

Abuja

Kano

Ogbomosho

Lagos

Porto-
Novo

Cotonou

BENIN

TOGO

Lomé

Niamey

Ouagadougou

BURKINA
FASO

GHANA

Accra

Yamoussoukro

Abidjan

CÔTE D'IVOIRE
(IVORY COAST)

LIBERIA

Monrovia

SIERRA
LEONE

Freetown

GUINEA

Conakry

THE GAMBIA

Banjul

GUINEA-
BISSAU

Bissau

Bamako

St. Helena
(U.K.)

Atlantic
Ocean

Ascension
(U.K.)

TROPIC OF CAPRICORN

EQUATOR

Azimuthal Equal-Area Projection

Map Key

⊛ National capital
• Other city
▲ Highest point
(above sea level)
▼ Lowest point
(below sea level)

800 Miles

800 Kilometers

ANTARCTICA

Humpback whale

There are active volcanoes in Antarctica.

In the summer months, humpback whales in Antarctica feed mostly on krill.

This frozen continent may be a cool place to visit, but unless you're a penguin, you probably wouldn't want to hang out in Antarctica for long. The fact that it's the coldest, windiest, and driest continent helps explain why humans never colonized this ice-covered land surrounding the South Pole.

Weddell seal

WARMER THAN EVER

With Antarctica experiencing record-breaking high temperatures, the continent as a whole is getting warmer. Temperatures reached a record high of nearly 65°F (18.3°C) in February 2020, making the area one of the fastest warming regions on Earth.

GOING THE DISTANCE

Each year, a few dozen runners from around the world compete in the Antarctic Ice Marathon, during which participants face an average temperature with windchill of minus 4°F (-20°C).

Annual Average Snowfall

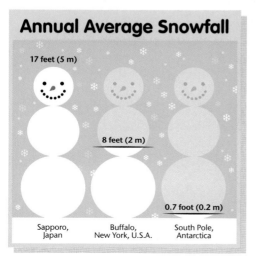

17 feet (5 m)

8 feet (2 m)

0.7 foot (0.2 m)

| Sapporo, Japan | Buffalo, New York, U.S.A. | South Pole, Antarctica |

WHAT LIES BENEATH

Researchers in Antarctica recently unearthed the totally intact remains of a ship that sank nearly 110 years ago. The H.M.S. *Endurance*, the ship of polar explorer Ernest Shackleton, sank in 1915 after it got stuck in the ice and was abandoned.

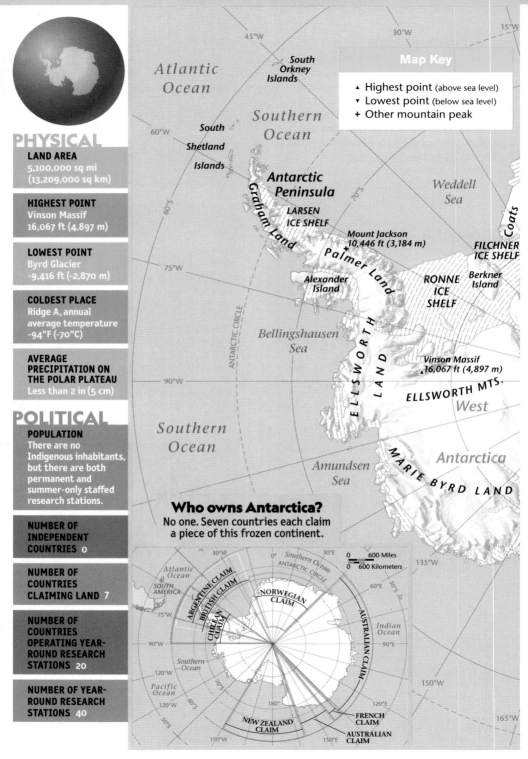

PHYSICAL

LAND AREA
5,100,000 sq mi
(13,209,000 sq km)

HIGHEST POINT
Vinson Massif
16,067 ft (4,897 m)

LOWEST POINT
Byrd Glacier
-9,416 ft (-2,870 m)

COLDEST PLACE
Ridge A, annual
average temperature
-94°F (-70°C)

**AVERAGE
PRECIPITATION ON
THE POLAR PLATEAU**
Less than 2 in (5 cm)

POLITICAL

POPULATION
There are no
Indigenous inhabitants,
but there are both
permanent and
summer-only staffed
research stations.

**NUMBER OF
INDEPENDENT
COUNTRIES** 0

**NUMBER OF
COUNTRIES
CLAIMING LAND** 7

**NUMBER OF
COUNTRIES
OPERATING YEAR-
ROUND RESEARCH
STATIONS** 20

**NUMBER OF YEAR-
ROUND RESEARCH
STATIONS** 40

*Atlantic
Ocean*

South
Orkney
Islands

Map Key

▲ Highest point (above sea level)
▼ Lowest point (below sea level)
+ Other mountain peak

*Southern
Ocean*

South
Shetland
Islands

**Antarctic
Peninsula**

*Weddell
Sea*

LARSEN
ICE SHELF

Mount Jackson
10,446 ft (3,184 m)

FILCHNER
ICE SHELF

Graham Land

Palmer Land

Alexander
Island

RONNE
ICE
SHELF

Berkner
Island

Coats

ANTARCTIC CIRCLE

*Bellingshausen
Sea*

Vinson Massif
▲16,067 ft (4,897 m)

ELLSWORTH LAND

ELLSWORTH MTS.

West

*Southern
Ocean*

*Amundsen
Sea*

MARIE BYRD LAND

Antarctica

Who owns Antarctica?

No one. Seven countries each claim
a piece of this frozen continent.

*Atlantic
Ocean*

Southern Ocean
ANTARCTIC CIRCLE

SOUTH
AMERICA

ARGENTINE CLAIM

BRITISH CLAIM

CHILEAN
CLAIM

NORWEGIAN
CLAIM

AUSTRALIAN CLAIM

*Indian
Ocean*

*Southern
Ocean*

*Pacific
Ocean*

NEW ZEALAND
CLAIM

FRENCH
CLAIM

AUSTRALIAN
CLAIM

0   600 Miles
0   600 Kilometers

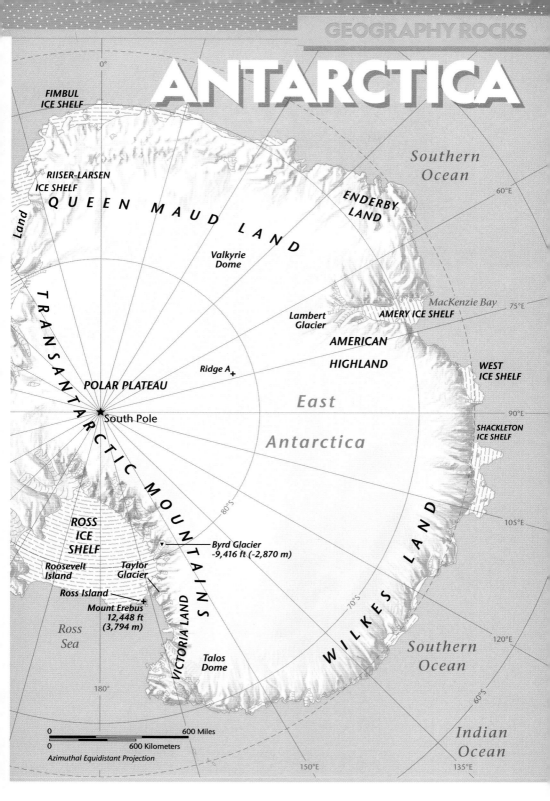

ANTARCTICA

0°

FIMBUL
ICE SHELF

RIISER-LARSEN
ICE SHELF

Land

Q U E E N   M A U D   L A N D

Valkyrie
Dome

Southern
Ocean

60°E

ENDERBY
LAND

MacKenzie Bay

75°E

Lambert
Glacier

AMERY ICE SHELF

AMERICAN

HIGHLAND

WEST
ICE SHELF

Ridge A +

T R A N S A N T A R C T I C   M O U N T A I N S

POLAR PLATEAU

★ South Pole

East

Antarctica

90°E

SHACKLETON
ICE SHELF

80°S

ROSS
ICE
SHELF

Byrd Glacier
-9,416 ft (-2,870 m)

105°E

Roosevelt
Island

Taylor
Glacier

Ross Island

Mount Erebus
12,448 ft
(3,794 m)

VICTORIA LAND

Ross
Sea

Talos
Dome

70°S

W I L K E S   L A N D

60°S

Southern
Ocean

120°E

180°

0   600 Miles

0   600 Kilometers

Azimuthal Equidistant Projection

150°E

135°E

Indian
Ocean

285

ASIA

Prayer flags in Tibet

The colors on Tibetan prayer flags represent different elements, such as air, fire, earth, and water.

Laos is the only landlocked country in Southeast Asia.

Made up of 46 countries, Asia is the world's largest continent. Just how big is it? From western Türkiye (Turkey) to the eastern tip of Russia, Asia spans nearly half the globe! Home to more than four billion citizens—that's three out of five people on the planet—Asia's population is bigger than that of all the other continents combined.

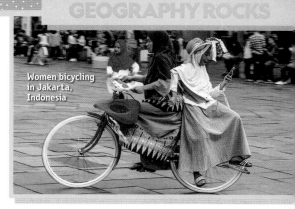

Women bicycling in Jakarta, Indonesia

TREES, PLEASE

Plans are underway for one million trees to be planted throughout Singapore by 2030. The hope? To improve air quality and add more parks, so that everyone in the city will one day be within a 10-minute walk to a green space.

CITY SCENTS

The name Hong Kong translates to "fragrant harbor" in Cantonese, the main language of the bustling city. Researchers think the name comes from Hong Kong's past as a trading post for oil and incense.

TIGERS ON THE RISE

After decades of dwindling numbers in China, tigers are steadily clawing back. Thanks to conservation efforts, the number of tigers in the wild of China is around 55, well up from just seven some 25 years ago. And Nepal has doubled its numbers in recent years, climbing to roughly 235 tigers.

World's Deepest Lakes

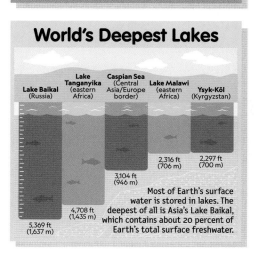

Lake Baikal (Russia)	**Lake Tanganyika** (eastern Africa)	**Caspian Sea** (Central Asia/Europe border)	**Lake Malawi** (eastern Africa)	**Ysyk-Köl** (Kyrgyzstan)
5,369 ft (1,637 m)	4,708 ft (1,435 m)	3,104 ft (946 m)	2,316 ft (706 m)	2,297 ft (700 m)

Most of Earth's surface water is stored in lakes. The deepest of all is Asia's Lake Baikal, which contains about 20 percent of Earth's total surface freshwater.

PHYSICAL

LAND AREA
17,208,000 sq mi
(44,570,000 sq km)

HIGHEST POINT
Mount Everest,
China–Nepal
29,032 ft (8,849 m)

LOWEST POINT
Dead Sea,
Israel–Jordan
-1,424 ft (-434 m)

LONGEST RIVER
Yangtze, China
3,880 mi (6,244 km)

**LARGEST LAKE
ENTIRELY IN ASIA**
Lake Baikal, Russia
12,200 sq mi
(31,500 sq km)

POLITICAL

POPULATION
4,666,831,000

**LARGEST
METROPOLITAN AREA**
Tokyo, Japan
Pop. 37,274,000

**LARGEST COUNTRY
ENTIRELY IN ASIA**
China
3,705,405 sq mi
(9,596,960 sq km)

**MOST DENSELY
POPULATED COUNTRY**
Singapore
21,300 people
per sq mi
(8,235 per sq km)

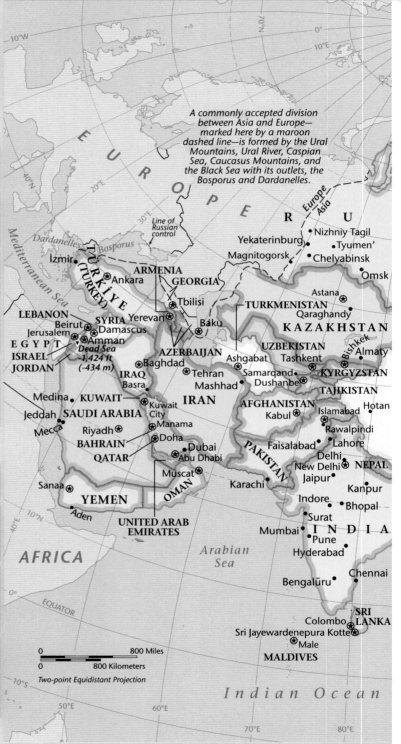

A commonly accepted division between Asia and Europe—marked here by a maroon dashed line—is formed by the Ural Mountains, Ural River, Caspian Sea, Caucasus Mountains, and the Black Sea with its outlets, the Bosporus and Dardanelles.

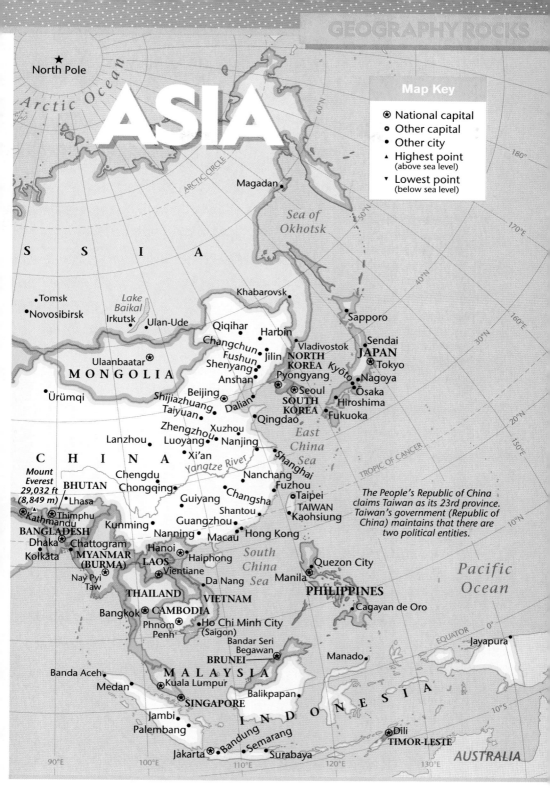

★ North Pole

Arctic Ocean

ASIA

Map Key

⊛ National capital
◉ Other capital
• Other city
▲ Highest point
(above sea level)
▼ Lowest point
(below sea level)

ARCTIC CIRCLE

Magadan

Sea of
Okhotsk

R S S I A

•Tomsk
•Novosibirsk

Lake
Baikal

Irkutsk •Ulan-Ude

Khabarovsk

Sapporo

Qiqihar
Changchun
Harbin
•Jilin
Vladivostok
Fushun
NORTH
KOREA

Sendai
JAPAN
•Tokyo
Kyōto
Nagoya

Ulaanbaatar ⊛

M O N G O L I A

Shenyang•
Anshan•
Pyongyang◉

Seoul
SOUTH
KOREA

Ōsaka
Hiroshima

•Ürümqi

Beijing
Shijiazhuang•
Taiyuan•

⊛
Dalian•
Qingdao•

Fukuoka

Zhengzhou•
Lanzhou•
Luoyang•

Xuzhou•
•Nanjing

East
China
Sea

C H I N A
•Xi'an
Yangtze River
Shanghai

Mount
Everest
29,032 ft
(8,849 m)

BHUTAN

Chengdu•
Chongqing•

Nanchang•
Fuzhou•

Lhasa•
⊛Kathmandu ⊛Thimphu

Guiyang•
Changsha•
Shantou•

•Taipei

TAIWAN
Kaohsiung

BANGLADESH
Dhaka◉
Kunming•
Guangzhou•

The People's Republic of China
claims Taiwan as its 23rd province.
Taiwan's government (Republic of
China) maintains that there are
two political entities.

Kolkata•
Chattogram•
Nanning•

•Macau •Hong Kong

MYANMAR
(BURMA)
Hanoi◉
Haiphong•

South
China
Sea

Nay Pyi
Taw

LAOS
•Vientiane

Quezon City
Manila⊛

THAILAND
Da Nang•

PHILIPPINES

VIETNAM

Bangkok ⊛ CAMBODIA

Pacific
Ocean

Phnom
Penh
•Ho Chi Minh City
(Saigon)

•Cagayan de Oro

Bandar Seri
Begawan

EQUATOR

•Jayapura

Banda Aceh•

BRUNEI
⊛
Manado•

Medan•
M A L A Y S I A
⊛Kuala Lumpur
Balikpapan•

I N D O N E S I A

⊛SINGAPORE

Jambi•

Palembang•
Bandung
Semarang•

⊛Dili
TIMOR-LESTE

Jakarta⊛
Surabaya•

AUSTRALIA

90°E   100°E   110°E   120°E   130°E

AUSTRALIA,
NEW ZEALAND, AND OCEANIA

A young red-legged pademelon stays in mom's pouch for its first six months of life.

More than 800 languages are spoken in Papua New Guinea.

Red-legged pademelon

G'day, mate! This vast region, covering almost 3.3 million square miles (8.5 million sq km), includes Australia—the world's smallest and flattest continent—and New Zealand, as well as a fleet of mostly tiny islands scattered across the Pacific Ocean. Also known as "down under," most of the countries in this region are in the Southern Hemisphere, below the Equator.

Maori children of New Zealand in ceremonial clothing

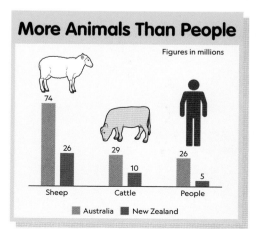

THE WANGARRU BOUNCES BACK

Good news for the wangarru: After a deluge of rain in Australia's outback, the species—also known as the yellow-footed rock wallaby—saw some growth in its dwindling numbers. It's a promising sign for the wild wangarru population, which had been shrinking due to drought.

ROCK ON

Western Australia's Mount Augustus, also called Burringurrah, is the world's largest rock. Actually made up of several different types of rocks, the reddish brown formation stands out against its barren desert surroundings, rising 2,346 feet (715 m) above the plain and stretching for five miles (8 km).

RAD RUINS

On a tiny island in the middle of the Pacific Ocean, you'll find Nan Madol, the only ancient city ever built atop a coral reef. What's left today—stone walls and columns—are the ruins of a once thriving civilization known as the Saudeleur, a dynasty that ruled the island of Pohnpei.

More Animals Than People

Figures in millions

74

26

29

10

26

5

| Sheep | Cattle | People |

■ Australia ■ New Zealand

PHYSICAL

LAND AREA
3,297,000 sq mi
(8,538,000 sq km)

HIGHEST POINT*
Mount Wilhelm,
Papua New Guinea
14,793 ft (4,509 m)
*Includes Oceania

LOWEST POINT
Lake Eyre, Australia
-49 ft (-15 m)

LONGEST RIVER
Murray,
Australia
1,558 mi (2,508 km)

LARGEST LAKE
Lake Eyre, Australia
3,741 sq mi
(9,690 sq km)

POLITICAL

POPULATION
44,285,000

**LARGEST
METROPOLITAN AREA**
Melbourne, Australia
Pop. 5,151,000

LARGEST COUNTRY
Australia
2,988,902 sq mi
(7,741,220 sq km)

**MOST DENSELY
POPULATED COUNTRY**
Nauru
1,250 people per sq mi
(476 per sq km)

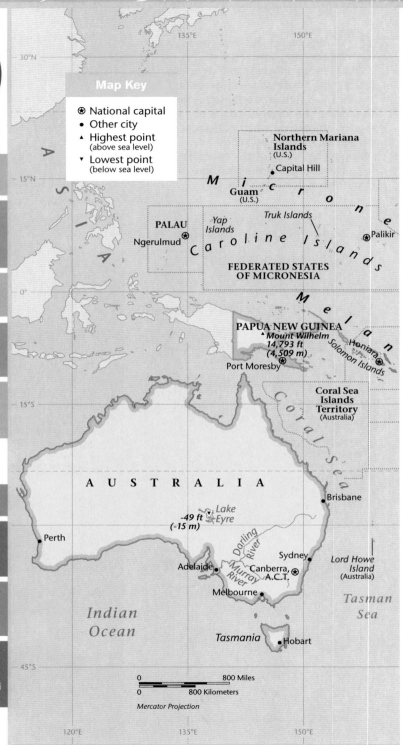

Map Key

⊛ National capital
● Other city
▲ Highest point
(above sea level)
▼ Lowest point
(below sea level)

A S I A

Northern Mariana
Islands
(U.S.)
● Capital Hill

Guam
(U.S.)

M i c r o n e

PALAU
Ngerulmud ⊛

Yap
Islands

Truk Islands

Caroline Islands

Palikir ⊛

FEDERATED STATES
OF MICRONESIA

M e l a n

PAPUA NEW GUINEA
▲ Mount Wilhelm
14,793 ft
(4,509 m)

Honiara ⊛
Solomon Islands

Port Moresby

Coral Sea
Islands
Territory
(Australia)

Coral Sea

A U S T R A L I A

● Brisbane

▼ Lake
Eyre
-49 ft
(-15 m)

● Perth

Darling
River

Sydney ●

Lord Howe
Island
(Australia)

Adelaide ●

Murray
River

Canberra, ⊛
A.C.T.

Melbourne ●

Tasman
Sea

Indian
Ocean

Tasmania
● Hobart

0   800 Miles
0   800 Kilometers

Mercator Projection

292

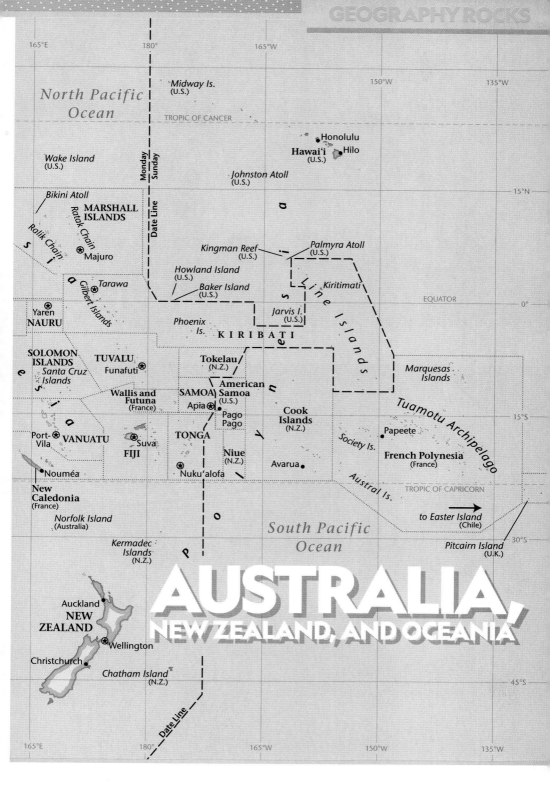

North Pacific
Ocean

Midway Is.
(U.S.)

TROPIC OF CANCER

165°E 180° 165°W 150°W 135°W

Honolulu

Hawai'i
(U.S.) Hilo

Wake Island
(U.S.)

Monday
Sunday

Johnston Atoll
(U.S.)

15°N

Bikini Atoll

MARSHALL
ISLANDS

Ratak Chain

Date Line

Rallik Chain

Majuro

Kingman Reef
(U.S.)

Palmyra Atoll
(U.S.)

Howland Island
(U.S.)

Kiritimati

a

Tarawa

Gilbert Islands

Baker Island
(U.S.)

Line Islands

Yaren
NAURU

Jarvis I.
(U.S.)

EQUATOR

0°

Phoenix
Is.

K I R I B A T I

s

SOLOMON
ISLANDS

TUVALU

Santa Cruz
Islands

Funafuti

Tokelau
(N.Z.)

Marquesas
Islands

Wallis and
Futuna
(France)

SAMOA

American
Samoa
(U.S.)

n

Tuamotu Archipelago

15°S

Apia

Port-
Vila

VANUATU

Suva

Pago
Pago

Cook
Islands
(N.Z.)

Society Is.

Papeete

TONGA

FIJI

Niue
(N.Z.)

Avarua

French Polynesia
(France)

Nouméa

Nuku'alofa

Austral Is.

TROPIC OF CAPRICORN

New
Caledonia
(France)

Norfolk Island
(Australia)

o

to Easter Island
(Chile)

South Pacific
Ocean

30°S

Kermadec
Islands
(N.Z.)

P

Pitcairn Island
(U.K.)

AUSTRALIA,
NEW ZEALAND, AND OCEANIA

Auckland
NEW
ZEALAND

Wellington

Christchurch

Chatham Island
(N.Z.)

45°S

Date Line

165°E 180° 165°W 150°W 135°W

EUROPE

A dachshund parade is held each September in Kraków, Poland.

There are no snakes in Ireland—except for those kept as pets.

Wawel Castle overlooks the Vistula River in Kraków, Poland.

A cluster of peninsulas and islands jutting west from Asia, Europe is bordered by the Atlantic and Arctic Oceans and more than a dozen seas. Here you'll find a variety of scenery, from mountains to countryside to coastlines. Europe is also known for its rich cultures and fascinating history, which make it one of the most visited continents on Earth.

Traditional dance performed in Greece

BUG OFF

One place you'll never have to worry about mosquito bites? Iceland! The country is totally mosquito free, likely because of its unique weather patterns that disrupt the life cycle from egg to pesky bug.

SEALED UP

Every fall, hundreds of gray seal pups are born on England's Farne Islands. For more than 70 years, rangers have been counting the seals in the colony. New pups are marked with rotating colors of a harmless dye to count and track the population.

CHOCOLATE, CHOCOLATE EVERYWHERE

Attention chocolate lovers! Switzerland is now home to a museum all about the sweet stuff. The Lindt Home of Chocolate offers a deep dive into the rich history of chocolate and features what may be the world's tallest chocolate fountain at a soaring three stories high.

Europe's Longest Rivers

Volga	2,294 mi (3,692 km)
Danube	1,770 mi (2,848 km)
Dnieper	1,420 mi (2,285 km)
Rhine	765 mi (1,230 km)
Elbe	724 mi (1,165 km)

PHYSICAL

LAND AREA
3,841,000 sq mi
(9,947,000 sq km)

HIGHEST POINT
El'brus, Russia
18,510 ft (5,642 m)

LOWEST POINT
Caspian Sea
-92 ft (-28 m)

LONGEST RIVER
Volga, Russia
2,294 mi
(3,692 km)

**LARGEST LAKE
ENTIRELY IN EUROPE**
Ladoga, Russia
6,900 sq mi
(17,872 sq km)

POLITICAL

POPULATION
764,189,000

**LARGEST
METROPOLITAN AREA**
Moscow, Russia
Pop. 12,641,000

**LARGEST COUNTRY
ENTIRELY IN EUROPE**
France
248,573 sq mi
(643,801 sq km)

**MOST DENSELY
POPULATED COUNTRY**
Monaco
31,400 people per sq
mi (15,700 per sq km)

Map Key

- ⊗ National capital
- ⊛ Capital of Northern Ireland, Scotland, or Wales
- ● Other capital
- • Other city
- ▫ Small country
- ▲ Highest point (above sea level)
- ▼ Lowest point (below sea level)

Jan Mayen (Norway)

Reykjavík
ICELAND

ARCTIC CIRCLE

Norwegian Sea

Faroe Islands (Denmark)

Shetland Islands

Orkney Islands

Oslo

Göteborg

SCOTLAND
Glasgow
Edinburgh
North Sea

N. IRELAND
Belfast
IRELAND (ÉIRE)
Dublin
UNITED KINGDOM
Liverpool • Manchester
WALES • Birmingham
Cardiff • ENGLAND
London ⊗
The Hague
NETH. Hamburg
Amsterdam • Berlin ⊗

DENMARK
Copenhagen ⊗
Kiel

Brussels ⊗
BELGIUM
—LUX.
GERMANY
Frankfurt
Prague

⊗ Paris

Nantes

Munich
LIECH.

Bay of Biscay

Bordeaux

F R A N C E Zürich
Bern ⊗ **SWITZ.**
Lyon
Milan
Turin Venice
AUSTRIA
Ljubljana
SLOV. ⊗

Toulouse

MONACO
Nice
Genoa
SAN MARINO ▫

Porto
PORTUGAL
Bilbao
Valladolid
ANDORRA
Zaragoza
Madrid ⊗
S P A I N
Barcelona
Valencia
Sevilla Murcia
Málaga
Gibraltar (U.K.)

Lisbon

Marseille

Corsica (France)
ITALY
VATICAN CITY ▫
Rome

Naples

Sardinia (Italy)

Balearic Is. (Spain)

M e d i t e r r a n e a n

Palermo
Messina
Catania
Sicily

Valletta
MALTA

Atlantic Ocean

0   400 Miles
0   400 Kilometers
Azimuthal Equidistant Projection

A F R I C A

10°E 20°E 30°E 40°E 50°E

60°E

Barents Sea

A commonly accepted division
between Asia and Europe—
marked here by a maroon
dashed line—is formed by the
Ural Mountains, Ural River, Caspian
Sea, Caucasus Mountains, and
the Black Sea with its outlets, the
Bosporus and Dardanelles.

Murmansk

60°N

Asia
Europe

•Arkhangel'sk

R U S S I A

EUROPE

Lake
Ladoga

Volga River Kazan'

•Ufa

60°N

⊛Helsinki

•St. Petersburg

•Yaroslavl' Nizhniy
Novgorod

•Tver'

Stockholm Tallinn•
⊛ ⊛ ESTONIA

⊛Moscow

Samara Orenburg

Ryazan'

50°N

S W E D E N

F I N L A N D

Rīga• LATVIA

LITHUANIA

Smolensk

Penza

KAZAKHSTAN

Russia ⊛Vilnius
Gdańsk• Kaunas

Vitsyebsk

Saratov

Baltic Sea

⊛Minsk

Bryansk

POLAND ⊛Warsaw
Bydgoszcz

BELARUS

Kursk

Volgograd•

Homyel'•

Łódź
•Wrocław Kraków

⊛Kyiv

Kharkiv

Astrakhan'

-92 ft
(-28 m)

CZECHIA
(CZECH REP.)

Poltava•

L'viv U K R A I N E Donets'k

Vienna SLOVAKIA
⊛ ⊛Bratislava
⊛Budapest

Vinnytsya

Dnipro

Rostov
na Donu

Line of
Russian
control

Boundary claimed
by Ukraine

El'brus Groznyy•

Sochi

Caspian Sea

HUNGARY

MOLDOVA

⊛Zagreb
CROATIA
BOSNIA &
HERZEGOVINA

ROMANIA

⊛Chisinau

Odesa
CRIMEA
Simferopol'

⊛Belgrade Bucharest

Sevastopol'

(5,642 m) 18,510 ft

GEORGIA

Baku
⊛

Sarajevo⊛ SERBIA
MONTENEGRO KOSOVO
Podgorica⊛ ⊛Prishtinë⊛

Varna

Black Sea

AZERBAIJAN

40°N

Tirana⊛ ⊛Sofia
ALBANIA N. MAC.

BULGARIA

Bosporus

⊛Skopje

Thessaloniki

•Istanbul

GREECE

⊛Athens

T
U
R
K
Dardanelles
İ
Y
E
(T U R K E Y)

CRIMEA
Russia invaded Crimea in 2014 and, after
secession from Ukraine was approved in a
disputed and boycotted referendum held in
Crimea, the Russian parliament voted to annex
Crimea into the Russian Federation. The
United Nations General Assembly subsequently
adopted a nonbinding resolution declaring
the annexation invalid and affirming Ukraine's
territorial jurisdiction. Russia administers and
controls the peninsula, while Ukraine continues
to maintain that Crimea is its sovereign territory.

Sea

Crete

NORTHERN CYPRUS
Nicosia⊛

CYPRUS

20°E 30°E 40°E

NORTH AMERICA

Flamingos are the national bird of the Bahamas.

Canada has more doughnut shops per person than any other country.

American flamingos

From the Great Plains of the United States and Canada to the rainforests of Panama, North America stretches 5,500 miles (8,850 km) from north to south. The third largest continent, North America can be divided into five regions: the mountainous west (including parts of Mexico and Central America's western coast), the Great Plains, the Canadian Shield, the varied eastern region (including Central America's lowlands and coastal plains), and the Caribbean.

A Day of the Dead (Día de los Muertos) parade in Mexico City, Mexico

CAVE OF CRYSTALS

Massive, milky white selenite crystals fill Mexico's Cave of Crystals, some 950 feet (290 m) below ground. Discovered in 2000, the cave was untouched by humans for hundreds of thousands of years, and its crystal contents grew big enough to walk on.

BRING BACK THE BEES

Efforts to boost honeybee numbers in the United States appear to be working. A recent study showed an increase in colonies across the country, which is good news for the buzzing pollinators, which have been threatened by climate change, habitat loss, and the use of harmful pesticides.

BLOW ON

For the first time in history, wind recently surpassed hydroelectricity as the top source of renewable energy in the United States. Currently, more than 71,000 wind turbines in the country provide some of the electricity used to power homes across at least 44 states.

World's Longest Coastlines

Canada	151,023 miles (243,048 km)
Indonesia	33,998 miles (54,716 km)
Russia	23,397 miles (37,653 km)
Philippines	22,549 miles (36,289 km)
Japan	18,486 miles (29,751 km)

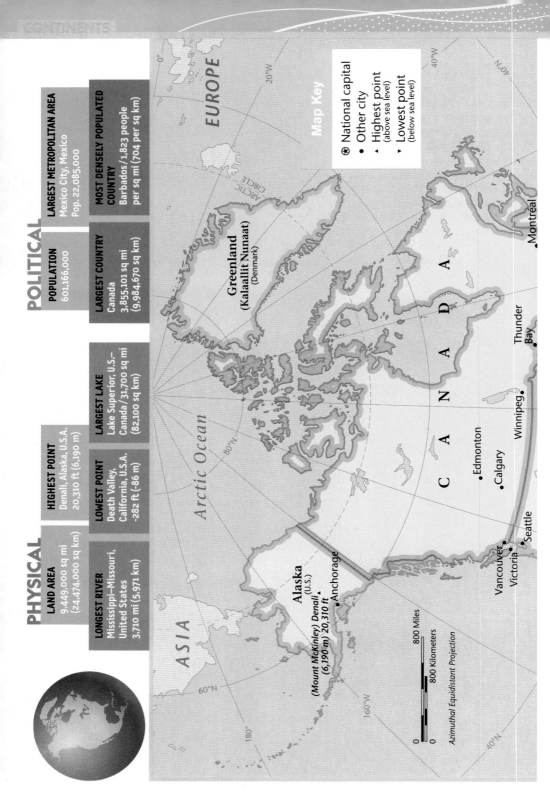

PHYSICAL

LAND AREA
9,449,000 sq mi
(24,474,000 sq km)

HIGHEST POINT
Denali, Alaska, U.S.A.
20,310 ft (6,190 m)

LOWEST POINT
Death Valley,
California, U.S.A.
-282 ft (-86 m)

LONGEST RIVER
Mississippi–Missouri,
United States
3,710 mi (5,971 km)

LARGEST LAKE
Lake Superior, U.S.–
Canada / 31,700 sq mi
(82,100 sq km)

POLITICAL

POPULATION
601,166,000

LARGEST COUNTRY
Canada
3,855,101 sq mi
(9,984,670 sq km)

LARGEST METROPOLITAN AREA
Mexico City, Mexico
Pop. 22,085,000

**MOST DENSELY POPULATED
COUNTRY**
Barbados / 1,823 people
per sq mi (704 per sq km)

Map Key

⊛ National capital
● Other city
▲ Highest point
   (above sea level)
▼ Lowest point
   (below sea level)

EUROPE

ASIA

Arctic Ocean

ARCTIC CIRCLE

Greenland
(Kalaallit Nunaat)
(Denmark)

C A N A D A

Alaska
(U.S.)

(Mount McKinley) Denali ▲
(6,190 m) 20,310 ft
● Anchorage

● Edmonton
● Calgary

● Winnipeg

Thunder
Bay ●

Montréal ●

Vancouver ●
Victoria ●
● Seattle

0   800 Miles
0   800 Kilometers
Azimuthal Equidistant Projection

20°W

40°W

80°N

60°N

180°

160°W

40°N

40°N

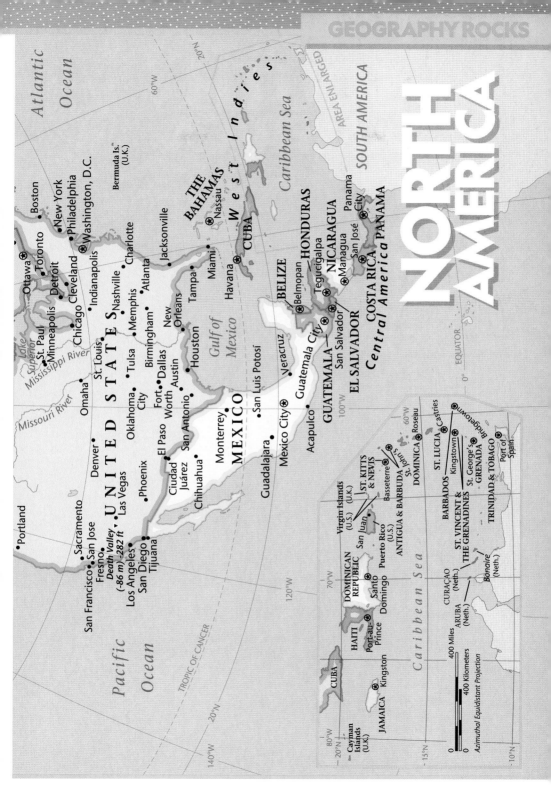

NORTH AMERICA

AREA ENLARGED

SOUTH AMERICA

Atlantic Ocean

West Indies

Bermuda Is.
(U.K.)

THE BAHAMAS

Nassau ⊗

Caribbean Sea

CUBA

Havana ⊗

HONDURAS

Tegucigalpa ⊗

NICARAGUA
Managua ⊗

Panama
City ⊗

Central America PANAMA

San José ⊗ COSTA RICA

BELIZE
Belmopan ⊗

EL SALVADOR
San Salvador ⊗

GUATEMALA
Guatemala City ⊗

Boston
New York
Philadelphia
Washington, D.C. ⊗

Charlotte
Jacksonville

Miami
Tampa

Atlanta

Nashville
Memphis

Birmingham

New
Orleans

Houston

*Gulf of
Mexico*

Veracruz

San Luis Potosí

Toronto
Detroit
Cleveland
Indianapolis
Chicago

Ottawa ⊗

Lake
Superior
St. Paul
Minneapolis

Mississippi River

St. Louis
Tulsa

Oklahoma
City

Dallas
Fort
Worth
Austin
San Antonio

El Paso

Ciudad
Juárez

Chihuahua

Monterrey

MEXICO

Guadalajara

Mexico City ⊗

Acapulco

UNITED STATES

Omaha
Denver

Missouri River

Portland

Sacramento
San Jose
San Francisco
Fresno
Las Vegas
Los Angeles
San Diego
Tijuana

Phoenix

Death Valley
(-86 m) -282 ft ▾

*Pacific
Ocean*

TROPIC OF CANCER

EQUATOR

20°N

60°W

20°W

120°W

70°W

80°W

100°W

Inset map (Caribbean)

Caribbean Sea

CUBA

JAMAICA
Kingston ⊗

Cayman
Islands
(U.K.)

HAITI
Port-au-
Prince ⊗

DOMINICAN
REPUBLIC
Santo
Domingo ⊗

Puerto Rico
(U.S.)
San Juan ⊗

Virgin Islands
(U.S.) (U.K.)

ST. KITTS
& NEVIS
Basseterre ⊗

St. John's ⊗
ANTIGUA & BARBUDA

DOMINICA
Roseau ⊗

ST. LUCIA
Castries ⊗

Kingstown ⊗
ST. VINCENT &
THE GRENADINES

Bridgetown ⊗
BARBADOS

St. George's ⊗
GRENADA

TRINIDAD & TOBAGO
Port of
Spain ⊗

CURAÇAO
(Neth.)

ARUBA
(Neth.)

Bonaire
(Neth.)

400 Miles
400 Kilometers

Azimuthal Equidistant Projection

15°N

10°N

60°W

60°W

301

SOUTH AMERICA

Kaieteur Falls, Guyana

Water flowing from Kaieteur Falls plunges 741 feet (226 m) down.

Capoeira, a sport combining martial arts and dance, was invented in Brazil.

South America is bordered by three major bodies of water—the Caribbean Sea, Atlantic Ocean, and Pacific Ocean. The world's fourth largest continent extends over a range of climates, from tropical in the north to subarctic in the south. South America produces a rich diversity of natural resources, including nuts, fruits, sugar, grains, coffee, and chocolate.

Santiago Cathedral in Santiago, Chile

RUNNING WILD

Guanacos, wild relatives of camels that look like small llamas with longer necks, are native to the grasslands of the Andes. Super-speedy animals that can run as fast as 35 miles an hour (56 km/h), guanacos are a protected species in Chile and Peru.

CHECKMATE

Chess has a long history in Montevideo, Uruguay. The game has been part of the cultural heritage for decades, and the capital city even hosted the World Youth Chess Championship in 2017. Today, you can usually spot people playing in parks or on the sidewalks of Montevideo.

Vast Watershed

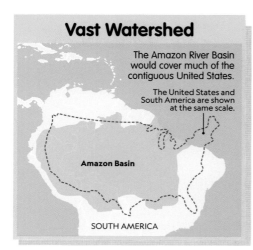

The Amazon River Basin would cover much of the contiguous United States.

The United States and South America are shown at the same scale.

Amazon Basin

SOUTH AMERICA

TALL FALLS

Venezuela's Angel Falls, also known as Salto Churún Merú, is the world's highest uninterrupted waterfall. With a height of 3,212 feet (979 m), the falls are named for American aviator Jimmie Angel, the first person to fly over them.

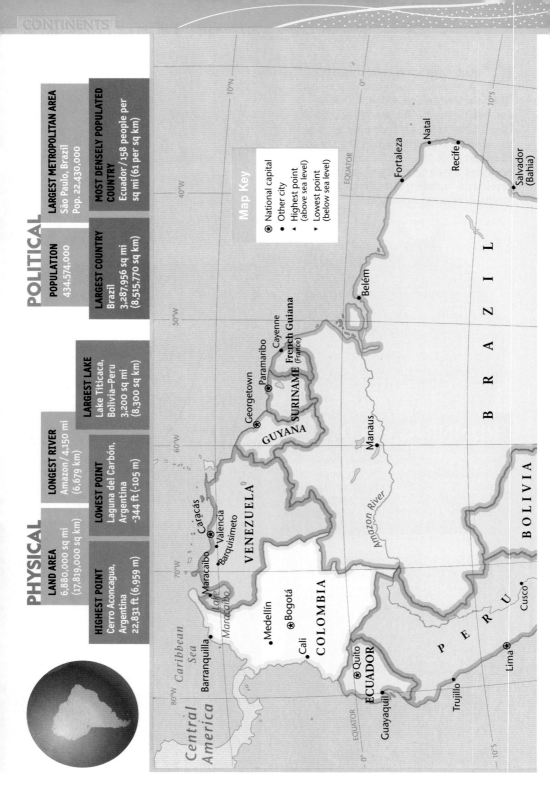

PHYSICAL

HIGHEST POINT
Cerro Aconcagua, Argentina
22,831 ft (6,959 m)

LAND AREA
6,880,000 sq mi
(17,819,000 sq km)

LONGEST RIVER
Amazon / 4,450 mi
(6,679 km)

LOWEST POINT
Laguna del Carbón, Argentina
-344 ft (-105 m)

LARGEST LAKE
Lake Titicaca, Bolivia–Peru
3,200 sq mi
(8,300 sq km)

POLITICAL

POPULATION
434,574,000

LARGEST METROPOLITAN AREA
São Paulo, Brazil
Pop. 22,430,000

LARGEST COUNTRY
Brazil
3,287,956 sq mi
(8,515,770 sq km)

MOST DENSELY POPULATED COUNTRY
Ecuador / 158 people per sq mi (61 per sq km)

Map Key

⊛ National capital
● Other city
▲ Highest point (above sea level)
▼ Lowest point (below sea level)

Central America

Caribbean Sea

Barranquilla
Maracaibo
Lake Maracaibo
Cali
Medellín
⊛ Bogotá
COLOMBIA
⊛ Quito
ECUADOR
Guayaquil

Caracas
⊛ Valencia
Barquisimeto
VENEZUELA

Georgetown
GUYANA
Paramaribo ⊛
SURINAME
Cayenne
French Guiana (France)

Manaus

Amazon River

Trujillo
⊛ Lima
Cusco
P E R U

B O L I V I A

B R A Z I L

Belém

Fortaleza
Natal
Recife
Salvador (Bahia)

EQUATOR

10°N
0°
10°S
80°W
70°W
60°W
50°W
40°W

304

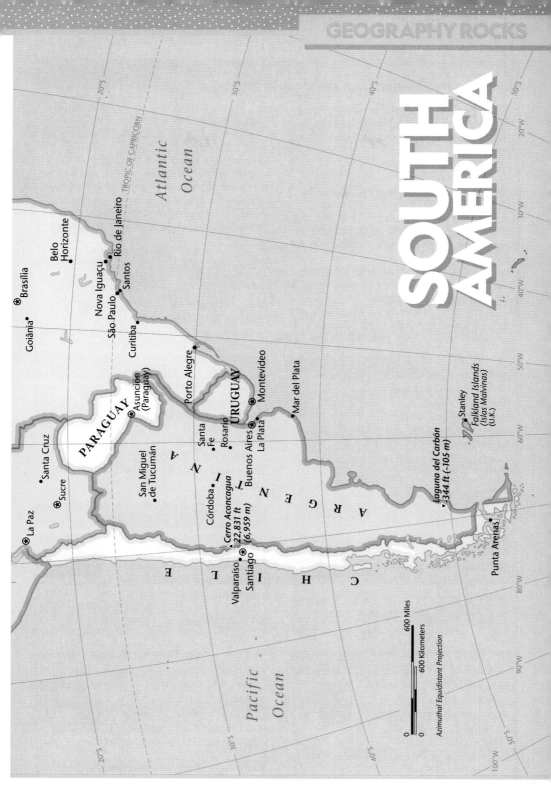

SOUTH AMERICA

Atlantic Ocean

Pacific Ocean

TROPIC OF CAPRICORN

PARAGUAY

ARGENTINA

URUGUAY

CHILE

La Paz
Sucre
Santa Cruz
Goiânia
Brasília
Belo Horizonte
Nova Iguaçu
Rio de Janeiro
São Paulo
Santos
Curitiba
Porto Alegre
Asunción (Paraguay)
San Miguel de Tucumán
Santa Fe
Rosario
Córdoba
Buenos Aires
La Plata
Montevideo
Mar del Plata
Valparaíso
Santiago
Cerro Aconcagua 22,831 ft (6,959 m)
Laguna del Carbón 344 ft (-105 m)
Punta Arenas
Stanley
Falkland Islands (Islas Malvinas) (U.K.)

600 Miles
600 Kilometers
Azimuthal Equidistant Projection

20°S
30°S
40°S
50°S

100°W
90°W
80°W
60°W
50°W
40°W
30°W
20°W

COUNTRIES OF THE WORLD

The following pages present a general overview of all 195 independent countries recognized by the National Geographic Society, including the newest nation, South Sudan, which gained independence in 2011.

The flags of each independent country symbolize diverse cultures and histories. The statistical data cover highlights of geography and demography and provide a brief overview of each country. They present general characteristics and are not intended to be comprehensive. For example, not every language spoken in a specific country can be listed. Thus, languages shown are the most representative of that area. This is also true of the religions mentioned.

A country is defined as a political body with its own independent government, geographical space, and, in most cases, laws, military, and taxes.

Disputed areas such as Northern Cyprus and Taiwan, and dependencies of independent nations, such as Bermuda and Puerto Rico, are not included in this listing.

Note the color key at the bottom of the pages and the locator map below, which assign a color to each country based on the continent on which it is located. Some capital city populations include that city's metro area. All information is accurate as of press time.

Color Key by Continent

Afghanistan

Area: 251,827 sq mi (652,230 sq km)
Population: 38,347,000
Capital: Kabul, pop. 4,458,000
Currency: afghani (AFN)
Religion: Muslim
Languages: Afghan Persian (Dari), Pashto, Uzbek, English

Andorra

Area: 181 sq mi (468 sq km)
Population: 86,000
Capital: Andorra la Vella, pop. 23,000
Currency: euro (EUR)
Religion: Roman Catholic
Languages: Catalan, French, Castilian, Portuguese

Albania

Area: 11,100 sq mi (28,748 sq km)
Population: 3,095,000
Capital: Tirana, pop. 512,000
Currency: lek (ALL)
Religions: Muslim, Roman Catholic, Eastern Orthodox
Language: Albanian

Angola

Area: 481,353 sq mi (1,246,700 sq km)
Population: 34,795,000
Capital: Luanda, pop. 8,952,000
Currency: kwanza (AOA)
Religions: Roman Catholic, Protestant
Languages: Portuguese, Umbundu, other African languages

Algeria

Area: 919,595 sq mi (2,381,740 sq km)
Population: 44,179,000
Capital: Algiers, pop. 2,854,000
Currency: Algerian dinar (DZD)
Religion: Muslim
Languages: Arabic, French, Berber (Tamazight)

Antigua and Barbuda

Area: 171 sq mi (443 sq km)
Population: 100,000
Capital: St. John's, pop. 21,000
Currency: East Caribbean dollar (XCD)
Religions: Protestant, Roman Catholic, other Christian
Languages: English, Antiguan creole

Argentina

Area: 1,073,518 sq mi
(2,780,400 sq km)
Population: 46,246,000
Capital: Buenos Aires,
pop. 15,370,000
Currency: Argentine peso (ARS)
Religion: Roman Catholic
Languages: Spanish, Italian, English, German, French

3 cool things about ARGENTINA

1. Both the highest (Mount Aconcagua) and lowest (Laguna del Carbón) points of the Southern Hemisphere are located in Argentina.

2. Pato, a polo-basketball hybrid played on horseback, is the national sport of Argentina.

3. Argentina has had two female presidents: Cristina Fernández de Kirchner and Isabel Martínez de Perón.

Armenia

Area: 11,484 sq mi
(29,743 sq km)
Population: 3,001,000
Capital: Yerevan,
pop. 1,092,000
Currency: dram (AMD)
Religion: Oriental Orthodox
Languages: Armenian, Russian

Australia

Area: 2,988,902 sq mi
(7,741,220 sq km)
Population: 26,141,000
Capital: Canberra, A.C.T.,
pop. 467,000
Currency: Australian dollar (AUD)
Religions: Protestant, Roman Catholic
Language: English

Austria

Area: 32,383 sq mi (83,871 sq km)
Population: 8,913,000
Capital: Vienna, pop. 1,960,000
Currency: euro (EUR)
Religions: Roman Catholic, Eastern Orthodox, Muslim
Languages: German, Croatian

Azerbaijan

Area: 33,436 sq mi
(86,600 sq km)
Population: 10,353,000
Capital: Baku, pop. 2,401,000
Currency: Azerbaijani manat (AZN)
Religion: Muslim
Languages: Azerbaijani (Azeri), Russian

Bahamas, The

Area: 5,359 sq mi
(13,880 sq km)
Population: 356,000
Capital: Nassau, pop. 280,000
Currency: Bahamian dollar (BSD)
Religions: Protestant, Roman Catholic, other Christian
Languages: English, Creole

Bahrain

Area: 293 sq mi (760 sq km)
Population: 1,541,000
Capital: Manama, pop. 689,000
Currency: Bahraini dinar (BHD)
Religions: Muslim, Christian
Languages: Arabic, English, Farsi, Urdu

Bangladesh

Area: 57,321 sq mi
(148,460 sq km)
Population: 165,650,000
Capital: Dhaka, pop. 22,478,000
Currency: taka (BDT)
Religions: Muslim, Hindu
Language: Bangla (Bengali)

● Asia　● Europe　● North America　● South America　　**307**

Barbados

Area: 166 sq mi (430 sq km)
Population: 303,000
Capital: Bridgetown, pop. 89,000
Currency: Barbadian dollar (BBD)
Religions: Protestant, other Christian
Languages: English, Bajan

Belgium

Area: 11,787 sq mi (30,528 sq km)
Population: 11,847,000
Capital: Brussels, pop. 2,110,000
Currency: euro (EUR)
Religions: Roman Catholic, Muslim
Languages: Dutch, French, German

Belarus

Area: 80,155 sq mi
(207,600 sq km)
Population: 9,414,000
Capital: Minsk, pop. 2,049,000
Currency: Belarusian ruble (BYN)
Religions: Eastern Orthodox, Roman Catholic
Languages: Russian, Belarusian

Belize

Area: 8,867 sq mi (22,966 sq km)
Population: 412,000
Capital: Belmopan, pop. 23,000
Currency: Belizean dollar (BZD)
Religions: Roman Catholic, Protestant
Languages: English, Spanish, Creole, Maya

SNAPSHOT
Botswana

A male African elephant faces the camera in Botswana, home to more elephants than any other country in the world.

COLOR KEY ● Africa ● Australia, New Zealand, and Oceania

Benin

Area: 43,484 sq mi (112,622 sq km)
Population: 13,755,000
Capitals: Porto-Novo, pop. 285,000;
Cotonou, pop. 709,000
Currency: CFA franc BCEAO (XOF)
Religions: Muslim, Roman Catholic, Protestant, Vodoun, other Christian
Languages: French, Fon, Yoruba, tribal languages

Bhutan

Area: 14,824 sq mi (38,394 sq km)
Population: 868,000
Capital: Thimphu, pop. 203,000
Currency: ngultrum (BTN)
Religions: Buddhist, Hindu
Languages: Sharchhopka, Dzongkha, Lhotshamkha

Bolivia

Area: 424,164 sq mi (1,098,581 sq km)
Population: 12,054,000
Capitals: La Paz, pop. 1,908,000;
Sucre, pop. 278,000
Currency: boliviano (BOB)
Religions: Roman Catholic, Protestant
Languages: Spanish, Quechua, Aymara, Guarani

Bosnia and Herzegovina

Area: 19,767 sq mi (51,197 sq km)
Population: 3,816,000
Capital: Sarajevo, pop. 344,000
Currency: convertible mark (BAM)
Religions: Muslim, Eastern Orthodox, Roman Catholic
Languages: Bosnian, Serbian, Croatian

Botswana

Area: 224,607 sq mi (581,730 sq km)
Population: 2,384,000
Capital: Gaborone, pop. 269,000
Currency: pula (BWP)
Religion: Christian
Languages: Setswana, Sekalanga, Shekgalagadi, English

Brazil

Area: 3,287,956 sq mi (8,515,770 sq km)
Population: 217,240,000
Capital: Brasília, pop. 4,804,000
Currency: real (BRL)
Religions: Roman Catholic, Protestant
Language: Portuguese

Brunei

Area: 2,226 sq mi (5,765 sq km)
Population: 478,000
Capital: Bandar Seri Begawan, pop. 241,000
Currency: Bruneian dollar (BND)
Religions: Muslim, Christian, Buddhist, Indigenous beliefs
Languages: Malay, English, Chinese

Bulgaria

Area: 42,811 sq mi (110,879 sq km)
Population: 6,873,000
Capital: Sofia, pop. 1,287,000
Currency: lev (BGN)
Religions: Eastern Orthodox, Muslim
Language: Bulgarian

Burkina Faso

Area: 105,869 sq mi (274,200 sq km)
Population: 21,935,000
Capital: Ouagadougou, pop. 3,056,000
Currency: CFA franc BCEAO (XOF)
Religions: Muslim, Roman Catholic, traditional or animist, Protestant
Languages: French, African languages

Burundi

Area: 10,745 sq mi (27,830 sq km)
Population: 12,696,000
Capitals: Bujumbura, pop. 1,139,000;
Gitega, pop. 135,000
Currency: Burundi franc (BIF)
Religions: Roman Catholic, Protestant
Languages: Kirundi, French, English, Swahili

Cabo Verde

Area: 1,557 sq mi (4,033 sq km)
Population: 597,000
Capital: Praia, pop. 168,000
Currency: Cabo Verdean escudo (CVE)
Religions: Roman Catholic, Protestant
Languages: Portuguese, Krioulo

Cambodia

Area: 69,898 sq mi (181,035 sq km)
Population: 16,713,000
Capital: Phnom Penh, pop. 2,211,000
Currency: riel (KHR)
Religion: Buddhist
Language: Khmer

Cameroon

Area: 183,568 sq mi (475,440 sq km)
Population: 29,322,000
Capital: Yaoundé, pop. 4,337,000
Currency: CFA franc BEAC (XAF)
Religions: Roman Catholic, Protestant, other Christian, Muslim
Languages: African languages, English, French

Canada

Area: 3,855,101 sq mi (9,984,670 sq km)
Population: 38,233,000
Capital: Ottawa, pop. 1,423,000
Currency: Canadian dollar (CAD)
Religions: Roman Catholic, Protestant, other Christian
Languages: English, French

Central African Republic

Area: 240,535 sq mi (622,984 sq km)
Population: 5,455,000
Capital: Bangui, pop. 933,000
Currency: CFA franc BEAC (XAF)
Religions: Christian, Muslim
Languages: French, Sangho, tribal languages

Chad

Area: 495,755 sq mi (1,284,000 sq km)
Population: 17,963,000
Capital: N'Djamena, pop. 1,533,000
Currency: CFA franc BEAC (XAF)
Religions: Muslim, Protestant, Roman Catholic
Languages: French, Arabic, Sara, Indigenous languages

Chile

Area: 291,932 sq mi (756,102 sq km)
Population: 18,430,000
Capital: Santiago, pop. 6,857,000
Currency: Chilean peso (CLP)
Religions: Roman Catholic, Protestant
Languages: Spanish, English

China

Area: 3,705,405 sq mi (9,596,960 sq km)
Population: 1,410,540,000
Capital: Beijing, pop. 21,333,000
Currency: Renminbi yuan (RMB)
Religions: folk religion, Buddhist, Christian
Languages: Standard Chinese (Mandarin), Yue (Cantonese), Wu, Minbei, Minnan, Xiang, Gan, regional official languages

Colombia

Area: 439,735 sq mi (1,138,910 sq km)
Population: 49,059,000
Capital: Bogotá, pop. 11,344,000
Currency: Colombian peso (COP)
Religions: Roman Catholic, Protestant
Language: Spanish

Comoros

Area: 863 sq mi (2,235 sq km)
Population: 876,000
Capital: Moroni, pop. 62,000
Currency: Comoran franc (KMF)
Religion: Muslim
Languages: Arabic, French, Shikomoro (Comorian)

COLOR KEY ● Africa ● Australia, New Zealand, and Oceania

Congo

Area: 132,047 sq mi (342,000 sq km)
Population: 5,546,000
Capital: Brazzaville, pop. 2,553,000
Currency: CFA franc BEAC (XAF)
Religions: Roman Catholic, other Christian, Protestant
Languages: French, Lingala, Monokutuba, Kikongo, local languages

Côte d'Ivoire (Ivory Coast)

Area: 124,504 sq mi (322,463 sq km)
Population: 28,713,000
Capitals: Abidjan, pop. 5,516,000; Yamoussoukro, pop. 231,000
Currency: CFA franc BCEAO (XOF)
Religions: Muslim, Roman Catholic, Protestant
Languages: French, Diola, Native dialects

Costa Rica

Area: 19,730 sq mi (51,100 sq km)
Population: 5,204,000
Capital: San José, pop. 1,441,000
Currency: Costa Rican colón (CRC)
Religions: Roman Catholic, Protestant
Languages: Spanish, English

Croatia

Area: 21,851 sq mi (56,594 sq km)
Population: 4,189,000
Capital: Zagreb, pop. 684,000
Currency: kuna (HRK)
Religion: Roman Catholic
Languages: Croatian, Serbian

SNAPSHOT
Colombia

From June to December, aquatic plants in Caño Cristales—also called the River of Five Colors—produce vibrant hues.

● Asia ● Europe ● North America ● South America

Cuba

Area: 42,803 sq mi
(110,860 sq km)
Population: 11,008,000
Capital: Havana, pop. 2,146,000
Currency: Cuban peso (CUP)
Religions: Christian, folk religion
Language: Spanish

Democratic Republic of the Congo

Area: 905,354 sq mi
(2,344,858 sq km)
Population: 108,408,000
Capital: Kinshasa, pop. 15,628,000
Currency: Congolese franc (CDF)
Religions: Roman Catholic, Protestant, other Christian
Languages: French, Lingala, Kingwana, Kikongo, Tshiluba

Cyprus

Area: 3,572 sq mi (9,251 sq km)
Population: 1,295,000
Capital: Nicosia, pop. 269,000
Currency: euro (EUR)
Religion: Eastern Orthodox
Languages: Greek, Turkish, English

Denmark

Area: 16,639 sq mi
(43,094 sq km)
Population: 5,921,000
Capital: Copenhagen, pop. 1,370,000
Currency: Danish krone (DKK)
Religions: Protestant, Muslim
Languages: Danish, Faroese, Greenlandic, English

3 cool things about CYPRUS

1. According to myth, Greek goddess of love Aphrodite was born in Cyprus, emerging from a rock at what's now called Aphrodite's Beach in the coastal city of Paphos.

2. Haloumi, a popular snack in Cyprus, is a salty cheese that's squeaky when eaten raw.

3. A shipwreck off the coast of Cyprus is one of the most popular scuba diving spots in the world.

Djibouti

Area: 8,958 sq mi
(23,200 sq km)
Population: 957,000
Capital: Djibouti, pop. 591,000
Currency: Djiboutian franc (DJF)
Religions: Muslim, Christian
Languages: French, Arabic, Somali, Afar

Dominica

Area: 290 sq mi (751 sq km)
Population: 75,000
Capital: Roseau, pop. 15,000
Currency: East Caribbean dollar (XCD)
Religions: Roman Catholic, Protestant
Languages: English, French patois

Czechia (Czech Republic)

Area: 30,451 sq mi (78,867 sq km)
Population: 10,705,000
Capital: Prague, pop. 1,318,000
Currency: koruna (CZK)
Religion: Roman Catholic
Languages: Czech, Slovak

Dominican Republic

Area: 18,792 sq mi
(48,670 sq km)
Population: 10,695,000
Capital: Santo Domingo, pop. 3,458,000
Currency: Dominican peso (DOP)
Religions: Roman Catholic, Protestant
Language: Spanish

Ecuador

Area: 109,483 sq mi
(283,561 sq km)
Population: 17,290,000
Capital: Quito, pop. 1,928,000
Currency: U.S. dollar (USD)
Religions: Roman Catholic, Protestant
Languages: Spanish, Amerindian languages

Egypt

Area: 386,662 sq mi
(1,001,450 sq km)
Population: 107,771,000
Capital: Cairo, pop. 21,750,000
Currency: Egyptian pound (EGP)
Religions: Muslim, Oriental Orthodox
Languages: Arabic, English, French

El Salvador

Area: 8,124 sq mi
(21,041 sq km)
Population: 6,569,000
Capital: San Salvador,
pop. 1,111,000
Currency: U.S. dollar (USD)
Religions: Roman Catholic, Protestant
Language: Spanish

TREES SOAR some NINE STORIES HIGH in the cloud forest of El Salvador's MONTECRISTO NATIONAL PARK.

Equatorial Guinea

Area: 10,831 sq mi (28,051 sq km)
Population: 1,679,000
Capital: Malabo, pop. 297,000
Currency: CFA franc BEAC (XAF)
Religions: Roman Catholic, Muslim, Baha'i, animist,
Indigenous beliefs
Languages: Spanish, Portuguese, French, Fang, Bubi

Eritrea

Area: 45,406 sq mi (117,600 sq km)
Population: 6,209,000
Capital: Asmara, pop. 1,035,000
Currency: nakfa (ERN)
Religions: Muslim, Oriental Orthodox, Roman Catholic,
Protestant
Languages: Tigrinya, Arabic, English, Tigre, Kunama,
Afar, other Cushitic languages

Estonia

Area: 17,463 sq mi (45,228 sq km)
Population: 1,212,000
Capital: Tallinn, pop. 452,000
Currency: euro (EUR)
Religions: Eastern Orthodox, Protestant
Languages: Estonian, Russian

Eswatini (Swaziland)

Area: 6,704 sq mi (17,364 sq km)
Population: 1,122,000
Capitals: Mbabane, pop. 68,000;
Lobamba, pop. 11,000
Currency: lilangeni (SZL)
Religions: Roman Catholic, other Christian
Languages: English, siSwati

Ethiopia

Area: 426,372 sq mi
(1,104,300 sq km)
Population: 113,657,000
Capital: Addis Ababa,
pop. 5,228,000
Currency: birr (ETB)
Religions: Oriental Orthodox, Muslim, Protestant
Languages: Oromo, Amharic, Somali, Tigrinya, Afar

Fiji

Area: 7,056 sq mi
(18,274 sq km)
Population: 944,000
Capital: Suva, pop. 178,000
Currency: Fijian dollar (FJD)
Religions: Protestant, Roman Catholic, other
Christian, Hindu, Muslim
Languages: English, Fijian, Hindustani

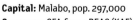

Finland

Area: 130,558 sq mi
(338,145 sq km)
Population: 5,602,000
Capital: Helsinki, pop. 1,328,000
Currency: euro (EUR)
Religion: Protestant
Languages: Finnish, Swedish

France

Area: 248,573 sq mi
(643,801 sq km)
Population: 68,305,000
Capital: Paris, pop. 11,142,000
Currency: euro (EUR)
Religions: Roman Catholic, Muslim
Language: French

Gabon

Area: 103,347 sq mi (267,667 sq km)
Population: 2,341,000
Capital: Libreville, pop. 857,000
Currency: CFA franc BEAC (XAF)
Religions: Roman Catholic, Protestant, other Christian, Muslim
Languages: French, Fang, Myene, Nzebi, Bapounou/Eschira, Bandjabi

Gambia, The

Area: 4,363 sq mi (11,300 sq km)
Population: 2,413,000
Capital: Banjul, pop. 470,000
Currency: dalasi (GMD)
Religion: Muslim
Languages: English, Mandinka, Wolof, Fula

Georgia

Area: 26,911 sq mi (69,700 sq km)
Population: 4,936,000
Capital: Tbilisi, pop. 1,080,000
Currency: lari (GEL)
Religions: Eastern Orthodox, Muslim
Language: Georgian

Germany

Area: 137,847 sq mi
(357,022 sq km)
Population: 84,317,000
Capital: Berlin, pop. 3,571,000
Currency: euro (EUR)
Religions: Roman Catholic, Protestant, Muslim
Language: German

Ghana

Area: 92,098 sq mi (238,533 sq km)
Population: 33,107,000
Capital: Accra, pop. 2,605,000
Currency: cedi (GHC)
Religions: Protestant, Roman Catholic, other Christian, Muslim, traditional
Languages: Assanta, Ewe, Fante, English

Gabon — Greece

Greece

Area: 50,949 sq mi (131,957 sq km)
Population: 10,534,000
Capital: Athens, pop. 3,154,000
Currency: euro (EUR)
Religion: Eastern Orthodox
Language: Greek

Grenada

Area: 133 sq mi (344 sq km)
Population: 114,000
Capital: St. George's, pop. 39,000
Currency: East Caribbean dollar (XCD)
Religions: Protestant, Roman Catholic
Languages: English, French patois

Guatemala

Area: 42,042 sq mi (108,889 sq km)
Population: 17,703,000
Capital: Guatemala City, pop. 3,036,000
Currency: quetzal (GTQ)
Religions: Roman Catholic, Protestant, Indigenous beliefs
Languages: Spanish, Maya languages

Guinea

Area: 94,926 sq mi (245,857 sq km)
Population: 13,238,000
Capital: Conakry, pop. 2,049,000
Currency: Guinean franc (GNF)
Religions: Muslim, Christian
Languages: French, African languages

Guyana

Area: 83,000 sq mi (214,969 sq km)
Population: 790,000
Capital: Georgetown, pop. 110,000
Currency: Guyanese dollar (GYD)
Religions: Hindu, Protestant, Roman Catholic, other Christian, Muslim
Languages: English, Guyanese Creole, Amerindian languages, Indian languages, Chinese

Guinea-Bissau

Area: 13,948 sq mi (36,125 sq km)
Population: 2,027,000
Capital: Bissau, pop. 643,000
Currency: CFA franc BCEAO (XOF)
Religions: Muslim, Christian, animist
Languages: Crioulu, Portuguese, Pular, Mandingo

Haiti

Area: 10,714 sq mi (27,750 sq km)
Population: 11,335,000
Capital: Port-au-Prince, pop. 2,915,000
Currency: gourde (HTG)
Religions: Roman Catholic, Protestant, voodoo
Languages: French, Creole

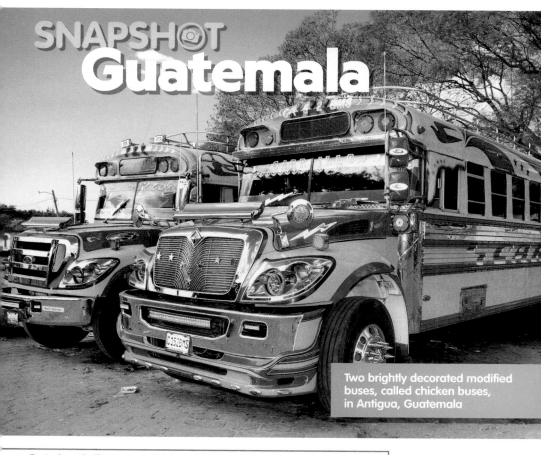

SNAPSHOT
Guatemala

Two brightly decorated modified buses, called chicken buses, in Antigua, Guatemala

Honduras

Area: 43,278 sq mi
(112,090 sq km)
Population: 9,459,000
Capital: Tegucigalpa,
pop. 1,527,000
Currency: lempira (HNL)
Religions: Roman Catholic, Protestant
Languages: Spanish, Amerindian dialects

Iceland

Area: 39,769 sq mi
(103,000 sq km)
Population: 358,000
Capital: Reykjavík, pop. 216,000
Currency: Icelandic krona (ISK)
Religion: Protestant
Languages: Icelandic, English, Nordic
languages, German

Hungary

Area: 35,918 sq mi (93,028 sq km)
Population: 9,700,000
Capital: Budapest, pop. 1,775,000
Currency: forint (HUF)
Religions: Roman Catholic, Protestant
Languages: Hungarian, English, German

India

Area: 1,269,219 sq mi (3,287,263 sq km)
Population: 1,389,637,000
Capital: New Delhi, pop. 32,066,000
Currency: Indian rupee (INR)
Religions: Hindu, Muslim
Languages: Hindi, English

SNAPSHOT
Japan

A group of Japanese macaques bathe
in a hot spring in a snow-covered valley
inside Joshin'etsu-Kogen National Park.

COLOR KEY ● Africa ● Australia, New Zealand, and Oceania

Indonesia

Area: 735,358 sq mi
(1,904,569 sq km)
Population: 277,329,000
Capital: Jakarta, pop. 11,075,000
Currency: Indonesian rupiah (IDR)
Religions: Muslim, Protestant
Languages: Bahasa Indonesia, English, Dutch, local dialects

Iran

Area: 636,371 sq mi
(1,648,195 sq km)
Population: 86,758,000
Capital: Tehran, pop. 9,382,000
Currency: Iranian rial (IRR)
Religion: Muslim
Languages: Persian (Farsi), Turkic dialects, Kurdish

Iraq

Area: 169,235 sq mi
(438,317 sq km)
Population: 40,463,000
Capital: Baghdad, pop. 7,512,000
Currency: Iraqi dinar (IQD)
Religion: Muslim
Languages: Arabic, Kurdish, Turkmen, Syriac, Armenian

Ireland (Éire)

Area: 27,133 sq mi
(70,273 sq km)
Population: 5,275,000
Capital: Dublin
(Baile Átha Cliath), pop. 1,256,000
Currency: euro (EUR)
Religion: Roman Catholic
Languages: English, Irish (Gaelic)

Israel

Area: 8,970 sq mi (23,232 sq km)
Population: 8,915,000
Capital: Jerusalem, pop. 957,000
Currency: new Israeli shekel (ILS)
Religions: Jewish, Muslim
Languages: Hebrew, Arabic, English

Italy

Area: 116,348 sq mi
(301,340 sq km)
Population: 61,096,000
Capital: Rome, pop. 4,298,000
Currency: euro (EUR)
Religion: Roman Catholic
Languages: Italian, German, French, Slovene

Jamaica

Area: 4,244 sq mi
(10,991 sq km)
Population: 2,819,000
Capital: Kingston, pop. 595,000
Currency: Jamaican dollar (JMD)
Religion: Protestant
Languages: English, English patois

Japan

Area: 145,914 sq mi (377,915 sq km)
Population: 124,215,000
Capital: Tokyo, pop. 37,274,000
Currency: yen (JPY)
Religions: Shinto, Buddhist
Language: Japanese

Jordan

Area: 34,495 sq mi
(89,342 sq km)
Population: 10,999,000
Capital: Amman, pop. 2,210,000
Currency: Jordanian dinar (JOD)
Religion: Muslim
Languages: Arabic, English

Kazakhstan

Area: 1,052,089 sq mi
(2,724,900 sq km)
Population: 19,398,000
Capital: Astana pop. 1,254,000
Currency: tenge (KZT)
Religions: Muslim, Eastern Orthodox
Languages: Kazakh (Qazaq), Russian, English

Kenya

Area: 224,081 sq mi (580,367 sq km)
Population: 55,865,000
Capital: Nairobi, pop. 5,119,000
Currency: Kenyan shilling (KES)
Religions: Protestant, Roman Catholic, other Christian, Muslim
Languages: English, Kiswahili, Indigenous languages

Kiribati

Area: 313 sq mi (811 sq km)
Population: 114,000
Capital: Tarawa, pop. 64,000
Currency: Australian dollar (AUD)
Religions: Roman Catholic, Protestant, Mormon
Languages: I-Kiribati, English

Kosovo

Area: 4,203 sq mi (10,887 sq km)
Population: 1,953,000
Capital: Pristina, pop. 217,000
Currency: euro (EUR)
Religion: Muslim
Languages: Albanian, Serbian, Bosnian

Kuwait

Area: 6,880 sq mi (17,818 sq km)
Population: 3,068,000
Capital: Kuwait City, pop. 3,239,000
Currency: Kuwaiti dinar (KWD)
Religions: Muslim, Christian
Languages: Arabic, English

Kyrgyzstan

Area: 77,201 sq mi (199,951 sq km)
Population: 6,072,000
Capital: Bishkek, pop. 1,082,000
Currency: Som (KGS)
Religions: Muslim, Eastern Orthodox
Languages: Kyrgyz, Uzbek, Russian

Laos

Area: 91,429 sq mi (236,800 sq km)
Population: 7,750,000
Capital: Vientiane, pop. 706,000
Currency: kip (LAK)
Religion: Buddhist
Languages: Lao, French, English, ethnic languages

Latvia

Area: 24,938 sq mi (64,589 sq km)
Population: 1,842,000
Capital: Riga, pop. 625,000
Currency: euro (EUR)
Religions: Protestant, Roman Catholic, Eastern Orthodox, Druze
Languages: Latvian, Russian

Lebanon

Area: 4,015 sq mi (10,400 sq km)
Population: 5,297,000
Capital: Beirut, pop. 2,433,000
Currency: Lebanese pound (LBP)
Religions: Muslim, Eastern Catholic
Languages: Arabic, French, English, Armenian

Lesotho

Area: 11,720 sq mi (30,355 sq km)
Population: 2,194,000
Capital: Maseru, pop. 202,000
Currency: loti (LSL)
Religions: Protestant, Roman Catholic, other Christian
Languages: Sesotho, English, Zulu, Xhosa

Liberia

Area: 43,000 sq mi (111,369 sq km)
Population: 5,358,000
Capital: Monrovia, pop. 1,623,000
Currency: Liberian dollar (LRD)
Religions: Christian, Muslim
Languages: English, Indigenous languages

Libya

Area: 679,362 sq mi (1,759,540 sq km)
Population: 7,138,000
Capital: Tripoli, pop. 1,176,000
Currency: Libyan dinar (LYD)
Religion: Muslim
Languages: Arabic, Italian, English, Berber

Lithuania

Area: 25,212 sq mi (65,300 sq km)
Population: 2,684,000
Capital: Vilnius, pop. 541,000
Currency: euro (EUR)
Religion: Roman Catholic
Language: Lithuanian

Liechtenstein

Area: 62 sq mi (160 sq km)
Population: 40,000
Capital: Vaduz, pop. 5,000
Currency: Swiss franc (CHF)
Religions: Roman Catholic, Protestant, Muslim
Language: German

Luxembourg

Area: 998 sq mi (2,586 sq km)
Population: 650,000
Capital: Luxembourg, pop. 120,000
Currency: euro (EUR)
Religion: Roman Catholic
Languages: Luxembourgish, Portuguese, French, German

SNAPSHOT Libya

Situated just off the Mediterranean Sea near downtown Tripoli, the Red Castle was an important fortress in the Byzantine era.

● Asia ● Europe ● North America ● South America

Madagascar

Area: 226,658 sq mi
(587,041 sq km)
Population: 28,172,000
Capital: Antananarivo,
pop. 3,700,000
Currency: Malagasy ariary (MGA)
Religions: Christian, Indigenous beliefs, Muslim
Languages: French, Malagasy, English

Madagascar is home to the INDRI, the WORLD'S LARGEST LEMUR SPECIES, which can GROW AS TALL AS A TODDLER.

Malawi

Area: 45,747 sq mi
(118,484 sq km)
Population: 20,794,000
Capital: Lilongwe, pop. 1,222,000
Currency: Malawian kwacha (MWK)
Religions: Protestant, Roman Catholic, other
Christian, Muslim
Languages: English, Chewa, other Bantu languages

Malaysia

Area: 127,355 sq mi (329,847 sq km)
Population: 33,871,000
Capital: Kuala Lumpur,
pop. 8,420,000
Currency: ringgit (MYR)
Religions: Muslim, Buddhist, Christian, Hindu
Languages: Bahasa Malaysia (Malay), English, Chinese,
Tamil, Telugu, Malayalam, Panjabi, Thai

Maldives

Area: 115 sq mi (298 sq km)
Population: 390,000
Capital: Male, pop. 177,000
Currency: rufiyaa (MVR)
Religion: Muslim
Languages: Dhivehi, English

Mali

Area: 478,841 sq mi (1,240,192 sq km)
Population: 20,742,000
Capital: Bamako, pop. 2,817,000
Currency: CFA franc BCEAO (XOF)
Religion: Muslim
Languages: French, Bambara, African languages

Malta

Area: 122 sq mi (316 sq km)
Population: 464,000
Capital: Valletta, pop. 213,000
Currency: euro (EUR)
Religion: Roman Catholic
Languages: Maltese, English

Marshall Islands

Area: 70 sq mi (181 sq km)
Population: 80,000
Capital: Majuro, pop. 31,000
Currency: U.S. dollar (USD)
Religions: Protestant, Roman Catholic, Mormon
Languages: Marshallese, English

Mauritania

Area: 397,955 sq mi
(1,030,700 sq km)
Population: 4,162,000
Capital: Nouakchott, pop. 1,432,000
Currency: ouguiya (MRU)
Religion: Muslim
Languages: Arabic, Pulaar, Soninke, Wolof, French

Mauritius

Area: 788 sq mi (2,040 sq km)
Population: 1,308,000
Capital: Port Louis, pop. 149,000
Currency: Mauritian rupee (MUR)
Religions: Hindu, Muslim,
Roman Catholic, other Christian
Languages: Creole, English

Mexico

Area: 758,449 sq mi
(1,964,375 sq km)
Population: 129,151,000
Capital: Mexico City,
pop. 22,085,000
Currency: Mexican peso (MXN)
Religions: Roman Catholic, Protestant
Language: Spanish

Micronesia, Federated States of

Area: 271 sq mi (702 sq km)
Population: 101,000
Capital: Palikir, pop. 7,000
Currency: U.S. dollar (USD)
Religions: Roman Catholic, Protestant
Languages: English, Chuukese, Kosrean, Pohnpeian,
other Indigenous languages

3 cool things about MICRONESIA

1. Micronesia is made up of some 600 islands and atolls, extending 1,700 miles (2,730 km) in the western Pacific Ocean.

2. In Micronesia's Truk Lagoon, divers can explore the shipwrecks of more than 60 Japanese vessels.

3. Traditional stone money called rai—which stands as tall as an adult human—is still exchanged during ceremonies, such as weddings, on the island of Yap, in Micronesia.

Moldova

Area: 13,070 sq mi
(33,851 sq km)
Population: 3,287,000
Capital: Chișinău,
pop. 491,000
Currency: Moldovan leu (MDL)
Religion: Eastern Orthodox
Languages: Moldovan, Romanian

Monaco

Area: 1 sq mi (2 sq km)
Population: 31,000
Capital: Monaco, pop. 31,000
Currency: euro (EUR)
Religion: Roman Catholic
Languages: French, English, Italian, Monegasque

Mongolia

Area: 603,908 sq mi
(1,564,116 sq km)
Population: 3,228,000
Capital: Ulaanbaatar,
pop. 1,645,000
Currency: tugrik (MNT)
Religion: Buddhist
Languages: Mongolian, Turkic, Russian

Montenegro

Area: 5,333 sq mi
(13,812 sq km)
Population: 605,000
Capital: Podgorica, pop. 177,000
Currency: euro (EUR)
Religions: Eastern Orthodox, Muslim
Languages: Serbian, Montenegrin

Morocco

Area: 276,662 sq mi
(716,550 sq km)
Population: 36,738,000
Capital: Rabat, pop. 1,932,000
Currency: Moroccan dirham (MAD)
Religion: Muslim
Languages: Arabic, Tamazight, other Berber
languages, French

Mozambique

Area: 308,642 sq mi
(799,380 sq km)
Population: 31,693,000
Capital: Maputo, pop. 1,139,000
Currency: metical (MZN)
Religions: Roman Catholic, Protestant, other
Christian, Muslim
Languages: Makhuwa, Portuguese, local languages

Myanmar (Burma)

Area: 261,228 sq mi
(676,578 sq km)
Population: 57,526,000
Capital: Nay Pyi Taw,
pop. 683,000
Currency: kyat (MMK)
Religions: Buddhist, Christian
Language: Burmese

Nauru

Area: 8 sq mi (21 sq km)
Population: 10,000
Capital: Yaren, pop. 800
Currency: Australian
dollar (AUD)
Religions: Protestant, Roman Catholic
Languages: Nauruan, English

Namibia

Area: 318,261 sq mi
(824,292 sq km)
Population: 2,727,000
Capital: Windhoek, pop. 461,000
Currency: Namibian dollar (NAD)
Religions: Protestant, Indigenous beliefs
Languages: Indigenous languages, Afrikaans, English

Nepal

Area: 56,827 sq mi
(147,181 sq km)
Population: 30,667,000
Capital: Kathmandu, pop. 1,521,000
Currency: Nepalese rupee (NPR)
Religions: Hindu, Buddhist
Languages: Nepali, Maithali

SNAPSHOT
North Korea

North Koreans participate in a
mass dance in a Pyongyang square.

COLOR KEY ● Africa ● Australia, New Zealand, and Oceania

Netherlands

Area: 16,040 sq mi
(41,543 sq km)
Population: 17,401,000
Capitals: Amsterdam, pop. 1,166,000;
The Hague, pop. 709,000
Currency: euro (EUR)
Religions: Roman Catholic, Protestant, Muslim
Language: Dutch

New Zealand

Area: 103,799 sq mi
(268,838 sq km)
Population: 5,053,000
Capital: Wellington, pop. 419,000
Currency: New Zealand dollar (NZD)
Religions: Roman Catholic, Protestant
Languages: English, Maori

Nicaragua

Area: 50,336 sq mi
(130,370 sq km)
Population: 6,302,000
Capital: Managua, pop. 1,083,000
Currency: cordoba oro (NIO)
Religions: Roman Catholic, Protestant
Language: Spanish

Niger

Area: 489,191 sq mi (1,267,000 sq km)
Population: 24,485,000
Capital: Niamey, pop. 1,384,000
Currency: CFA franc BCEAO (XOF)
Religion: Muslim
Languages: French, Hausa, Djerma

Nigeria

Area: 356,669 sq mi
(923,768 sq km)
Population: 225,082,000
Capital: Abuja, pop. 3,652,000
Currency: naira (NGN)
Religions: Muslim, Roman Catholic, other Christian
Languages: English, Indigenous languages

North Korea

Area: 46,540 sq mi
(120,538 sq km)
Population: 25,955,000
Capital: Pyongyang,
pop. 3,133,000
Currency: North Korean won (KPW)
Religions: Buddhist, Confucianist, Christian,
syncretic Chondogyo
Language: Korean

North Macedonia

Area: 9,928 sq mi
(25,713 sq km)
Population: 2,131,000
Capital: Skopje, pop. 606,000
Currency: Macedonian denar (MKD)
Religions: Macedonian Orthodox, Muslim
Languages: Macedonian, Albanian

Norway

Area: 125,021 sq mi
(323,802 sq km)
Population: 5,554,000
Capital: Oslo, pop. 1,071,000
Currency: Norwegian krone (NOK)
Religion: Protestant
Languages: Bokmal Norwegian, Nynorsk Norwegian

Oman

Area: 119,499 sq mi
(309,500 sq km)
Population: 3,764,000
Capital: Muscat, pop. 1,623,000
Currency: Omani rial (OMR)
Religions: Muslim, Christian, Hindu
Languages: Arabic, English, Baluchi, Swahili, Urdu,
Indian dialects

Pakistan

Area: 307,374 sq mi
(796,095 sq km)
Population: 242,924,000
Capital: Islamabad, pop. 1,198,000
Currency: Pakistan rupee (PKR)
Religion: Muslim
Languages: Punjabi, Sindhi, Saraiki, Urdu, English

● Asia ● Europe ● North America ● **South America**

Palau

Area: 177 sq mi (459 sq km)
Population: 22,000
Capital: Ngerulmud, pop. 300
Currency: U.S. dollar (USD)
Religions: Roman Catholic, Protestant, Modekngei
Languages: Palauan, English, Filipino

Philippines

Area: 115,831 sq mi (300,000 sq km)
Population: 114,597,000
Capital: Manila, pop. 14,406,000
Currency: Philippine peso (PHP)
Religions: Roman Catholic, Protestant, Muslim
Languages: Filipino (Tagalog), English, Indigenous languages

Panama

Area: 29,120 sq mi (75,420 sq km)
Population: 4,338,000
Capital: Panama City, pop. 1,938,000
Currency: balboa (PAB)
Religions: Roman Catholic, Protestant
Languages: Spanish, Indigenous languages, English

Poland

Area: 120,728 sq mi (312,685 sq km)
Population: 38,093,000
Capital: Warsaw, pop. 1,795,000
Currency: zloty (PLN)
Religion: Roman Catholic
Language: Polish

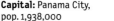

Area: 178,703 sq mi (462,840 sq km)
Population: 9,593,000
Capital: Port Moresby, pop. 400,000
Currency: kina (PGK)
Religions: Protestant, Roman Catholic, other Christian
Languages: Tok Pisin, English, Hiri Motu, other Indigenous languages

Portugal

Area: 35,556 sq mi (92,090 sq km)
Population: 10,242,000
Capital: Lisbon, pop. 2,986,000
Currency: euro (EUR)
Religion: Roman Catholic
Languages: Portuguese, Mirandese

Paraguay

Area: 157,048 sq mi (406,752 sq km)
Population: 7,356,000
Capital: Asunción (Paraguay), pop. 3,452,000
Currency: Guarani (PYG)
Religions: Roman Catholic, Protestant
Languages: Spanish, Guarani

Qatar

Area: 4,473 sq mi (11,586 sq km)
Population: 2,508,000
Capital: Doha, pop. 652,000
Currency: Qatari rial (QAR)
Religions: Muslim, Christian, Hindu
Languages: Arabic, English

Peru

Area: 496,224 sq mi (1,285,216 sq km)
Population: 32,276,000
Capital: Lima, pop. 11,045,000
Currency: nuevo sol (PEN)
Religions: Roman Catholic, Protestant
Languages: Spanish, Quechua, Aymara

Romania

Area: 92,043 sq mi (238,391 sq km)
Population: 18,520,000
Capital: Bucharest, pop. 1,785,000
Currency: leu (RON)
Religions: Eastern Orthodox, Protestant
Language: Romanian

COLOR KEY ● Africa ● Australia, New Zealand, and Oceania

Russia

Area: 6,601,665 sq mi
(17,098,242 sq km)
Population: 142,022,000
Capital: Moscow, pop. 12,641,000
Currency: Russian ruble (RUB)
Religions: Eastern Orthodox, Muslim
Language: Russian
Note: Russia is in both Europe and Asia, but its capital is in Europe, so it is classified here as a European country.

Samoa

Area: 1,093 sq mi
(2,831 sq km)
Population: 206,000
Capital: Apia, pop. 36,000
Currency: tala (SAT)
Religions: Protestant, Roman Catholic, Mormon
Languages: Samoan (Polynesian), English

Rwanda

Area: 10,169 sq mi
(26,338 sq km)
Population: 13,174,000
Capital: Kigali, pop. 1,208,000
Currency: Rwandan franc (RWF)
Religions: Protestant, Roman Catholic
Languages: Kinyarwanda, French, English, Kiswahili (Swahili)

San Marino

Area: 24 sq mi (61 sq km)
Population: 35,000
Capital: San Marino, pop. 4,000
Currency: euro (EUR)
Religion: Roman Catholic
Language: Italian

SNAPSHOT Palau

A saltwater crocodile, which can grow up to 17 feet (5 m) long, lurks below the surface in waters off the coast of Palau.

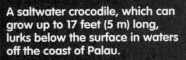

Asia ● Europe ● North America ● **South America**

325

Sao Tome and Principe

Area: 372 sq mi (964 sq km)
Population: 217,000
Capital: São Tomé, pop. 80,000
Currency: dobra (STN)
Religion: Roman Catholic
Languages: Portuguese, Forro

Saudi Arabia

Area: 830,000 sq mi (2,149,690 sq km)
Population: 35,354,000
Capital: Riyadh, pop. 7,538,000
Currency: Saudi riyal (SAR)
Religion: Muslim
Language: Arabic

Senegal

Area: 75,955 sq mi (196,722 sq km)
Population: 17,923,000
Capital: Dakar, pop. 3,326,000
Currency: CFA franc BCEAO (XOF)
Religion: Muslim
Languages: French, Wolof, other Indigenous languages

Serbia

Area: 29,913 sq mi (77,474 sq km)
Population: 6,739,000
Capital: Belgrade, pop. 1,405,000
Currency: Serbian dinar (RSD)
Religions: Eastern Orthodox, Roman Catholic
Language: Serbian

Seychelles

Area: 176 sq mi (455 sq km)
Population: 97,000
Capital: Victoria, pop. 28,000
Currency: Seychelles rupee (SCR)
Religions: Roman Catholic, Protestant
Languages: Seychellois Creole, English, French

Sierra Leone

Area: 27,699 sq mi (71,740 sq km)
Population: 8,693,000
Capital: Freetown, pop. 1,272,000
Currency: leone (SLL)
Religions: Muslim, Christian
Languages: English, Mende, Temne, Krio

Singapore

Area: 278 sq mi (719 sq km)
Population: 5,921,000
Capital: Singapore, pop. 5,921,000
Currency: Singapore dollar (SGD)
Religions: Buddhist, Christian, Muslim, Taoist, Hindu
Languages: English, Mandarin, other Chinese dialects, Malay, Tamil

3 cool things about SINGAPORE

1. Singapore's mascot is the merlion, a half-fish, half-lion mythical creature said to represent Singapore's name in Malay—Singapura—which means "Lion City."

2. The country's Changi Airport features a butterfly garden, an indoor waterfall, a movie theater, and Singapore's tallest slide at four stories high.

3. Singapore's Night Safari, the world's first nighttime zoo, welcomes guests to check out animals in the dark.

Slovakia

Area: 18,933 sq mi (49,035 sq km)
Population: 5,431,000
Capital: Bratislava, pop. 439,000
Currency: euro (EUR)
Religions: Roman Catholic, Protestant
Language: Slovak

Slovenia

Area: 7,827 sq mi
(20,273 sq km)
Population: 2,101,000
Capital: Ljubljana,
pop. 286,000
Currency: euro (EUR)
Religion: Roman Catholic
Language: Slovenian

Solomon Islands

Area: 11,157 sq mi
(28,896 sq km)
Population: 703,000
Capital: Honiara, pop. 82,000
Currency: Solomon Islands dollar (SBD)
Religions: Protestant, Roman Catholic
Languages: Melanesian pidgin, English,
Indigenous languages

Somalia

Area: 246,201 sq mi
(637,657 sq km)
Population: 12,386,000
Capital: Mogadishu, pop. 2,497,000
Currency: Somali shilling (SOS)
Religion: Muslim
Languages: Somali, Arabic, Italian, English

South Africa

Area: 470,693 sq mi (1,219,090 sq km)
Population: 57,517,000
Capitals: Pretoria (Tshwane),
pop. 2,740,000; Cape Town, pop.
4,801,000; Bloemfontein, pop. 588,000
Currency: rand (ZAR)
Religions: Christian, traditional or animist
Languages: isiZulu, isiXhosa, other Indigenous languages,
Afrikaans, English

South Korea

Area: 38,502 sq mi
(99,720 sq km)
Population: 51,845,000
Capital: Seoul, pop. 9,976,000
Currency: South Korean won (KRW)
Religions: Protestant, Buddhist, Roman Catholic
Languages: Korean, English

South Sudan

Area: 248,777 sq mi
(644,329 sq km)
Population: 11,545,000
Capital: Juba, pop. 440,000
Currency: South Sudanese pound (SSP)
Religions: animist, Christian, Muslim
Languages: English, Arabic, Dinka, Nuer, Bari,
Zande, Shilluk

Spain

Area: 195,124 sq mi (505,370 sq km)
Population: 47,163,000
Capital: Madrid, pop. 6,714,000
Currency: euro (EUR)
Religion: Roman Catholic
Languages: Castilian Spanish, Catalan,
Galician, Basque

Sri Lanka

Area: 25,332 sq mi
(65,610 sq km)
Population: 23,188,000
Capitals: Colombo, pop. 626,000
Sri Jayewardenepura Kotte, pop. 103,000
Currency: Sri Lankan rupee (LKR)
Religions: Buddhist, Hindu, Muslim, Roman Catholic
Languages: Sinhala, Tamil, English

St. Kitts and Nevis

Area: 101 sq mi (261 sq km)
Population: 54,000
Capital: Basseterre, pop. 14,000
Currency: East Caribbean
dollar (XCD)
Religions: Protestant, Roman Catholic
Language: English

St. Lucia

Area: 238 sq mi (616 sq km)
Population: 167,000
Capital: Castries,
pop. 22,000
Currency: East Caribbean dollar (XCD)
Religions: Roman Catholic, Protestant
Languages: English, French patois

St. Vincent and the Grenadines

Area: 150 sq mi (389 sq km)
Population: 101,000
Capital: Kingstown, pop. 27,000
Currency: East Caribbean dollar (XCD)
Religions: Protestant, Roman Catholic
Languages: English, Vincentian Creole English, French patois

Sudan

Area: 718,723 sq mi (1,861,484 sq km)
Population: 47,959,000
Capital: Khartoum, pop. 6,160,000
Currency: Sudanese pound (SDG)
Religion: Muslim
Languages: Arabic, English, Nubian, Ta Bedawie, Fur

Suriname

Area: 63,251 sq mi (163,820 sq km)
Population: 633,000
Capital: Paramaribo, pop. 239,000
Currency: Surinamese dollar (SRD)
Religions: Protestant, Hindu, Roman Catholic, Muslim
Languages: Dutch, English, Sranang Tongo, Caribbean Hindustani, Javanese

SURINAME is one of the world's few CARBON NEGATIVE COUNTRIES, meaning they absorb more greenhouse gases than they emit from human activities.

Sweden

Area: 173,860 sq mi (450,295 sq km)
Population: 10,484,000
Capital: Stockholm, pop. 1,679,000
Currency: Swedish krona (SEK)
Religion: Protestant
Language: Swedish

Switzerland

Area: 15,937 sq mi (41,277 sq km)
Population: 8,509,000
Capital: Bern, pop. 437,000
Currency: Swiss franc (CHF)
Religions: Roman Catholic, Protestant, other Christian, Muslim
Languages: German (Swiss German), French, Italian, Romansch

Syria

Area: 71,870 sq mi (186,142 sq km)
Population: 21,564,000
Capital: Damascus, pop. 2,503,000
Currency: Syrian pound (SYP)
Religions: Muslim, Eastern Orthodox, Oriental Orthodox, Eastern Catholic, other Christian
Languages: Arabic, Kurdish, Armenian, Aramaic, Circassian, French, English

Tajikistan

Area: 55,637 sq mi (144,100 sq km)
Population: 9,119,000
Capital: Dushanbe, pop. 962,000
Currency: Tajikistani somoni (TJS)
Religion: Muslim
Languages: Tajik, Uzbek

Tanzania

Area: 365,754 sq mi (947,300 sq km)
Population: 63,853,000
Capitals: Dar es Salaam, pop. 7,405,000; Dodoma, pop. 262,000
Currency: Tanzanian shilling (TZS)
Religions: Christian, Muslim
Languages: Kiswahili (Swahili), Kiunguja, English, Arabic, local languages

Thailand

Area: 198,117 sq mi (513,120 sq km)
Population: 69,648,000
Capital: Bangkok, pop. 10,900,000
Currency: baht (THB)
Religion: Buddhist
Languages: Thai, English

COLOR KEY ● Africa ● Australia, New Zealand, and Oceania

Timor-Leste

Area: 5,743 sq mi
(14,874 sq km)
Population: 1,445,000
Capital: Dili, pop. 281,000
Currency: U.S. dollar (USD)
Religion: Roman Catholic
Languages: Tetun, Mambai, Makasai, Portuguese, Indonesian, English

Togo

Area: 21,925 sq mi (56,785 sq km)
Population: 8,492,000
Capital: Lomé, pop. 1,926,000
Currency: CFA franc BCEAO (XOF)
Religions: Christian, folk religion, Muslim
Languages: French, Ewe, Mina, Kabye, Dagomba

Tonga

Area: 288 sq mi (747 sq km)
Population: 106,000
Capital: Nuku´alofa,
pop. 23,000
Currency: pa'anga (TOP)
Religions: Protestant, Mormon, Roman Catholic
Languages: Tongan, English

Trinidad and Tobago

Area: 1,980 sq mi (5,128 sq km)
Population: 1,406,000
Capital: Port of Spain,
pop. 545,000
Currency: Trinidad and Tobago dollar (TTD)
Religions: Protestant, Roman Catholic, Hindu, Muslim
Languages: English, Creole, Caribbean Hindustani, Spanish, Chinese

Tunisia

Area: 63,170 sq mi
(163,610 sq km)
Population: 11,897,000
Capital: Tunis, pop. 2,439,000
Currency: Tunisian dinar (TND)
Religion: Muslim
Languages: Arabic, French, Berber

Türkiye (Turkey)

Area: 302,535 sq mi
(783,562 sq km)
Population: 83,048,000
Capital: Ankara, pop. 5,310,000
Currency: Turkish lira (TRY)
Religion: Muslim
Languages: Turkish, Kurdish

Turkmenistan

Area: 188,456 sq mi
(488,100 sq km)
Population: 5,636,000
Capital: Ashgabat, pop. 883,000
Currency: Turkmenistani manat (TMT)
Religions: Muslim, Eastern Orthodox
Languages: Turkmen, Russian

Tuvalu

Area: 10 sq mi (26 sq km)
Population: 12,000
Capital: Funafuti,
pop. 7,000
Currency: Australian dollar (AUD)
Religion: Protestant
Languages: Tuvaluan, English, Samoan, Kiribati

Uganda

Area: 93,065 sq mi
(241,038 sq km)
Population: 46,206,000
Capital: Kampala, pop. 3,652,000
Currency: Ugandan shilling (UGX)
Religions: Protestant, Roman Catholic, Muslim
Languages: English, Ganda (Luganda), local languages, Swahili, Arabic

FOSSILS of a SCHOOL BUS–SIZE ANCIENT REPTILE were unearthed in TUNISIA.

Ukraine

Area: 233,032 sq mi (603,550 sq km)
Population: 43,528,000
Capital: Kyiv, pop. 3,010,000
Currency: hryvnia (UAH)
Religions: Eastern Orthodox, Eastern Catholic, Roman Catholic, Protestant
Languages: Ukrainian, Russian

United Kingdom

Area: 94,058 sq mi (243,610 sq km)
Population: 67,791,000
Capital: London, pop. 9,541,000
Currency: pound sterling (GBP)
Religions: Protestant, Roman Catholic
Languages: English, Scots, Scottish Gaelic, Welsh, Irish, Cornish

United Arab Emirates

Area: 32,278 sq mi (83,600 sq km)
Population: 9,916,000
Capital: Abu Dhabi, pop. 1,540,000
Currency: UAE dirham (AED)
Religions: Muslim, Christian
Languages: Arabic, English, Hindi, Malayam, Urdu, Pashto, Tagalog, Persian

United States

Area: 3,796,741 sq mi (9,833,517 sq km)
Population: 337,342,000
Capital: Washington, D.C., pop. 670,000
Currency: U.S. dollar (USD)
Religions: Protestant, Roman Catholic
Languages: English, Spanish, Native American languages

SNAPSHOT
United Arab Emirates

The Burj Khalifa, the world's tallest building, soars above Dubai, U.A.E.

COLOR KEY ● Africa ● Australia, New Zealand, and Oceania

Uruguay

Area: 68,037 sq mi
(176,215 sq km)
Population: 3,407,000
Capital: Montevideo, pop. 1,767,000
Currency: Uruguayan peso (UYU)
Religions: Roman Catholic, other Christian
Language: Spanish

Uzbekistan

Area: 172,742 sq mi
(447,400 sq km)
Population: 31,105,000
Capital: Tashkent,
pop. 2,574,000
Currency: Uzbekistan sum (UZS)
Religions: Muslim, Eastern Orthodox
Languages: Uzbek, Russian, Tajik

Vanuatu

Area: 4,706 sq mi (12,189 sq km)
Population: 308,000
Capital: Port-Vila, pop. 53,000
Currency: Vatu (VUV)
Religions: Protestant, Roman Catholic
Languages: local languages, Bislama, English, French

Vatican City

Area: 0.2 sq mi (0.4 sq km)
Population: 1,000
Capital: Vatican City, pop. 1,000
Currency: euro (EUR)
Religion: Roman Catholic
Languages: Italian, Latin, French

Venezuela

Area: 352,144 sq mi
(912,050 sq km)
Population: 29,790,000
Capital: Caracas, pop. 2,957,000
Currency: bolivar soberano (VES)
Religion: Roman Catholic
Languages: Spanish, Indigenous languages

Vietnam

Area: 127,881 sq mi
(331,210 sq km)
Population: 103,808,000
Capital: Hanoi, pop. 5,067,000
Currency: dong (VND)
Religions: Buddhist, Roman Catholic
Languages: Vietnamese, English, French, Chinese,
Khmer, Mon-Khmer, Malayo-Polynesian

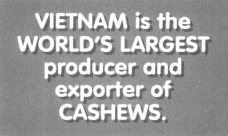

VIETNAM is the WORLD'S LARGEST producer and exporter of CASHEWS.

Yemen

Area: 203,850 sq mi
(527,968 sq km)
Population: 30,985,000
Capital: Sanaa, pop. 3,182,000
Currency: Yemeni rial (YER)
Religion: Muslim
Language: Arabic

Zambia

Area: 290,587 sq mi
(752,618 sq km)
Population: 19,642,000
Capital: Lusaka, pop. 3,042,000
Currency: Zambian kwacha (ZMW)
Religions: Protestant, Roman Catholic
Languages: Bembe, Nyanja, Tonga, other Indigenous
languages, English

Zimbabwe

Area: 150,872 sq mi
(390,757 sq km)
Population: 15,121,000
Capital: Harare, pop. 1,558,000
Currency: Zimbabwean dollar (ZWL)
Religions: Protestant, Roman Catholic, other Christian
Languages: Shona, Ndebele, English,
Indigenous languages

● Asia ● Europe ● North America ● **South America**

THE POLITICAL
UNITED STATES

9:00 AM PACIFIC TIME

10:00 AM

MOUNTAIN TIME

Cape Flattery

Seattle
Olympia ⊛ Tacoma
Columbia
WASHINGTON   Spokane
Yakima
Portland   Great Falls   Minot
Columbia   Lewiston
Salem   MONTANA   NORTH DAKOTA
Butte Helena   Bismarck
Eugene
OREGON   Billings
Medford   Aberdeen
Klamath Falls   Cody
Snake   Idaho   Yellowstone L.   SOUTH DAKOTA
Eureka   Boise   Falls   Pierre
Redding   Pocatello   WYOMING   Rapid
                                                        City
                                    Casper   N. Platte   Missouri
                        Great   Ogden   Cheyenne
                        Salt   Laramie   NEBRASKA
                Reno   Lake   Salt Lake   Grand
                Carson City   City   Fort Collins   Island
Sacramento   Lake Tahoe   Basin   Provo   Platte
San   Oakland   NEVADA   UTAH   Grand   Boulder
Francisco San Jose   Junction   Denver
Salinas   COLORADO
Fresno   Mojave   Lake   Pueblo
                Las   Powell   Colorado   KANSA
Bakersfield   Vegas Lake   Colorado Springs   Dodge City
Point   Mead   Arkansas   Wichita
Conception   Desert   Grand Canyon
Los Angeles   Flagstaff   Santa Fe
Long Beach   Riverside   Albuquerque   Amarillo   OKLAH
                Salton   ARIZONA   Oklahoma City
San Diego   Sea   Phoenix Mesa   NEW MEXICO   Lawton
                Yuma   Wichita Falls
                                                    Lubbock
                    Tucson   Roswell   Fort Worth
                                    Las Cruces   Midland   Abilene
                North Slope   Odessa   Waco
                Brooks Range   El Paso   TEXAS
7:00 AM   Yukon   Austin
HAWAI'I-   Alaska Range   San Antonio
ALEUTIAN   Juneau
TIME   Anchorage   Kaua'i   Corpus
                                Ni'ihau O'ahu   Christi
            ALASKA   Honolulu   Moloka'i   Laredo
                            0   400 miles   Lāna'i Maui
        ALEUTIAN ISLANDS   Alaska Peninsula   0   400 kilometers   HAWAI'I   Kaho'olawe Hilo Hawai'i   Brownsville
                                            0   150 mi   HAWAI'I-
8:00 AM   0   150 km   ALEUTIAN
ALASKA TIME   **7:00 AM**   TIME

The United States is made up of 50 states joined like a giant quilt. Each is unique, but together they make a national fabric held together by a constitution and a federal government. State boundaries, outlined in dotted lines on the map, set apart internal political units within the country. The national capital—Washington, D.C.—is marked by a star in a double circle. The capital of each state is marked by a star in a single circle.

11:00 AM
CENTRAL TIME

12:00 NOON
EASTERN TIME

TIME ZONES: Earth is divided into 24 time zones, each about 15 degrees of longitude wide, reflecting the distance Earth turns from west to east each hour. The U.S. is divided into six time zones, indicated by red dotted lines on the map.

THE PHYSICAL UNITED STATES

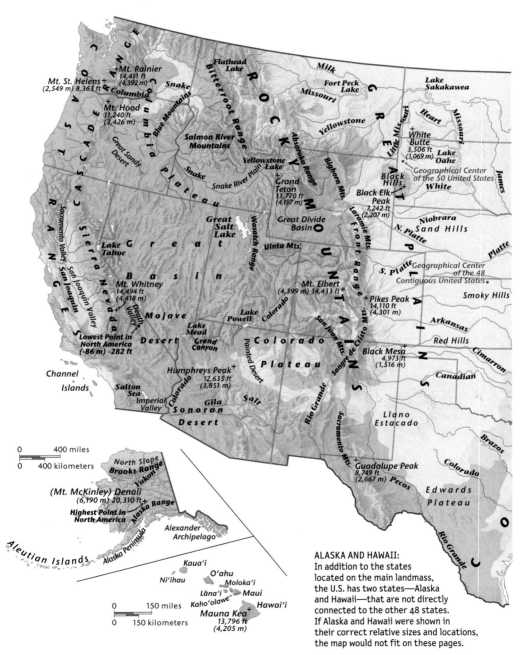

Mt. St. Helens+
(2,549 m) 8,363 ft
+Mt. Rainier
14,411 ft
(4,392 m)
+Mt. Hood
11,240 ft
(3,426 m)

Flathead Lake

Snake

Milk

Fort Peck Lake

Missouri

Lake Sakakawea

COLUMBIA

Columbia

Blue Mountains

ROCKY

Great Sandy Desert

Bitterroot Range

Salmon River Mountains

Columbia Plateau

Snake River Plain

Snake

Yellowstone Lake

Yellowstone

Absaroka Range

Bighorn Mts.

Little Missouri

Heart

Missouri

White Butte
3,506 ft
(1,069 m)

Lake Oahe

Geographical Center of the 50 United States

White

James

CASCADE RANGE

Grand Teton
13,770 ft
(4,197 m)

GREAT

Black Hills

Black Elk Peak
7,242 ft
(2,207 m)

Great Salt Lake

Great Divide Basin

Laramie Mts.

Niobrara

Sand Hills

N. Platte

Platte

Sierra Nevada

Lake Tahoe

Great

Wasatch Range

Uinta Mts.

Front Range

Sacramento Valley

San Joaquin

Basin

Mt. Whitney
14,494 ft
(4,418 m)

Mt. Elbert
(4,399 m) 14,433 ft

S. Platte

Geographical Center of the 48 Contiguous United States

Smoky Hills

San Joaquin Valley

Death Valley

Mojave

Lake Powell

Colorado

+Pikes Peak
14,110 ft
(4,301 m)

Arkansas

Lowest Point in North America
(−86 m) −282 ft

Desert

Lake Mead

Grand Canyon

Colorado

San Juan Mts.

Sangre de Cristo

MOUNTAINS

Red Hills

Channel Islands

Salton Sea

Imperial Valley

Humphreys Peak+
12,635 ft
(3,851 m)

Painted Desert

Plateau

Black Mesa
4,973 ft
(1,516 m)

Canadian

Cimarron

Colorado

Gila

Salt

Rio Grande

Llano Estacado

Brazos

Sonoran Desert

PLAINS

GREAT

0   400 miles
0   400 kilometers

North Slope

Brooks Range

Yukon

(Mt. McKinley) Denali
(6,190 m) 20,310 ft+
Highest Point in North America

Alaska Range

Alexander Archipelago

Aleutian Islands

Alaska Peninsula

Sacramento Mts.

+Guadalupe Peak
8,749 ft
(2,667 m)

Pecos

Edwards Plateau

Rio Grande

Colorado

Kaua'i

O'ahu

Ni'ihau

Moloka'i

Lāna'i   Maui

Kaho'olawe

Hawai'i

0   150 miles
0   150 kilometers

Mauna Kea+
13,796 ft
(4,205 m)

ALASKA AND HAWAII:
In addition to the states located on the main landmass, the U.S. has two states—Alaska and Hawaii—that are not directly connected to the other 48 states. If Alaska and Hawaii were shown in their correct relative sizes and locations, the map would not fit on these pages.

Stretching from the Atlantic Ocean in the east to the Pacific Ocean in the west, the United States is the third largest country (by area) in the world. Its physical diversity ranges from mountains to fertile plains to dry deserts. Shading on the map indicates changes in elevation, while colors show different vegetation patterns.

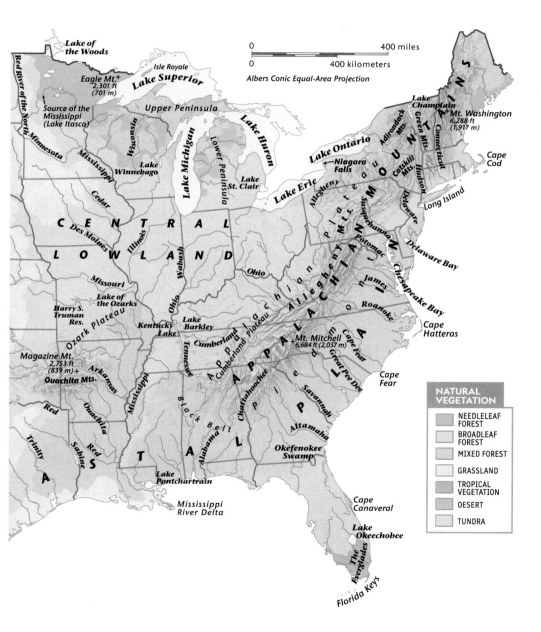

0   400 miles
0   400 kilometers
Albers Conic Equal-Area Projection

NATURAL VEGETATION

- NEEDLELEAF FOREST
- BROADLEAF FOREST
- MIXED FOREST
- GRASSLAND
- TROPICAL VEGETATION
- DESERT
- TUNDRA

Lake of the Woods
Red River of the North
Eagle Mt. 2,301 ft (701 m)
Isle Royale
Lake Superior
Upper Peninsula
Source of the Mississippi (Lake Itasca)
Minnesota
Mississippi
Wisconsin
Lake Winnebago
Lake Michigan
Lower Peninsula
Lake Huron
Lake St. Clair
Cedar
Des Moines
CENTRAL LOWLAND
Illinois
Wabash
Ohio
Missouri
Lake of the Ozarks
Harry S. Truman Res.
Ozark Plateau
Kentucky Lake
Lake Barkley
Tennessee
Magazine Mt. 2,753 ft (839 m)
Ouachita Mts.
Arkansas
Ouachita
Mississippi
Black Belt
Red
Trinity
Sabine
Red
COASTAL PLAIN
Alabama
Chattahoochee
Lake Pontchartrain
Mississippi River Delta
Lake Champlain
Adirondack Mts.
Green Mts.
Mt. Washington 6,288 ft (1,917 m)
Connecticut
Hudson
Catskill Mts.
Lake Ontario
Niagara Falls
Lake Erie
Allegheny
Allegheny Plateau
Susquehanna
Delaware
Cape Cod
Long Island
Delaware Bay
Potomac
APPALACHIAN MOUNTAINS
James
Chesapeake Bay
Roanoke
Cape Hatteras
Cumberland Mts.
Cumberland Plateau
Mt. Mitchell 6,684 ft (2,037 m)
Cape Fear
Great Pee Dee
Cape Fear
Piedmont
Savannah
Altamaha
Okefenokee Swamp
Cape Canaveral
Lake Okeechobee
The Everglades
Florida Keys

335

THE STATES

From sea to shining sea, the United States of America is a nation of diversity. In the 248 years since its creation, the nation has grown to become home to a wide range of peoples, industries, and cultures. The following pages present a general overview of all 50 states in the United States.

The country is generally divided into five large regions: the Northeast, the Southeast, the Midwest, the Southwest, and the West. Though loosely defined, these zones tend to share important similarities, including climate, history, and geography. The color key below provides a guide to which states are in each region.

The flag of each state and highlights of demography and industry are also included. These details offer a brief overview of each state.

In addition, each state's official flower and bird are identified.

Color Key by Region

Alabama

Nickname: Heart of Dixie
Area: 52,420 sq mi (135,767 sq km)
Population: 5,040,000
Capital: Montgomery; population 196,000
Statehood: December 14, 1819; 22nd state
State flower/bird: Camellia/yellowhammer (northern flicker)

Alaska

Nickname: Last Frontier
Area: 665,384 sq mi (1,723,337 sq km)
Population: 733,000
Capital: Juneau; population 32,000
Statehood: January 3, 1959; 49th state
State flower/bird: Forget-me-not/ willow ptarmigan

Arizona

Nickname: Grand Canyon State
Area: 113,990 sq mi (295,234 sq km)
Population: 7,276,000
Capital: Phoenix; population 1,708,000
Statehood: February 14, 1912; 48th state
State flower/bird: Saguaro cactus blossom/ cactus wren

YUMA, ARIZONA, is the SUNNIEST SPOT in the United States, with 91 PERCENT of its DAYLIGHT HOURS SOAKED IN SUN.

Arkansas

Nickname: Natural State
Area: 53,179 sq mi (137,732 sq km)
Population: 3,026,000
Capital: Little Rock; population 198,000
Statehood: June 15, 1836; 25th state
State flower/bird: Apple blossom/ mockingbird

California

Nickname: Golden State
Area: 163,695 sq mi (423,967 sq km)
Population: 39,238,000
Capital: Sacramento; population 513,000
Statehood: September 9, 1850; 31st state
State flower/bird: California poppy/ California quail

Colorado

Nickname: Centennial State
Area: 104,094 sq mi (269,601 sq km)
Population: 5,812,000
Capital: Denver; population 736,000
Statehood: August 1, 1876; 38th state
State flower/bird: Rocky Mountain columbine/ lark bunting

Connecticut

Nickname: Constitution State
Area: 5,543 sq mi (14,357 sq km)
Population: 3,606,000
Capital: Hartford; population 122,000
Statehood: January 9, 1788; 5th state
State flower/bird: Mountain laurel/ American robin

Delaware

Nickname: First State
Area: 2,489 sq mi (6,446 sq km)
Population: 1,003,000
Capital: Dover; population 38,000
Statehood: December 7, 1787; 1st state
State flower/bird: Peach blossom/ blue hen chicken

Florida

Nickname: Sunshine State
Area: 65,758 sq mi (170,312 sq km)
Population: 21,781,000
Capital: Tallahassee; population 196,000
Statehood: March 3, 1845; 27th state
State flower/bird: Orange blossom/ mockingbird

Georgia

Nickname: Peach State
Area: 59,425 sq mi (153,910 sq km)
Population: 10,800,000
Capital: Atlanta; population 513,000
Statehood: January 2, 1788; 4th state
State flower/bird: Cherokee rose/brown thrasher

Hawaii

Nickname: Aloha State
Area: 10,932 sq mi (28,313 sq km)
Population: 1,442,000
Capital: Honolulu; population 342,000
Statehood: August 21, 1959; 50th state
State flower/bird: Pua aloalo/ nene (Hawaiian goose)

Idaho

Nickname: Gem State
Area: 83,569 sq mi (216,443 sq km)
Population: 1,901,000
Capital: Boise; population 230,000
Statehood: July 3, 1890; 43rd state
State flower/bird: Syringa/ mountain bluebird

Illinois

Nickname: Prairie State
Area: 57,914 sq mi (149,995 sq km)
Population: 12,671,000
Capital: Springfield; population 114,000
Statehood: December 3, 1818; 21st state
State flower/bird: Violet/northern cardinal

Indiana

Nickname: Hoosier State
Area: 36,420 sq mi (94,326 sq km)
Population: 6,806,000
Capital: Indianapolis; population 888,000
Statehood: December 11, 1816; 19th state
State flower/bird: Peony/northern cardinal

The INFIELD of the **INDIANAPOLIS MOTOR SPEEDWAY** could fit 42 ROMAN COLOSSEUMS.

Iowa

Nickname: Hawkeye State
Area: 56,273 sq mi (145,746 sq km)
Population: 3,193,000
Capital: Des Moines; population 212,000
Statehood: December 28, 1846; 29th state
State flower/bird: Wild prairie rose/ American goldfinch

Kansas

Nickname: Sunflower State
Area: 82,278 sq mi (213,100 sq km)
Population: 2,935,000
Capital: Topeka; population 125,000
Statehood: January 29, 1861; 34th state
State flower/bird: Wild native sunflower/western meadowlark

Kentucky

Nickname: Bluegrass State
Area: 40,408 sq mi
(104,656 sq km)
Population: 4,509,000
Capital: Frankfort; population 28,000
Statehood: June 1, 1792; 15th state
State flower/bird: Goldenrod/northern cardinal

> # Roughly 50 PERCENT of the LAND in KENTUCKY is COVERED IN FORESTS.

Louisiana

Nickname: Pelican State
Area: 52,378 sq mi
(135,659 sq km)
Population: 4,624,000
Capital: Baton Rouge; population 219,000
Statehood: April 30, 1812; 18th state
State flower/bird: Magnolia/brown pelican

Maine

Nickname: Pine Tree State
Area: 35,380 sq mi (91,633 sq km)
Population: 1,372,000
Capital: Augusta; population 19,000
Statehood: March 15, 1820; 23rd state
State flower/bird: White pine cone and tassel/black-capped chickadee

Maryland

Nickname: Old Line State
Area: 12,406 sq mi (32,131 sq km)
Population: 6,165,000
Capital: Annapolis; population 40,000
Statehood: April 28, 1788; 7th state
State flower/bird: Black-eyed Susan/Baltimore oriole

Massachusetts

Nickname: Bay State
Area: 10,554 sq mi (27,336 sq km)
Population: 6,985,000
Capital: Boston; population 692,000
Statehood: February 6, 1788; 6th state
State flower/bird: Mayflower/black-capped chickadee

Michigan

Nickname: Wolverine State
Area: 96,714 sq mi (250,487 sq km)
Population: 10,051,000
Capital: Lansing; population 118,000
Statehood: January 26, 1837; 26th state
State flower/bird: Apple blossom/American robin

Minnesota

Nickname: North Star State
Area: 86,936 sq mi (225,163 sq km)
Population: 5,707,000
Capital: Saint Paul; population 307,000
Statehood: May 11, 1858; 32nd state
State flower/bird: Pink and white lady slipper/common loon

Mississippi

Nickname: Magnolia State
Area: 48,432 sq mi (125,438 sq km)
Population: 2,950,000
Capital: Jackson; population 158,000
Statehood: December 10, 1817; 20th state
State flower/bird: Magnolia/mockingbird

COLOR KEY ● Northeast ● Southeast

Missouri

Nickname: Show-Me State
Area: 69,707 sq mi (180,540 sq km)
Population: 6,168,000
Capital: Jefferson City; population 42,000
Statehood: August 10, 1821; 24th state
State flower/bird: Hawthorn blossom/ eastern bluebird

Montana

Nickname: Treasure State
Area: 147,040 sq mi (380,831 sq km)
Population: 1,104,000
Capital: Helena; population 34,000
Statehood: November 8, 1889; 41st state
State flower/bird: Bitterroot/ western meadowlark

Nebraska

Nickname: Cornhusker State
Area: 77,348 sq mi (200,330 sq km)
Population: 1,964,000
Capital: Lincoln; population 291,000
Statehood: March 1, 1867; 37th state
State flower/bird: Goldenrod/ western meadowlark

> A ZOO in OMAHA, NEBRASKA, features the LARGEST INDOOR RAINFOREST in the United States, covering 1.5 acres (0.6 ha) of land in an eight-story building.

Nevada

Nickname: Silver State
Area: 110,572 sq mi (286,380 sq km)
Population: 3,144,000
Capital: Carson City; population 56,000
Statehood: October 31, 1864; 36th state
State flower/bird: Sagebrush/ mountain bluebird

New Hampshire

Nickname: Granite State
Area: 9,349 sq mi (24,214 sq km)
Population: 1,389,000
Capital: Concord; population 44,000
Statehood: June 21, 1788; 9th state
State flower/bird: Purple lilac/purple finch

New Jersey

Nickname: Garden State
Area: 8,723 sq mi (22,591 sq km)
Population: 9,267,000
Capital: Trenton; population 83,000
Statehood: December 18, 1787; 3rd state
State flower/bird: Violet/Eastern goldfinch

New Mexico

Nickname: Land of Enchantment
Area: 121,590 sq mi (314,917 sq km)
Population: 2,116,000
Capital: Santa Fe; population 85,000
Statehood: January 6, 1912; 47th state
State flower/bird: Yucca/greater roadrunner

New York

Nickname: Empire State
Area: 54,555 sq mi (141,297 sq km)
Population: 19,836,000
Capital: Albany; population 95,000
Statehood: July 26, 1788; 11th state
State flower/bird: Rose/eastern bluebird

North Carolina

Nickname: Tar Heel State
Area: 53,819 sq mi (139,391 sq km)
Population: 10,551,000
Capital: Raleigh; population 474,000
Statehood: November 21, 1789; 12th state
State flower/bird: Flowering dogwood/ northern cardinal

● Midwest ● Southwest ● West

North Dakota

Nickname: Peace Garden State
Area: 70,698 sq mi (183,108 sq km)
Population: 775,000
Capital: Bismarck; population 74,000
Statehood: November 2, 1889; 39th state
State flower/bird: Wild prairie rose/
western meadowlark

Ohio

Nickname: Buckeye State
Area: 44,826 sq mi (116,098 sq km)
Population: 11,780,000
Capital: Columbus; population 904,000
Statehood: February 19, 1803; 17th state
State flower/bird: Scarlet carnation/
northern cardinal

Oklahoma

Nickname: Sooner State
Area: 69,899 sq mi (181,037 sq km)
Population: 3,987,000
Capital: Oklahoma City; population 662,000
Statehood: November 16, 1907; 46th state
State flower/bird: Oklahoma rose/
scissor-tailed flycatcher

Oregon

Nickname: Beaver State
Area: 98,379 sq mi (254,799 sq km)
Population: 4,246,000
Capital: Salem; population 176,000
Statehood: February 14, 1859; 33rd state
State flower/bird: Oregon grape/
western meadowlark

Pennsylvania

Nickname: Keystone State
Area: 46,054 sq mi (119,280 sq km)
Population: 12,964,000
Capital: Harrisburg; population 49,000
Statehood: December 12, 1787; 2nd state
State flower/bird: Mountain laurel/
ruffed grouse

Rhode Island

Nickname: Ocean State
Area: 1,545 sq mi (4,001 sq km)
Population: 1,096,000
Capital: Providence; population 179,000
Statehood: May 29, 1790; 13th state
State flower/bird: Violet/
Rhode Island red

South Carolina

Nickname: Palmetto State
Area: 32,020 sq mi (82,933 sq km)
Population: 5,191,000
Capital: Columbia; population 132,000
Statehood: May 23, 1788; 8th state
State flower/bird: Yellow jessamine/
Carolina wren

South Dakota

Nickname: Mount Rushmore State
Area: 77,116 sq mi (199,729 sq km)
Population: 895,000
Capital: Pierre; population 14,000
Statehood: November 2, 1889; 40th state
State flower/bird: American pasque/
ring-necked pheasant

3 cool things about PENNSYLVANIA

1. Pennsylvania is home to its own "Grand Canyon," a gorge that spans more than 45 miles (72 km) with depths of nearly 1,500 feet (457 m).

2. A firefly is Pennsylvania's state insect.

3. Not to be outdone by the Times Square Ball drop, Kennett Square, Pennsylvania—known as the "Mushroom Capital of the World"—has a mushroom drop every New Year's Eve.

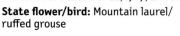

COLOR KEY ● Northeast ● Southeast

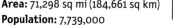

Tennessee

Nickname: Volunteer State
Area: 42,144 sq mi (109,153 sq km)
Population: 6,975,000
Capital: Nashville; population 694,000
Statehood: June 1, 1796; 16th state
State flower/bird: Iris/mockingbird

Texas

Nickname: Lone Star State
Area: 268,596 sq mi (695,662 sq km)
Population: 29,528,000
Capital: Austin; population 995,000
Statehood: December 29, 1845; 28th state
State flower/bird: Bluebonnet/mockingbird

Utah

Nickname: Beehive State
Area: 84,897 sq mi
(219,882 sq km)
Population: 3,338,000
Capital: Salt Lake City; population 204,000
Statehood: January 4, 1896; 45th state
State flower/bird: Sego lily/California gull

Vermont

Nickname: Green Mountain State
Area: 9,616 sq mi (24,906 sq km)
Population: 646,000
Capital: Montpelier; population 7,000
Statehood: March 4, 1791; 14th state
State flower/bird: Red clover/hermit thrush

Virginia

Nickname: Old Dominion
Area: 42,775 sq mi (110,787 sq km)
Population: 8,642,000
Capital: Richmond; population 232,000
Statehood: June 25, 1788; 10th state
State flower/bird: American dogwood/
northern cardinal

Washington

Nickname: Evergreen State
Area: 71,298 sq mi (184,661 sq km)
Population: 7,739,000
Capital: Olympia; population 54,000
Statehood: November 11, 1889; 42nd state
State flower/bird: Coast rhododendron/
American goldfinch

West Virginia

Nickname: Mountain State
Area: 24,230 sq mi (62,756 sq km)
Population: 1,783,000
Capital: Charleston; population 46,000
Statehood: June 20, 1863; 35th state
State flower/bird: Rhododendron/
northern cardinal

Wisconsin

Nickname: Badger State
Area: 65,496 sq mi (169,635 sq km)
Population: 5,896,000
Capital: Madison; population 263,000
Statehood: May 29, 1848; 30th state
State flower/bird: Wood violet/
American robin

Wyoming

Nickname: Equality State
Area: 97,813 sq mi (253,335 sq km)
Population: 579,000
Capital: Cheyenne; population 65,000
Statehood: July 10, 1890; 44th state
State flower/bird: Indian paintbrush/
western meadowlark

Wyoming's JACKSON HOLE AIRPORT is the ONLY U.S. AIRPORT fully LOCATED WITHIN A NATIONAL PARK.

● Midwest ● Southwest ● West

THE TERRITORIES

The United States has 14 territories— political divisions that are not states. Three of these are in the Caribbean Sea, and the other 11 are in the Pacific Ocean.

St. John, U.S. Virgin Islands

Convention Center, San Juan, Puerto Rico

Talofofo Falls, Guam

U.S. CARIBBEAN TERRITORIES

Puerto Rico

Area: 5,325 sq mi (13,791 sq km)
Population: 3,264,000
Capital: San Juan; population 2,443,000
Languages: Spanish, English

U.S. Virgin Islands
Area: 733 sq mi (1,898 sq km)
Population: 106,000
Capital: Charlotte Amalie; population 52,000
Languages: English, Spanish, French

U.S. PACIFIC TERRITORIES

American Samoa

Area: 581 sq mi (1,505 sq km)
Population: 46,000
Capital: Pago Pago; population 3,000
Language: Samoan, English

Guam

Area: 571 sq mi (1,478 sq km)
Population: 169,000
Capital: Hagåtña (Agana); population 147,000
Languages: English, Filipino, Chamorro, other Pacific island and Asian languages

Northern Mariana Islands

Area: 1,976 sq mi (5,117 sq km)
Population: 52,000
Capital: Capital Hill; population 51,000
Languages: Philippine languages, Chinese, Chamorro, English

Other U.S. Territories

Baker Island, Howland Island, Jarvis Island, Johnston Atoll, Kingman Reef, Midway Islands, Palmyra Atoll, Wake Island, Navassa Island (in the Caribbean)

Figures for capital cities vary widely between sources because of differences in the way areas are defined and other projection methods.

THE U.S. CAPITAL

District of Columbia
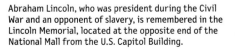
Area: 68 sq mi (177 sq km)
Population: 670,000

Abraham Lincoln, who was president during the Civil War and an opponent of slavery, is remembered in the Lincoln Memorial, located at the opposite end of the National Mall from the U.S. Capitol Building.

The Lincoln Memorial celebrated its 100th anniversary in 2022.

COLOR KEY ● Territories ● Northeast

weird but true!

Check out these outrageous U.S.A. facts.

The **Virginia opossum** can have **20 babies** in a litter.

California's **San Andreas Fault** moves at about **the same rate as your fingernails grow.**

In Massachusetts, it's illegal to have **exploding golf balls.**

There is a **toilet-seat** art museum in The Colony, Texas.

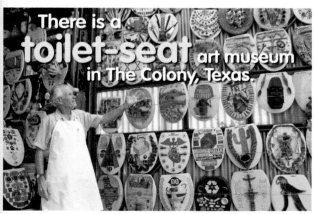

A **restaurant in Connecticut gives away FREE BOOKS** to every customer.

You can **DIG** for **DIAMONDS** in a crater in Arkansas and **KEEP** what **YOU FIND.**

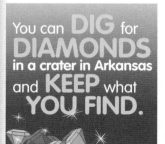

One in eight Americans eats pizza on any given day.

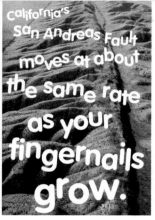

10 WONDERFUL FACTS ABOUT WACKY ATTRACTIONS

In Wahiawa, Hawaii, you can get lost in a **GIANT BOTANICAL MAZE,** a dizzying series of paths through some **14,000 pineapple plants.**

Taller than a two-story building, the Big Boxing Crocodile makes a giant statement outside a gas station in Humpty Doo, Australia, **home to many (real-life) saltwater crocs.**

IN TILLAMOOK, OREGON, U.S.A., YOU CAN OGLE AT THE **OCTOPUS TREE,** A 250-YEAR-OLD SITKA SPRUCE TREE WITH **TENTACLE-LIKE LIMBS** THAT REACH 100 FEET (30 M) IN THE AIR.

Featuring one of South Africa's largest art murals, the colorfully painted **SOWETO TOWERS** also offer a launching spot for fearless bungee jumpers, who scale to the top to take a leap from 33 stories up.

The **Witches Garden** in Mitta Mitta, Australia, doubles as a **broomstick gallery.**

You can explore an **UPSIDE-DOWN HOUSE** in Szymbark, Poland—enter through a window near the roof, then stroll along the ceilings instead of the floors!

Check out a **100-year-old house made almost entirely out of newspaper**—furniture included!—at the Paper House in Rockport, Massachusetts, U.S.A.

Learn about an ancient Chinese scholar and get your fill of fried chicken at the Du Fu KFC in Chengdu, China. The fast-food spot features framed writings of a famed eighth-century poet and holograms of his house.

The **SNAIL HOUSE** in Sofia, Bulgaria, doesn't just stand out for its rainbow-colored paint job: At five stories tall, this building—which has **NO STRAIGHT WALLS OR CORNERS**—was built entirely out of energy-efficient materials.

A POPULAR SITE IN HEADINGTON, ENGLAND, IS **THE 25-FOOT** (7.6-M) **FIBERGLASS SHARK** SCULPTURE JUTTING OUT FROM THE ROOF OF A COTTAGE.

awes8me

NO FILTER NEEDED! THESE EIGHT BRIGHT SPOTS AROUND THE WORLD HAVE ALL-NATURAL HUES.

1 BANDS OF BLOOMS

Tulips grow in neat rows in the Netherlands, where millions of the buds pop up each spring. Originally a wildflower from Asia, tulips were brought to Europe by a botanist in the 17th century. Today, billions of flowers are exported from the Netherlands every year.

COLORFUL CORNERS OF EARTH

2 RAINBOW ROCKS

Natural zigzag formations in Argentina's **Hornocal mountain range** appear to change color depending on the shade of the sky. A rainbow of rock layers glows in fiery shades of orange and red, plus purple and pink.

4 MARBLE MARVEL

Thanks to centuries of erosion, the underbelly of this towering rock formation found in Chile's **General Carrera Lake** is pure marble. The white-rock caves feature swirling details that appear blue as they reflect the glacier-fed lake. One part is even known as Capillas de Marmol, or "marble chapel."

5 CRIMSON TIDE

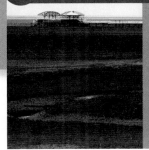

This wetland has visitors sea-ing red! China's **Panjin Red Beach** is covered by masses of seepweed, a plant that turns a scarlet shade each autumn. The result? Crimson as far as the eye can see.

SHADE-SHIFTERS 6

You never know what hue you're going to see at the crater lakes in Indonesia's **Kelimutu National Park**. Because of chemical reactions triggered by volcanic activity, the crater lakes here are constantly changing color—from navy blue to emerald green to shocking white.

3 FLY HIGH

The gorgeous **Fly Geyser** in Nevada, U.S.A. was the accidental outcome of humans drilling for geothermic energy. But its radiant reddish green glow is all natural—a result of being covered by colorful algae that grow only at extreme temperatures.

7 COOL CORAL

Dive into Australia's **Great Barrier Reef** to experience the world's most amazing aquarium: Thousands of coral and tropical fish in an array of bold colors cover more than 1,400 miles (2,253 km), creating the planet's largest living ecosystem.

Each spring, a carpet of pink wildflowers spreads below the base of Japan's **Mount Fuji**. Tourists flock to the mountain for the annual Festival of Flowers, where they can view the blooms—also known as moss phlox—growing in stunning shades of magenta and blush.

8 BRIGHT BLOSSOMS

WHAT WEIRD DESTINATION IS RIGHT FOR YOU?

Do you like your weirdness from a distance?

Lake Hillier, Middle Island, Western Australia
Researchers think that bacteria in this pink lake give it its rosy color. But because the island is used only for research, your visit will be from the air.

Spotted Lake, British Columbia, Canada
The water of this lake evaporates in summer, leaving behind small mineral pools of varying colors. They're best viewed from far enough away that you can see all the quirky circles at once.

Skylodge Adventure Suites, Cusco, Peru
Get cozy in your transparent bedroom capsule 1,000 feet (305 m) up—hanging from the side of a cliff in Peru's Sacred Valley.

Or do you prefer your weirdness up close?

Bonne Terre Mine, Missouri, U.S.A.
Scuba dive to your heart's content in this flooded underground lead mine—now the world's largest freshwater dive resort.

INTERNATIONAL PEDAL POWER

Want to go on a bike ride? With some one billion bicycles on the road worldwide, bikes are one of the most popular ways to get around. Strap on your helmet and pedal your way around 10 of the most bike-friendly cities in the world.

1. COPENHAGEN, DENMARK

In Copenhagen, 42 percent of people bike to school or work. Only 10 percent drive a car!

2. AMSTERDAM, NETHERLANDS

In the Netherlands, 26.8 percent of all trips are by bike.

3. UTRECHT, NETHERLANDS

In Utrecht, 96 percent of households have one or more bikes.

4. STRASBOURG, FRANCE

In Strasbourg, 370 miles (600 km) of bike paths wind through the city.

5. EINDHOVEN, NETHERLANDS

6. MALMÖ, SWEDEN

7. NANTES, FRANCE

8. BORDEAUX, FRANCE

9. ANTWERP, BELGIUM

10. SEVILLE, SPAIN

91.5% of American households have a car, but only **half** have a **bike.**

EUROPE

THE COLOR OF THE BOX BEHIND EACH NUMBER MATCHES THE COLOR OF ITS LOCATION TAG.

Bizarre Beaches

THE WORLD'S COOLEST COASTLINES OFFER SO MUCH MORE THAN SANDY SHORES.

BLACK-OUT

WHAT: Punalu'u Black Sand Beach
WHERE: Big Island, Hawaii, U.S.A.
WHY IT'S BIZARRE: The jet-black sand on this skinny stretch of beach is made up of tiny bits of hardened lava, produced over centuries by the nearby (and still active) Kilauea volcano. This cool spot is also a popular nesting place for hawksbill and green sea turtles.

GLASS FROM THE PAST

WHAT: Glass Beach
WHERE: Fort Bragg, California, U.S.A.
WHY IT'S BIZARRE: Decades ago, the water along this beach was a dumping ground for glass bottles and other debris. Now what was once tossed into the ocean has washed up as a rainbow of shimmering sea glass covering the coves.

FOR THE BIRDS

WHAT: Boulders Beach
WHERE: Harbour Island, The Bahamas
WHY IT'S BIZARRE: You might expect to see penguins on an icy coast. But these birds like it hot! African penguins splash in the warm waters of this national park next to 540-million-year-old granite boulders.

TIP-OFF

WHAT: Zlatni Rat
WHERE: Bol, Croatia
WHY IT'S BIZARRE: This narrow beach is a real shape-shifter. Its tip—which sticks out as much as 1,640 feet (500 m) into the crystal blue water—shifts in different directions as a result of wind, waves, and currents.

THE ORIGINAL 7 WONDERS of the WORLD

More than 2,000 years ago, many travelers wrote about sights they had seen on their journeys. Over time, seven of those places made history as the "wonders of the ancient world." There are seven because the Greeks, who made the list, believed the number seven to be magical.

THE PYRAMIDS OF GIZA, EGYPT
BUILT: ABOUT 2600 B.C.
MASSIVE TOMBS OF EGYPTIAN PHARAOHS LIE INSIDE THIS ANCIENT WONDER—THE ONLY ONE STILL STANDING TODAY.

HANGING GARDENS OF BABYLON, IRAQ
BUILT: DATE UNKNOWN
LEGEND HAS IT THAT THIS GARDEN PARADISE WAS PLANTED ON AN ARTIFICIAL MOUNTAIN, BUT MANY EXPERTS SAY IT NEVER REALLY EXISTED.

TEMPLE OF ARTEMIS AT EPHESUS, TÜRKİYE
BUILT: SIXTH CENTURY B.C.
THIS TOWERING TEMPLE WAS BUILT TO HONOR ARTEMIS, THE GREEK GODDESS OF THE HUNT.

STATUE OF ZEUS, GREECE
BUILT: FIFTH CENTURY B.C.
THIS 40-FOOT (12-M) STATUE DEPICTED THE KING OF THE GREEK GODS.

MAUSOLEUM AT HALICARNASSUS, TÜRKİYE
BUILT: FOURTH CENTURY B.C.
THIS ELABORATE TOMB WAS BUILT FOR KING MAUSOLUS.

COLOSSUS OF RHODES, RHODES (AN ISLAND IN THE AEGEAN SEA)
BUILT: FOURTH CENTURY B.C.
THE 110-FOOT (34-M) STATUE HONORED THE GREEK SUN GOD HELIOS.

LIGHTHOUSE OF ALEXANDRIA, EGYPT
BUILT: THIRD CENTURY B.C.
THE WORLD'S FIRST LIGHTHOUSE, IT USED MIRRORS TO REFLECT SUNLIGHT FOR MILES OUT TO SEA.

THE NEW 7 WONDERS of the WORLD

Why name new wonders of the world? Most of the original ancient wonders no longer exist. To be eligible for the new list, the wonders had to be human-made before the year 2000 and in preservation. They were selected through a poll of more than 100 million voters!

TAJ MAHAL, INDIA
COMPLETED: 1648
THIS LAVISH TOMB WAS BUILT AS A FINAL RESTING PLACE FOR MUMTAZ MAHAL, THE BELOVED WIFE OF EMPEROR SHAH JAHAN.

PETRA, SOUTHWEST JORDAN
COMPLETED: ABOUT 200 B.C.
SOME 30,000 PEOPLE ONCE LIVED IN THIS ROCK CITY CARVED INTO CLIFF WALLS.

MACHU PICCHU, PERU
COMPLETED: ABOUT 1450
OFTEN CALLED THE "LOST CITY IN THE CLOUDS," MACHU PICCHU IS PERCHED 7,710 FEET (2,350 M) HIGH IN THE ANDES.

THE COLOSSEUM, ITALY
COMPLETED: A.D. 80
WILD ANIMALS—AND HUMANS—FOUGHT EACH OTHER TO THE DEATH BEFORE 50,000 SPECTATORS IN THIS ARENA.

CHRIST THE REDEEMER STATUE, BRAZIL
COMPLETED: 1931
TOWERING ATOP CORCOVADO MOUNTAIN, THIS STATUE IS TALLER THAN A 12-STORY BUILDING AND WEIGHS ABOUT 2.5 MILLION POUNDS (1.1 MILLION KG).

CHICHÉN ITZÁ, MEXICO
COMPLETED: 10TH CENTURY
ONCE THE CAPITAL CITY OF THE ANCIENT MAYA EMPIRE, CHICHÉN ITZÁ IS HOME TO THE FAMOUS PYRAMID OF KUKULCÁN.

GREAT WALL OF CHINA, CHINA
COMPLETED: 1644
THE LONGEST HUMAN-MADE STRUCTURE EVER BUILT, IT WINDS OVER AN ESTIMATED 4,500 MILES (7,200 KM).

QUIZ WHIZ

Is your geography knowledge off the map? Quiz yourself to find out!

Write your answers on a piece of paper. Then check them below.

1 Where in the world is the Cave of Crystals?
a. England
b. Mexico
c. New Zealand
d. Uruguay

2 Steep-sided valleys called _____ are created mainly by running water.
a. rivers
b. glaciers
c. canyons
d. waterfalls

3 In Nepal, tiger numbers have recently doubled to roughly _____ individuals thanks to conservation efforts.
a. 235
b. 2,350
c. 23,500
d. 235,000

4 True or false? Researchers in Antarctica unearthed the ship of polar explorer Ernest Shackleton.

5 Which flower grows by the millions in neat rows in the Netherlands each spring?
a. daisy
b. lily
c. rose
d. tulip

Not **STUMPED** yet? Check out the *NATIONAL GEOGRAPHIC KIDS QUIZ WHIZ* collection for more crazy **GEOGRAPHY** questions!

ANSWERS: 1. b; 2. c; 3. a; 4. True; 5. d

HOMEWORK HELP

Finding Your Way Around

LATITUDE AND LONGITUDE lines help us determine locations on Earth. Every place on Earth has a special address called absolute location. Imaginary lines called lines of latitude run west to east, parallel to the Equator. These lines measure distance in degrees north or south from the Equator (0° latitude) to the North Pole (90° N) or to the South Pole (90° S). One degree of latitude is approximately 70 miles (113 km).

Lines of longitude run north to south, meeting at the poles. These lines measure distance in degrees east or west from 0° longitude (prime meridian) to 180° longitude. The prime meridian runs through Greenwich, England.

ABSOLUTE LOCATION. Suppose you are using latitude and longitude to play a game of global scavenger hunt. The clue says the prize is hidden at absolute location 30° S, 60° W. You know that the first number is south of the Equator, and the second is west of the prime meridian. On the map at right, find the line of latitude labeled 30° S. Now find the line of longitude labeled 60° W. Trace these lines with your fingers until they meet. Identify this spot. The prize must be located in northern Argentina (see arrow, right).

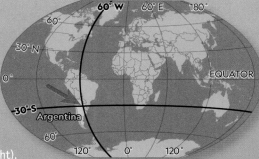

CHALLENGE!

1. Look at the map of Africa on pp. 280–281. Which country can you find at 10° S, 20° E?

2. Look at the map of Asia on pp. 288–289. Which country can you find at 20° N, 80° E?

3. On the map of Europe on pp. 296–297, which country is found at 50° N, 30° E?

4. Look at the map of North America on pp. 300–301. Which country can you find at 20° N, 100° W?

ANSWERS: 1. Angola; 2. India; 3. Ukraine; 4. Mexico

GAME

ANSWERS

Animal Fun House
page 132

1. flamingo
2. African elephant
3. macaroni penguin
4. Siberian tiger
5. red panda
6. chameleon
7. cheetah

What in the World?
page 134

Top row: **cat whiskers, camel hump, moose antler**
Middle row: **snake tongue, whale tail, gecko foot**
Bottom row: **octopus arms, blue-footed booby foot, rooster comb**

Stump Your Parents
page 135

1. D, 2. D, 3. B, 4. C, 5. B, 6. D, 7. C, 8. B, 9. B, 10. A

Find the Hidden Animals
page 137

1. C, 2. E, 3. F, 4. D, 5. A, 6. B

What in the World?
page 138

Top row: **sea stars, octopus, seahorse**
Middle row: **angelfish, stingray, sea slug**
Bottom row: **blowfish, sea urchin, lobster**

Signs of the Times
page 140

Signs **2** and **6** are fake.

What in the World?
page 141

Top row: **ice cream, sun, snowy creek**
Middle row: **lava, frozen fruit, stove burner**
Bottom row: **glacier, chili peppers, ice rink**

Stump Your Parents
page 142

1. B, 2. B, 3. D, 4. A, 5. B, 6. A, 7. A, 8. C, 9. D, 10. B

What in the World?
page 145

Top row: **lava lamp, neon sign, firefly**
Middle row: **lightning, sparklers, crosswalk sign**
Bottom row: **lightbulb, northern lights, night-light**

Find the Hidden Animals
page 146

1. A, 2. D, 3. B, 4. E, 5. F, 6. C

Signs of the Times
page 147

Signs **1** and **4** are fake.

Want to Learn More?

Find more information about topics in this book in these National Geographic Kids resources.

Weird But True! series

Just Joking series

5,000 Awesome Facts (About Everything!) series

1,000 Facts series

Critter Chat
Rosemary Mosco
May 2022

Ultimate Book of the Future
Stephanie Warren Drimmer
June 2022

Break Down
Mara Grunbaum
August 2022

Weird But True! World 2023
National Geographic Kids
August 2022

The Ultimate Book of Big Cats
Sharon Guynup and Steve Winter
September 2022

Not-So-Common Cents
Sarah Wassner Flynn
January 2023

That's Fact-tastic!
National Geographic
February 2023

How to Survive in the Age of Dinosaurs
Stephanie Warren Drimmer
April 2023

Abbreviations:
AL: Alamy Stock Photo
AS: Adobe Stock
DS: Dreamstime
GI: Getty Images
IS: iStockphoto
MP: Minden Pictures
NGIC: National Geographic Image Collection
SS: Shutterstock

All Maps
By National Geographic

Front Cover
(wolf), Art Wolfe/Art Wolfe Inc.;(CTR RT), pixel-liebe/SS;(LO RT), Leonard Zhukovsky/SS;(LO LE), Science RF/AS

Spine
(wolf), Art Wolfe/Art Wolfe Inc.

Back Cover
Back cover (wolf), ixpert/SS;(owl), Tatiana/AS;(LO RT), Chris Hill;(CTR RT), jerbarber/IS/GI;(CTR LE), Eric Gevaert/AL;(LO LE), Overflightstock/AS;(butterfly), Steven Russell Smith/AL

Front Matter (2–7)
2-3, Ward Poppe/SS; 5 (UP), dsaimages/AS; 5 (UP CTR), Photo by Dan Nocera; 5 (LO CTR), Marc Casanovas - UW Photography/GI; 5 (LO), NASA, ESA, CSA, STScI, Webb ERO Production Team; 5 (LO RT), Science RF/AS; 6 (UP), Stephen Frink/GI; 6 (UP CTR LE), mlorenzphotography/GI; 6 (UP CTR RT), Dan Sipple; 6 (CTR LE), John M Lund Photography Inc/GI; 6 (CTR RT), reptiles4all/SS; 6 (LO CTR LE), day2505/AS; 6 (LO CTR RT), Tubol Evgeniya/SS; 6 (LO LE), phonlamaiphoto/AS; 6 (LO RT), Noriko Hayashi/Bloomberg via GI; 7 (UP LE), Han/AS; 7 (UP RT), Stephen Hummel, McDonald Observatory; 7 (UP CTR LE), aphotos/AL; 7 (LO CTR LE), Tim Fitzharris/MP

Your World 2024 (8–17)
8-9, dsaimages/AS; 10 (UP), AP Photo/Efrem Lukatsky; 10 (LO), evgeniy/AS; 10 (INSET), NASA/Desiree Stover; 11 (UP), Jaime Culebras; 11 (LO), Victor Habbick/DS; 12 (UP), Matthew Power Photography/Cover Images via Zuma Press; 12 (INSET), Michael Rosskothen/AS; 12 (LO), VANO SHLAMOV/GI; 13 (UP), Benjamin Tapley/ZSL; 13 (UP RT), Soulivanh Lanorsavanh; 13 (CTR RT), WWF - Malaysia; 13 (LO), Parinya Pawangkhanant; 14 (UP LE), Gavran333/AS; 14 (LO), Dimas Ardian/Bloomberg via GI; 15 (UP), Chaithanya/AS; 15 (LO LE), NASA/JSC; 15 (LO RT), NASA/JSC; 16 (UP), NorthShoreSurfPhotos/AS; 16 (UP RT), Stephen Rudolph/DS; 16 (CTR RT), CroMary/SS; 16 (Aug19), Robert,/AS; 16 (LO RT), Cienpies Design/AS; 16 (LO LE), Olga Moonlight/SS; 16 (Mar21), Gavran333/SS; 16 (CTR LE), katet/AS; 16 (UP LE), halfbottle/AS; 17 (UP), AP Photo/Ariel Schalit); 17 (CTR), Kelsie Lambert, Bush Heritage Australia; 17 (LO), Lucas Bustamante

Kids vs. Plastic (18–33)
18-19, Photo by Dan Nocera; 20-21 (BACKGROUND), trialartinf/AS; 20 (BACKGROUND), Chones/SS; 21 (UP), Jacobs Stock Photography Ltd/GI; 21 (CTR RT), SeeCee/SS; 21 (CTR LE), Norbert Pouchain/EyeEm/GI; 22-23 (BACKGROUND), Steve de Neef/NGIC; 22 (LO), Pete Atkinson/GI; 22 (RT), Aflo/SS; 23 (UP RT),

photka/SS; 23 (CTR), NG Maps; 24 (UP LE), Elena Veselova/SS; 24 (UP RT), Maks Narodenko/SS; 24 (LO), Melica/SS; 25 (UP LE), eurobanks/AS; 25 (UP RT), Odua Images/AS; 25 (CTR), aryfahmed/AS; 25 (1), Dmytro/AS; 25 (2), Inga/AS; 25 (3), Tatiana/AS; 25 (4), lindaoqian/AS; 26 (UP), Nastia M/AL; 26 (CTR), Mr. Mendis Wickramasinghe; 26 (LO RT), John Nacion/SOPA Images/LightRocket via GI; 26 (LO LE), Tone Holmen; 27 (UP), Robyn Beck/AFP via GI; 27 (CTR), Friend Productions; 27 (LO), James D. Morgan/GI; 28-29 (BACKGROUND), Tory Kallman/SS; 28 (LO), Manta Ray Advocates; 29 (UP), NG Maps; 29 (LO), The Ocean Cleanup; 30 (UP), Hilary Andrews/NG Staff; 30 (CTR LE), Jane Kelly/SS; 30 (ALL STEPS), Hilary Andrews/NG Staff; 32 (UP LE), Norbert Pouchain/EyeEm/GI; 32 (UP RT), Dmytro/AS; 32 (CTR RT), Robyn Beck/AFP via GI; 32 (LO LE), Hilary Andrews/NG Staff; 33, Alboo03/SS

Amazing Animals (34–85)
34-35, Marc Casanovas - UW Photography/GI; 36 (ALL), 4ocean; 37 (UP LE), Anna Hager/GI; 37 (UP RT), FocusMaster/SS; 37 (LO), Zackrydz Rodzi; 38 (UP), James Warwick/GI; 38 (pottery), Richard Brown and Giselle Eagle; 38 (pebble), Richard Brown and Giselle Eagle; 38 (LE), Richard Brown and Giselle Eagle; 39 (ALL), Dean MacAdam; 40 (UP LE), Guy Bryant/AS; 40 (CTR RT), Wild Wonders of Europe/Zankl/Nature Picture Library; 40 (LO LE), Marie Hickman/GI; 41 (UP LE), Paul/AS; 41 (UP RT), Cyril Ruoso/MP; 41 (CTR LE), sergioboccardo/GI; 41 (LO RT), Ryan M. Bolton/AL; 42 (UP LE), Karl Ammann/npl/MP; 42 (UP RT), Masatsugu Ohashi/SS; 42 (LO RT), Heather Burditt/GI; 42 (LO LE), Randy Kokesch; 43 (UP RT), Fiona McAllister Photography/GI; 43 (CTR LE), Christian Musat/SS; 43 (CTR RT), Roni Kurniawan/EyeEm/GI; 43 (LO LE), John Shaw/Nature Picture Library; 44 (UP RT), Shin Yoshino/MP; 44 (CTR), DioGen/SS; 44 (LO), Nick Garbutt; 45 (UP CTR), Kant Liang/EyeEm/GI; 45 (UP RT), reptiles4all/SS; 45 (CTR), Hiroya Minakuchi/MP; 45 (CTR RT), FP media/SS; 45 (LO), Ziva_K/IS/GI; 46, Eric Gevaert/AL; 47 (UP RT), AP Photo/Martin Meissner; 47 (CTR RT), Haroldo Palo Jr./Avalon; 47 (CTR), NG Maps; 48-49 (ALL), Ami Vitale; 50, Fred Olivier/NPL/MP; 51 (UP), Jay Dickman/GI; 51 (LO), Breck P. Kent/Animals Animals/Earth Scenes/NGIC; 52 (UP), Dan Costa/UC Santa Cruz; 52 (LO), Sara Labrousse WAPITI cruise JR16004; 53 (UP), Mauricio Handler/NGIC; 53 (CTR RT), S. Rohrlach/GI; 53 (CTR RT), WaterFrame/AL; 53 (LO), WaterFrame/AL; 54 (BACKGROUND), Paul Nicklen/NGIC; 54 (UP), Paul Nicklen/NGIC; 54 (UP RT), Paul Nicklen/NGIC; 54 (LO RT), Russ Kinne/age fotostock; 54 (LO CTR), Flip Nicklin/MP; 55, Emily M. Eng/NG Staff; 56 (UP), WaterFrame/AL; 56 (CTR), Andy Murch/Blue Planet Archive; 56 (LO), David Gruber; 57 (UP), Masa Ushioda/Blue Planet Archive; 57 (CTR), Saul Gonor/Blue Planet Archive; 57 (LO), Richard Carey/AS; 58, Edward Myles/MP; 59 (UP), Claudio Contreras/MP; 59 (LO), Claudio Contreras/MP; 60 (UP), Martin van Lokven/MP; 60 (closed), Ingo Arndt/MP; 60 (open), Ingo Arndt/MP; 60 (LO), Chien Lee/MP; 61 (UP), Stu Porter/SS; 61 (CTR), Stephen Dalton/MP; 61 (LO), reptiles4all/GI; 62 (UP LE), Sahara Frost/SS; 62 (CTR RT), Lizgiv/DS; 62 (LO LE), Damian Lugowski/GI; 63 (UP LE), Tezzah32/SS/SS; 63 (CTR RT), Kevin Schafer/MP; 63 (LO LE), Kevin Schafer/

MP; 64 (UP), Michael D. Kern; 64 (CTR), Hitendra Sinkar Photography/Alamy; 64 (CTR LE), Stephen Dalton/MP; 64 (CTR RT), AtSkwongPhoto/SS; 64 (LO), Heidi & Hans-Juergen Koch/MP; 65 (UP), Andrew Walmsley/Nature Picture Library; 65 (LO), Andrew Walmsley/Nature Picture Library/AL; 66, Michael Durham/MP; 67, Mircea Costina/SS; 68, Beverly Joubert/NGIC; 69 (snow leopard fur), Eric Isselée/SS; 69 (jaguar fur), worldswildlifewonders/SS; 69 (tiger fur), Kesu/SS; 69 (leopard fur), WitR/SS; 69 (lion fur), Eric Isselée/SS; 69 (jaguar), DLILLC/Corbis/GI; 69 (lion), Eric Isselée/SS; 69 (tiger), Eric Isselée/SS; 69 (snow leopard), Eric Isselée/SS; 69 (leopard), Eric Isselée/SS; 70 (LE), Gerard Lacz/Science Source; 70 (CTR), FionaAyerst/GI; 70 (RT), Suzi Eszterhas/MP; 71 (UP), Henner Damke/AS; 71 (CTR LE), Nick Garbutt/MP; 71 (LO LE), Kris Wiktor/SS; 71 (LO RT), Jak Wonderly/NGIC; 72 (UP), Wayne Marinovich/GI; 72 (CTR), Andyworks/GI; 73 (UP), sduben/GI; 73 (LO), Pavel Glazkov/GI; 74 (UP LE), age fotostock/SuperStock; 74 (UP RT), smrm1977/GI; 74 (LO RT), Corbis/SuperStock; 74 (LO LE), Eva Blanco/EyeEm/GI; 75 (UP LE), Lori Epstein; 75 (UP RT), Lori Epstein; 75 (LO RT), The Sun\News Licensing; 76 (ring), Tsurukame Design/SS; 76 (cat), Ermolaev Alexander/SS; 76 (dog), Eric Isselee/SS; 76 (gloves), xmee/SS; 78 (UP), Chris Butler/Science Photo Library/Photo Researchers, Inc.; 78 (CTR), Publiphoto/Photo Researchers, Inc.; 78 (LO), Pixeldust Studios/NGIC; 79 (A), Publiphoto/Photo Researchers, Inc.; 79 (B), Laurie O'Keefe/Photo Researchers, Inc.; 79 (C), Chris Butler/Science Photo Library/Photo Researchers, Inc.; 79 (D), Publiphoto/Photo Researchers, Inc.; 79 (E), image courtesy of Project Exploration; 80 (ALL), Franco Tempesta; 81 (UP LE), Lucas Jaymez/dinoesculturas; 81 (UP RT), Xinhua/AL; 81 (LO RT), Shundong Bi; 81 (LO LE), James Kuether; 82-83 (ALL), Davide Bonadonna; 84 (UP RT), Edward Myles/MP; 84 (CTR RT), Lori Epstein; 84 (LO LE), Anna Hager/GI; 84 (CTR LE), sduben/GI; 85, GOLFX/SS

Space and Earth (86–107)
86-87, NASA, ESA, CSA, STScI, Webb ERO Production Team; 88 (1), NASA, ESA, J. Hester and A. Loll (Arizona State University); 88 (2), NASA, ESA, and E. Karkoschka (University of Arizona); 88 (3), NASA/JSC; 88 (4), NASA, ESA, and The Hubble Heritage Team (STScI/AURA); 88 (5), NASA, H. Ford (JHU), G. Illingworth (UCSC/LO), M.Clampin (STScI), G. Hartig (STScI), the ACS Science Team, and ESA; 89, Johan Swanepoel/SS; 90-91, David Aguilar; 92 (Haumea), David Aguilar; 92 (Eris), David Aguilar; 92 (Pluto), NASA/JHUAPL/SwRI; 93 (UP), EHT Collaboration/NASA; 93 (LO), Joe Rocco; 94 (UP LE), Evan Dalen/Stocksy/AS; 94 (UP RT), cosmicvue/AS; 94 (LO RT), Tandem Stock/AS; 94 (LO LE), Peter/AS; 95 (UP), Mark Garlick/Science Source; 95 (CTR), KEENPRESS/NGIC; 95 (LO), Science RF/AS; 96, Mondolithic Studios; 96 (INSET), NASA/Goddard/University of Arizona; 97, Allexxandar/IS/GI; 98 (UP), NGIC; 98 (LO), Joe Rocco; 99 (UP), Ralph Lee Hopkins/NGIC; 99 (andesite), MarekPhotoDesign/AS; 99 (granite), losmandarinas/SS; 99 (mica), Yeso58 Montree Nanta/SS; 99 (gneiss), Dirk Wiersma/Science Source; 99 (limestone), Charles D. Winters/Photo Researchers, Inc.; 99 (halite), Theodore Clutter/Science Source; 100 (LO LE), Albert Russ/SS; 100 (UP RT), MarcelC/IS; 100 (CTR RT), Anatoly Maslennikov/SS; 100 (LO RT), IS; 100

(UP LE), raiwa/IS; 101 (UP RT), Mark A. Schneider/ Science Source; 101 (CTR LE), didyk/IS; 101 (talc), Ben Johnson/Science Source; 101 (gypsum), Meetchum/DS; 101 (calcite), Kazakovmaksim/ DS; 101 (fluorite), Albertruss/DS; 101 (apatite), Ingemar Magnusson/DS; 101 (orthoclase), Joel Arem/Science Source; 101 (topaz), Igorkali/ DS; 101 (corundum), oldeez/DS; 101 (diamond), 123dartist/DS; 102, Frank Ippolito; 103 (UP LE), Gary Fiegehen/All Canada Photos/Alamy; 103 (UP RT), Salvatore Gebbia/NGIC; 103 (CTR LE), NASA/ JSC; 103 (CTR RT), Diane Cook & Len Jenshel/ NGIC; 103 (LO RT), NG Maps; 104, andersen_oys-tein/GI; 105, Vulkanette/DS; 106 (UP LE), Albert Russ/SS; 106 (UP RT), Vulkanette/DS; 106 (LO RT), NASA, ESA, and E. Karkoschka (University of Arizona); 106 (LO LE), NASA/JSC; 107, pixhook/ E+/GI

Awesome Exploration (108–129)

108-109, Stephen Frink/GI; 110 (UP), Courtesy of Tiassa Mutunkei; 110 (CTR RT), Ermolaev Alexander/SS; 110 (CTR LE), Ursula Page/AS; 110 (LO), Four Oaks/SS; 111 (UP), Singkham/SS; 111 (CTR LE), lalalululala/AS; 111 (CTR RT), Tom/AS; 111 (LO), Ariel Skelley/DI; 112 (UP LE), Lvcas Fiat; 112-113 (ALL), Leo Lanna; 114 (UP CTR), Mariela Biondi; 114 (UP RT), Morales/age fotostock; 114 (CTR RT), Vanessa Bézy/NGIC; 114 (LO LE), Vanessa Bézy/NGIC; 114 (UP LE), Lydia Gibson; 115 (UP RT), Maurice Oniango; 115 (CTR RT), Zach Bolton/National Geographic Staff; 115 (LO LE), Surapon Gawee; 115 (LO CTR LE), Mark Thiessen/ National Geographic Staff; 115 (CTR), Lydia Gibson; 115 (CTR LE), Lydia Gibson; 116-117 (ALL), Joel Sartore, National Geographic Photo Ark/ NGIC; 118, Mattias Klum/NGIC; 119 (UP), Brian J. Skerry/NGIC; 119 (LO), Michael Nichols/NGIC; 120, Ralph Pace/MP; 121, NG Maps; 122 (UP LE), Gabby Wild; 122 (UP RT), Rebecca Hale/NG Staff; 122 (LO RT), Theo Allofs/MP; 123 (BACKGROUND), Arctic-Images/Corbis/GI; 123 (UP RT), Arctic Images/AL; 123 (LO LE), Arctic Images/AL; 124 (UP), Keystone View Co/NGIC; 124 (LO RT), NASA; 124 (LO LE), Visions of America/Education Images/Universal Images Group via GI; 125 (UP LE), Imaginechina/ AL; 125 (UP RT), Frank Hurley/Scott Polar Research Institute, University of Cambridge/GI; 125 (CTR RT), Kon-Tiki on its epic voyage, English School, (20th century)/Private Collection/ Look and Learn/Bridgeman Images; 125 (LO LE), © INTERFOTO/AL; 125 (CTR LE), Captain Roald Amundsen at the South Pole, 1912, from 'The Year 1912', published London, 1913 (litho)/Private Collection/Photo © Ken Welsh/Bridgeman Images; 126 (UP), Charlie Hamilton James/NGIC; 126 (CTR), Denis-Huot/Nature Picture Library; 126 (LO), 663highland/AS; 127 (Adam), Adam Amir Belmezouar; 127 (Abby), Abby Kress; 128 (UP RT), © Keystone View Co/NGIC; 128 (LO RT), Surapon Gawee; 128 (LO LE), Leo Lanna; 128 (CTR LE), Ralph Pace/MP; 129, Grady Reese/IS

Fun and Games (130–149)

130-131, mlorenzphotography/GI; 132 (UP LE), FocusStocker/SS; 132 (UP CTR), NightOwlZA/IS; 132 (UP RT), Leksele/SS; 132 (CTR RT), Jerryway/ DS; 132 (LO RT), Bildagentur Zoonar GmbH/SS; 132 (LO LE), Jan/AS; 132 (CTR LE), Nick Biemans/ DS; 133 (ALL), Dan Sipple; 134 (UP LE), kapulya/ GI; 134 (UP CTR), Kenneth W. Fink/ARDEA; 134 (UP RT), Exactostock/SuperStock; 134 (CTR

RT), Klein-Hubert/Kimball Stock; 134 (LO RT), Irynarasko/DS; 134 (LO CTR), Kevin Schafer; 134 (LO LE), Jeff Griffin/EyeEm/GI; 134 (CTR LE), Martin Harvey/GI; 134 (CTR), Joe & Mary Ann McDonald/Kimball Stock; 135 (UP RT), Luca Bruno/AP/SS; 135 (UP CTR), PK6289/GI; 135 (CTR RT), Maks Narodenko/SS; 135 (LO CTR), Bill Kennedy/SS; 135 (LO LE), Grisha Bruev/SS; 136 (UP), Paul Nicklen/NGIC; 136 (WetUnicorn), Paul Nicklen/NGIC; 136 (SlowJaws), Doug Perrine/ Blue Planet Archive; 136 (Tusky), Ken Watkins/ GI; 136 (IceTeddy), Marion Vollborn/MP; 136 (BaffinBay), Flip Nicklin/MP; 136 (CTR RT), Steven Kazlowski/MP; 136 (LO CTR), zanskar/GI; 136 (LO LE), Ole Jorgen Liodden/NPL/MP; 137 (UP CTR), Scott McCusker/GI; 137 (UP RT), David Laurent/ GI; 137 (CTR RT), Chico Sanchez/GI; 137 (LO RT), Placebo365/GI; 137 (LO LE), Sava Ivanov/GI; 137 (CTR LE), Matteo Colombo/GI; 138 (UP LE), Junda/ DS; 138 (UP CTR), Planctonvideo/DS; 138 (UP RT), Hannu Viitanen/DS; 138 (CTR RT), Kelpfish/ DS; 138 (LO RT), John Anderson/DS; 138 (LO CTR), Derek Holzapfel/DS; 138 (LO LE), Ernst Daniel Scheffler/DS; 138 (CTR LE), Mayama/DS; 138 (CTR), Annette Boettcher/DS; 139 (ALL), Dan Sipple; 140 (1), Photograph by Devon OpdenDries/GI; 140 (2), Jennifer Chen/AL; 140 (3), Alan Schein Photography/GI; 140 (4), H. Mark Weidman Photography/AL; 140 (5), Dee Kay Photos/AL; 140 (6), Zoonar GmbH/AL; 140 (7), Peter Unger/GI; 141 (UP LE), Dmitry Ternovoy/DS; 141 (UP CTR), Serban Enache/DS; 141 (UP RT), Ventura69/DS; 141 (CTR RT), Brad Calkins/DS; 141 (LO RT), Lorraine Swanson/DS; 141 (LO CTR), Vitaly Korovin/DS; 141 (LO LE), Pablo Caridad/DS; 141 (CTR LE), Jason Yoder/DS; 141 (CTR), Alena Brozova/DS; 142 (UP RT), Suzi Eszterhas/MP; 142 (CTR), mbbirdy/ GI; 142 (LO CTR), Leena Robinson/SS; 142 (LO LE), yevgeniy11/SS; 143 (UP RT), Raghupathi K.V./500px/GI; 143 (RedDog), ePhotocorp/GI; 143 (MonkeyAround), Pete Oxford/MP; 143 (MoHawk), Lucas Bustamante/NPL/MP; 143 (LongLizard), Yashpal Rathore/NPL/MP; 143 (CTR RT), Mary McDonald/NPL/MP; 143 (CTR), Mary McDonald/ MP; 143 (CTR LE), Martin Chapman/AL; 143 (LO LE), Ashish and Shanthi Chandola/MP; 144 (ALL), Dan Sipple; 145 (UP LE), Dave Pattinson/ AL; 145 (UP CTR), D. Hurst/AL; 145 (UP RT), Atsuo Fujimaru/MP; 145 (CTR), Evannovostro/SS; 145 (LO RT), Flirt/SuperStock; 145 (LO CTR), Radius/ SuperStock; 145 (LO LE), Kelly Redinger/Design Pics; 145 (CTR LE), alexandre/AS; 145 (CTR), Gunnar Pippel/SS; 146 (A), Chien Lee/MP; 146 (B), Martin Harvey/MP; 146 (C), Chris Newbert/MP; 146 (D), Thomas Marent/MP; 146 (E), Chien Lee/MP; 146 (F), Paul Bertner/MP; 147 (1), Tommy (Louth)/ AL; 147 (2), Rolf Adlercreutz/AL; 147 (3), Colin Monteath/age fotostock; 147 (4), Kim Hammar/ AL; 147 (5), Joseph Sohm/age fotostock; 147 (6), Lawrence Wiles/AL; 147 (7), Philip J Hill/AL; 148-149, Strika Entertainment

Laugh Out Loud (150–165)

150-151, John M Lund Photography Inc/ GI; 152 (CTR), reptiles4all/SS; 152 (LO RT), VVCephei/IS; 152 (LO LE), EM Karuna/SS; 153 (ALL), Chris Ware; 155 (UP LE), jHannamariah/ SS; 155 (UP RT), hobbit/SS; 155 (bamboo), leungchopan/SS; 155 (UP LE), Nagel Photography/SS; 155 (CTR RT), anueing/SS; 155 (LO RT), StevenRussellSmithPhotos/SS; 155 (LO LE), Waseef Akhtar/SS; 155 (CTR LE), Strahil Dimitrov/SS; 155 (CTR), jo Crebbin/

SS; 156 (UP RT), Rasulovs/IS; 156 (CTR RT), Stephanie Zieber/IS; 156 (LO RT), Linn Currie/ SS; 156 (LO LE), © Sarkao/DS.com; 156 (CTR LE), Linn Currie/SS; 157 (UP LE), nicolecedik/AS; 157 (phone), Boonthida Srijak/SS; 157 (UP RT), eva_blanco/SS; 157 (CTR RT), halfmax/SS; 157 (LO RT), Everita Pane/SS; 157 (LO LE), Robynrg/ SS; 157 (hat), Richard Peterson/SS; 157 (CTR LE), Dora Zett/SS; 157 (CTR), Aneta Jungerova/ SS; 158 (ALL), Chris Ware; 160 (UP RT), M. Unal Ozmen/SS; 160 (CTR RT), Brenda Carson/SS; 160 (LO RT), Melica/SS; 160 (LO CTR), Denis Larkin/ SS; 160 (LO LE), margouillat photo/SS; 161 (ALL), Chris Ware; 162 (UP LE), Strahil Dimitrov/SS; 162 (UP RT), Stokkete/SS; 162 (CTR RT), Aleksei Verhovski/SS; 162 (LO RT), SomPhoto/SS; 162 (LO LE), Peter Gudella/SS; 162 (CTR LE), Volodymyr Burdiak/SS; 162 (CTR), Sergey Uryadnikov/SS; 163 (BACKGROUND), Herschel Hoffmeyer/SS; 163 (LO RT), Ozja/SS; 163 (napkin), Olyina/SS; 164 (UP LE), Kletr/SS; 164 (porcupinefish), Eric Isselee/ SS; 164 (UP RT), S.Borisov/SS; 164 (CTR RT), vvoe/SS; 164 (LO RT), Milkovasa/SS; 164 (CTR LE), Netfalls Remy Musser/SS; 165 (ALL), Chris Ware

Culture Connection (166–189)

166-167, day2505/AS; 168 (UP LE), CreativeNature. nl/SS; 168 (UP RT), SL-Photography/SS; 168 (LO RT), Johan Roux/AL; 168 (LO LE), Tubol Evgeniya/ SS; 168 (CTR LE), nungning20/AS; 169 (UP), New Africa/AS; 169 (CTR RT), Dinodia Photos; 169 (CTR LE), Zee/Alamy; 169 (LO), wacpan/SS; 170 (UP), Scott Keeler/Tampa Bay Times/ZUMA Wire/AL; 170 (LO), Marie1969/SS; 171 (UP LE), VisitBritain/ John Coutts/GI; 171 (UP RT), lev radin/SS; 171 (CTR RT), Viviane Ponti/GI; 171 (LO RT), Carol M. Highsmith/Library of Congress Prints and Photographs Division; 171 (LO LE), epa european pressphoto agency b.v./AL; 171 (CTR LE), CR Shelare/GI; 173 (BACKGROUND), Olga Rom/SS; 173 (UP CTR), Elena Blokhina/SS; 173 (LO CTR), Tiger Images/SS; 173 (LO RT), Photastic/SS; 173 (LO LE), Astral232/SS; 174, Chris Hill/NGIC; 175 (UP), M6 Mega Jump/ABACAPRESS/Newscom; 175 (CTR LE), © John Harper/Photolibrary/GI; 175 (CTR RT), NG Maps; 175 (LO), Mark Campbell/ REX/SS; 176 (UP LE), The camvalleys/SS; 176 (UP RT), PictureSyndicate/AS; 176 (LO LE), poco_bw/ AS; 177 (UP LE), Richard Peterson/SS; 177 (CTR LE), Ekaterina Mikhaïlova/AS; 177 (CTR RT), ExQuisine/AS; 177 (LO RT), Successo images/AS; 178-179, Joe Rocco; 178 (CTR RT), Denis Tabler/ SS; 178 (LO), The Art Archive/SS; 179 (LO), PVDE/ Bridgeman Images; 180 (UP LE), US Mint; 180 (UP RT), Stack's Bowers Galleries; 180 (CTR RT), Jack Guez/AFP/GI; 180 (LO RT), Brian Hagiwara/GI; 180 (LO LE), dpa picture alliance/AL; 181 (UP LE), money & coins @ ian sanders/AL; 181 (UP RT), Richard Du Toit/MP; 181 (CTR RT), Sepia Times/ Universal Images Group via GI; 181 (CTR), ZU_09/ GI; 181 (LO RT), Kelley Miller/NGS Staff; 181 (LO LE), Colin Hampden-White 2010; 181 (LO CTR LE), Mohamed Osama/DS; 181 (UP CTR LE) Courtesy Gabriel Vandervort/Ancientresource; 182 (Ton), Nguyen Dai Duong; 182 (CTR RT), Ho Trung Lam; 182 (Narayanan), Randall Scott/NGIC; 182 (LO LE), Mark Thiessen/NG Staff; 183 (UP LE), Jeremy Fahringer; 183 (Harrison), Mark Thiessen/NG Staff; 183 (Barfield), Robert Masser; 183 (CTR RT), Catherine Cofré; 183 (CTR LE), K. Bista; 183 (Perlin), Mark Thiessen/NGS Staff; 183 (LO RT), Jeevan Sunuwar Kirat; 183 (Rapacha), Jeevan

Sunuwar Kirat; 184 (UP LE), liquidlibrary/GI Plu/GI; 184 (UP RT), Jose Ignacio Soto/SS; 185 (LE), Corey Ford/DS; 185 (RT), IS; 186 (UP), Randy Olson; 186 (LO RT), Sam Panthaky/AFP/GI; 186 (LO LE), Martin Gray/NGIC; 187 (UP), Humba Frame/SS; 187 (LO RT), Richard Nowitz/NGIC; 187 (LO LE), Reza/NGIC; 188 (UP LE), money & coins @ ian sanders/AL; 188 (UP RT), John Harper/Photolibrary/GI; 188 (LO RT), Joe Rocco; 188 (LO LE), poco_bw/AS; 189 (bird stamp), spatuletail/SS; 189 (Brazil stamp), PictureLake/E+/AL; 189 (money), cifotart/SS; 189 (flag), zydesign/SS

Science and Technology (190–213)

190-191, phonlamaiphoto/AS; 192 (UP), LucasFilm; 192 (CTR LE), Abaca Press/AL; 192 (LO RT), Randy Hayashi/Bloomberg via GI; 193 (UP), Paul Marotta/GI; 193 (CTR RT), Dibyangshu Sarkar/AFP via GI; 193 (LO), Diligent Robotics; 193 (CTR LE), Todd Taulman/DS; 194 (UP), Shenzhen Elephant Robotics Technology Co., Ltd; 194 (LO), Arcade1Up; 195 (3), Little Tikes; 195 (4), Cutecircuit; 195 (5), REX USA; 195 (6), Origami Labs; 196, Ted Kinsman/Science Source; 197 (1), Sebastian Kaulitzki/SS; 197 (2), Eye of Science/Photo Researchers, Inc.; 197 (3), Volker Steger/Christian Bardele/Photo Researchers, Inc.; 197 (fungi), ancelpics/GI; 197 (protists), sgame/SS; 197 (animals), kwest/SS; 197 (plants), puwanai/SS; 198 (ALL), Alejandro Mesa; 199, Reinhard, H./Arco Images/AL; 200, SciePro/SS; 201, Andrey_Kuzmin/SS; 202 (UP LE), Adam Taylor/GI; 202 (UP RT), Taleseedum/AS; 202 (LO RT), Krakenimages/AS; 203 (UP LE), juan moyano/AL; 203 (UP RT), William West/AFP via GI; 203 (LO RT), Pasieka/Science Source; 203 (LO LE), VikramRaghuvanshi/GI; 204 (UP), WavebreakMediaMicro/AS; 204 (UP CTR), Rost9/SS; 204 (CTR RT), alswart/AS; 204 (CTR), Maxximmm/DS; 206 (LE), Eric Isselee/SS; 206 (RT), Route66Photography/AS; 207 (UP), Jean-Pierre Clatot/AFP/GI; 207 (CTR), kryzhov/SS; 207 (LO), Lane V. Erickson/SS; 208-209, Mondolithic Studios; 210-211, Mondolithic Studios; 212 (UP LE), Ted Kinsman/Science Source; 212 (CTR RT), Rost9/SS; 212 (LO RT), Diligent Robotics; 212 (LO LE), Alejandro Mesa; 213, Klaus Vedfelt/GI

Wonders of Nature (214–235)

214-215, Han/AS; 216 (LE), AVTG/IS; 216 (RT), Brad Wynnyk/SS; 217 (UP LE), Rich Carey/SS; 217 (UP RT), Richard Walters/IS; 217 (LO RT), Michio Hoshino/MP/NGIC; 217 (LO LE), Karen Graham/IS; 218-219 (BACKGROUND), Al'fred/SS; 218, NG Maps; 219 (river), Curioso.Photography/AS; 219 (fish), David Shale/Nature Picture Library; 219 (jaguar), Hans Wagemaker/SS; 219 (monkey), W. Orfeno Fotografia/AS; 219 (RT), Rudzhan/AS; 220-221 (BACKGROUND), Chris Anderson/SS; 220-221 (globes), NG Maps; 220 (LE), cbpix/SS; 220 (RT), Mike Hill/Photographer's Choice/GI; 221 (CTR RT), Wil Meinderts/Buiten-beeld/MP; 221 (CTR RT), Paul Nicklen/NGIC; 221 (LO RT), Jan Vermeer/MP; 222, NG Maps; 223 (UP), Stuart Armstrong; 223 (LO), Franco Tempesta; 224 (UP), tobiasjo/GI; 224 (LO), NG Maps; 225 (UP), Chasing Light - Photography by James Stone/GI; 225 (RT), James Balog/NGIC; 226 (UP LE), Richard T. Nowitz/Corbis; 226 (UP RT), gevende/IS/GI; 226 (CTR RT), Brand X; 226 (LO RT), Eric Nguyen/Corbis; 226 (LO LE), Alan and Sandy Carey/GI; 227 (1), Leonid Tit/SS; 227 (2), Frans Lanting/

NGIC; 227 (3), Lars Christensen/SS; 227 (4), Daniel Loretto/SS; 227 (LO), Richard Peterson/SS; 228 (UP LE), Dennis Hallinan/AL; 228 (UP RT), Robynrg/SS; 228 (LO RT), jerbarber/GI; 228 (LO LE), lavizzara/AS; 229 (UP), Ryszard Stelmacho/SS; 229 (CTR RT), Stephen Hummel, McDonald Observatory; 229 (LO), JSirlin/AS; 229 (CTR LE), Jason Persoff Stormdoctor/GI; 230, 3dmotus/SS; 231 (UP LE), Lori Mehmen/Associated Press; 231 (EFo), Susan Law Cain/SS; 231 (EF1), Brian Nolan/IS.com; 231 (EF2), Susan Law Cain/SS; 231 (EF3), Judy Kennamer/SS; 231 (EF4), jam4travel/SS; 231 (EF5), jam4travel/SS; 231 (LO LE), Jim Reed; 232 (UP LE), Mary Lyn Fonua/Matangi Tonga/AFP via GI; 232 (CTR LE), Pesi Fonua/GI; 232 (LO CTR), Hilary Andrews/NG Staff; 232 (LO RT), Jeff Herge/SS; 233 (UP), California Department of Fish and Wildlife; 233 (CTR), CDFW photo by Travis VanZant; 233 (LO), Lior Rubin/GI; 234 (UP RT), Curioso.Photography/AS; 234 (CTR RT), Jan Vermeer/MP; 234 (LO LE), Richard Walters/IS.com; 234 (CTR LE), JSirlin/AS

History Happens (236–267)

236-237, Japhotos/AL; 238 (UP LE), dbvirago/AS; 238 (UP RT), alona_s/AS; 238 (LO RT), AFP/AFP via GI; 238 (LO LE), Reuters/Mohamed Abd El Ghany; 239 (UP), sebastienlemyre/SS; 239 (CTR RT), Hendrik Schmidt/picture-alliance/dpa/AP Images; 239 (LO RT), SIPA USA/SIPA/Newscom; 240-241 (UP), Brian Jannsen/Alamy; 241 (CTR), NG Maps; 241 (LO RT), 4D News; 242, Alberto Loyo/SS; 243 (ALL), Alice Brereton; 244-245 (ALL), Art by Gloria Felix; 246 (UP), Jim Zuckerman/GI; 246 (CTR), Dinodia Photo/GI; 247 (UP), David Keith Jones/AL; 247 (CTR), NG Maps; 247 (LO), Afateev/GI; 248-249 (BACKGROUND), Matjaz Slanic/E+/GI; 248-249 (square frames), Iakov Filimonov/SS; 248-249 (oval frame), Winterling/DS; 248 (portraits), Marí Lobos; 250, Vera/AS; 251, akg-images; 252, Scott Rothstein/SS; 253 (UP), SS; 253 (CTR), Zack Frank/SS; 253 (LO), Gary Blakely/SS; 254 (UP), grandriver/E+/GI; 254 (CTR), Stan Honda/AFP via GI; 254 (LO), grandriver/E+/GI; 255-259 (portraits), White House Historical Association; 255 (LO), Heritage Auctions, Dallas; 258 (CTR LE), Shaper/AS; 259 (CTR LE), Serg64/SS; 259 (Obama), Pete Souza/The White House; 259 (Trump), Shealah Craighead/The White House; 259 (Biden), David Lienemann/The White House; 259 (LO LE), Elisabeth Aardema/SS; 260-261 (CTR), Speculator27/DS; 260-261 (LO), piotr_pabijan/SS; 262 (UP), Bettmann/CORBIS/GI; 262 (INSET), Science Source/GI; 263 (UP), Charles Kogod/NGIC; 263 (LO), Saul Loeb/AFP via GI; 264, Bettmann Archive/GI; 265 (UP LE), Kent Nishimura/Los Angeles Times via GI; 265 (UP RT), Bill Stafford/NASA/JSC; 265 (LO), Warren K Leffler/US News & World Report Magazine Photograph Collection/PhotoQuest/GI; 266 (UP LE), Brian Jannsen/Alamy; 266 (CTR LE), Art by Gloria Felix; 266 (CTR RT), Alberto Loyo/SS; 266 (LO RT), Speculator27/DS; 267, Christopher Furlong/GI

Geography Rocks (268–353)

268-269, Tim Fitzharris/MP; 270-271, NG Maps; 272-273, NG Maps; 274, NG Maps; 275 (UP), Mark Thiessen/NGP; 275 (LO), NASA; 276 (ALL), NG Maps; 277 (BACKGROUND), Fabiano Rebeque/Moment/GI; 277 (UP LE), Thomas J. Abercrombie/NGIC; 277 (UP CTR), Maria Stenzel/NGIC; 277 (UP RT), Gordon Wiltsie/NGIC; 277 (LO RT), Carsten Peter/

NGIC; 277 (LO CTR), Bill Hatcher/NGIC; 277 (LO LE), James P. Blair/NGIC; 278, Londolozi Images/Mint Images/GI; 279 (UP RT), AdemarRangel/GI; 279 (CTR RT), imageBROKER/SS; 279 (LO RT), David Havel/SS; 279 (CTR LE), Frank Glaw; 280-281, NG Maps; 282, heckepics/GI; 283 (UP RT), Achim Baque/SS; 283 (CTR RT), Flipser/SS; 283 (Shackleton), Keystone-France/Gamma-Keystone via GI; 283 (LO RT), Frank Hurley/Scott Polar Research Institute, University of Cambridge/GI; 283 (CTR LE), Mark Conlon, Antarctic Ice Marathon; 284-285, NG Maps; 286, Tim on Tour/AS; 287 (UP), Grant Rooney Premium/AL; 287 (CTR RT), Nate Allen/EyeEm/GI; 287 (LO RT), Tom Brakefield/GI; 287 (CTR LE), estherpoon/AS; 288-289, NG Maps; 290, Dave Watts/Nature Picture Library; 291 (UP RT), Andrew Watson/John Warburton-Lee Photography Ltd/GI; 291 (CTR RT), WITTE-ART/AS; 291 (LO RT), Dmitry/AS; 291 (CTR LE), Ken/AS; 292-293, NG Maps; 294, Yasonya/AS; 295 (UP RT), Roy Pedersen/SS; 295 (CTR RT), sucharat/AS; 295 (LO RT), Cover Images via AP Images; 295 (CTR LE), drhfoto/AS; 296-297, NG Maps; 298, John A. Anderson/SS; 299 (UP RT), Dina Julayeva/SS; 299 (CTR RT), Daniel Prudek/AS; 299 (LO), Mint Images RF/GI; 299 (CTR LE), Javier Trueba/MSF/Science Source; 300-301, NG Maps; 302, Overflightstock/AS; 303 (UP), Soberka Richard/hemis.fr/GI; 303 (CTR RT), Ernesto Ryan/Getty Image; 303 (LO RT), Jacek Warsaw PL/AS; 303 (LO LE), NG Maps; 303 (CTR LE), buteo/AS; 304-305, NG Maps; 308, Cheryl Ramalho/AS; 311, JorgeIvan/AS; 315, Aleksandar Todorovic/SS; 316, eyetronic/AS; 319, Mohamed I Khalid/SS; 322, Adam Howard/AL; 325, Giordano Cipriani/GI; 330, dblight/GI; 342 (UP), SeanPavonePhoto/IS/GI; 342 (CTR RT), Harold G Herradura/GI; 342 (CTR LE), TexPhoto/E+/GI; 342 (LO), PhotoDisc; 343 (UP LE), Photolibrary RM/GI; 343 (UP CTR), Stocktrek/GI; 343 (UP RT), Dan Thornberg/SS; 343 (LO RT), studiovin/SS; 343 (plate), AlenKadr/SS; 343 (LO CTR), adidas4747/SS; 343 (CTR LE), Dan Leeth/AL; 344 (UP LE), Andy Caulfield/AL; 344 (UP RT), Bedh Yadav/SS; 344 (CTR RT), Anna Munoz/GI; 344 (LO RT), Martin Kemp/SS; 344 (LO LE), Gil.K/SS; 345 (UP LE), vivooo/SS; 345 (CTR RT), Ognyan Trifonov/AL; 345 (LO LE), Velirina/AS; 346 (UP), Frans Lemmens/AL; 346 (LO), Kevin Zaouali/Caters News Agency; 347 (3), blickwinkel/AL; 347 (4), imageBROKER/AL; 347 (5), Xinhua/Tao Ming/Newscom; 347 (6), AsianDream/GI; 347 (7), Debra James/SS; 347 (8), The Asahi Shimbun via GI; 348 (UP), Auscape International Pty Ltd/AL; 348 (CTR LE), Bruce Obee/Newscom; 348 (CTR RT), CB2/ZOB/Supplied by WENN/Newscom; 348 (LO), Alastair Pollock Photography/GI; 350 (UP LE), Danita Delimont/AL; 350 (UP RT), ArtyAlison/IS/GI; 350 (LO RT), Gardel Bertrand/GI; 350 (LO LE), Ian Cumming/ZUMApress/Newscom; 351 (A), sculpies/GI; 351 (B), Archives Charmet/Bridgeman Images; 351 (C), Archives Charmet/Bridgeman Images; 351 (D), Archives Charmet/Bridgeman Images; 351 (E), Bridgeman Images; 351 (F), Archives Charmet/Bridgeman Images; 351 (G), DEA PICTURE LIBRARY/GI; 351 (H), Holger Mette/SS; 351 (I), Holger Mette/SS; 351 (J), Jarno Gonzalez Zarraonandia/SS; 351 (K), David Iliff/SS; 351 (L), ostill/SS; 351 (M), Hannamariah/SS; 351 (N), Jarno Gonzalez Zarraonandia/SS; 352 (UP LE), Bill Hatcher/NGIC; 352 (UP RT), Javier Trueba/MSF/Science Source; 352 (CTR LE), Tom Brakefield/SS; 352 (LO), Frans Lemmens/AL; 353, NG Maps

NATIONAL GEOGRAPHIC and Yellow Border Design are trademarks of the
National Geographic Society, used under license.

Since 1888, the National Geographic Society has funded more than
14,000 research, conservation, education, and storytelling projects around
the world. National Geographic Partners distributes a portion of the funds
it receives from your purchase to National Geographic Society to support
programs including the conservation of animals and their habitats.
To learn more, visit natgeo.com/info.

For more information, visit nationalgeographic.com,
call 1-877-873-6846, or write to the following address:

National Geographic Partners, LLC
1145 17th Street N.W.
Washington, DC 20036-4688 U.S.A.

For librarians and teachers:
nationalgeographic.com/books/librarians-and-educators

More for kids from National Geographic: natgeokids.com

National Geographic Kids magazine inspires children to explore their world
with fun yet educational articles on animals, science, nature, and more.
Using fresh storytelling and amazing photography, *Nat Geo Kids* shows kids
ages 6 to 14 the fascinating truth about the world—and why they should care.
natgeo.com/subscribe

For rights or permissions inquiries, please contact National Geographic
Books Subsidiary Rights: bookrights@natgeo.com

Designed by Kathryn Robbins and Ruthie Thompson

The publisher would like to thank everyone who worked to make this book
come together: Rose Davidson, project editor; Lisa Gerry, editor; Angela Modany,
editor; Sarah Wassner Flynn, writer; Michelle Harris, researcher; Sarah J. Mock,
senior photo editor; Mike McNey, map production; Lauren Sciortino and
David Marvin, design production assistants; Joan Gossett, editorial production
manager; and Molly Reid, production editor.

Trade paperback ISBN: 978-1-4263-7387-9
Reinforced library binding ISBN: 978-1-4263-7531-6

Printed in the United States of America
23/WOR/1